STRATEGIES OF
POLITICAL
EMANCIPATION

Loyola Lecture Series
in Political Analysis

Richard Shelley Hartigan
Editor and Director

CHRISTIAN BAY

STRATEGIES OF POLITICAL EMANCIPATION

University of Notre Dame Press
Notre Dame • London

Copyright © 1981 by
University of Notre Dame Press
Notre Dame, Indiana 46556

Library of Congress Cataloging in Publication Data

Bay, Christian, 1921-
   Strategies of political emancipation.

   (Loyola lecture series in political analysis)
   Includes bibliographical references and index.
   1. Liberty. 2. Liberalism. 3. Need (Psychology)
4. Oppression (Psychology) I. Title. II. Series.
JC571.B377   323.44   80-53117
ISBN 0-268-01702-6

Manufactured in the United States of America

for Juanita
with my gratitude, admiration, and love

Contents

Series Editor's Preface

In the past decade much has been written about the "post-behavioral" revolution in political science. The general theme has been that this academic discipline has modified a two generation long obsession with excessively empirical, data-oriented and value free study, and has now returned, like a wayward spouse, to the consideration of philosophical issues. Though in some instances valid, this current revisionism generally oversimplifies one fact and ignores another.

In the first instance it tends to falsely distinguish "empirical" from "normative" in political study, implying that the former pretends to be value-free, while the latter approach is subjective and largely unencumbered by objective data and analysis. In truth, of course, the tradition of Western political philosophy has always been an attempt to philosophize about the real world—in effect to speculate on the relationships between facts and values.

So too, the recent critique overlooks the fact that this traditional perspective of political philosophy has never been abandoned, but rather, has been carefully cultivated and refined in spite of some modern social science methodology which had declared such an effort to be obsolete. In "fact," normative political analysis, that is, political philosophy, has continued to engage the attention of thoughtful intellects, now as before.

Unfortunately, it is true that in recent years normative political scientists have not enjoyed an extensive public forum which would enable them to test their insights and reach a wide audience with their conclusions. It was in an effort to partially remedy this that the Loyola Lecture Series in Political Analysis was founded.

Strategies of Political Emancipation is the most recent publication of the Loyola Lecture Series. It is the outgrowth of six public lectures, delivered by Professor Christian Bay, of the University of Toronto, during his two-week stay at Loyola in 1977. In this work Professor Bay demonstrates, as in his previous extensive writings, a breadth of scholarship, a sensitivity to the human predicament, and an intellectual integrity which has earned him the well deserved respect of his professional colleagues. Such a work of obvious merit cannot by itself, however, convey the human warmth and dedication which the author extended to students and faculty at Loyola. For that previous extension of himself, and for his continuing support and friendship, all associated with the Series, and I in particular, are deeply grateful.

With the publication of this work, the Loyola Lecture Series in Political Analysis is pleased to begin an association with the University of Notre Dame Press. I would like to express my appreciation to its Director, James R. Langford, for his cooperation and encouragement.

Richard Shelley Hartigan
Editor and Director,
Loyola Lecture Series
in Political Analysis

Acknowledgments

This work owes its inception to Richard S. Hartigan and to Loyola University of Chicago, where he directs its annual program of Lectures in Political Analysis. The chapters were first presented as six lectures, in November 1977, on that campus. The task of turning the lectures into chapters was aided by the thoughtful criticism of Professors Hartigan and James L. Wiser, and indeed by the exceptionally searching questions addressed to me after each lecture, mainly by faculty and students at Loyola University.

Friends and colleagues have been helpful at every stage of the work. Andrew Baines, then Principal of New College at the University of Toronto, gave me an opportunity to try out the earliest version of Chapter 1 as a Centennial Lecture in the college, which was followed up by a discussion-session in its futures-debating Gnu Society. Yet my biggest debt, outside my always supportive immediate family, is to several friends who read and criticized the whole manuscript, some of them twice, at different stages of its development: Ben Agger, David J. Baugh, Joseph F. Fletcher, Gad Horowitz, and Wolf-Dieter Narr.

Others have responded just as generously, when I requested critiques of one chapter-draft or another: Robert E. Agger, Gregory Baum, John Burton, Frances Herring, Patrick Neal, Mark Roelofs, and Mark Warren. Useful leads to ideas and sources were given by Cranford Pratt, Marek Thee, and Alan Wolfe; and surely by others also, in the course of everyday discussions of the plight of the world and what should be done about it.

Three highly skilled, intelligent and thoughtful typists helped to make the work fit for publication: Marilyn French, Anne Lee, and Ina Omar.

None of the people named above should be expected to share all of my views, let alone my preferred style of writing. It is possible that the reader will find a less than complete fit between his or her views and mine, regarding matters of substance or style. If so, I want the ire directed at myself only.

Amsterdam   Christian Bay
February 23, 1981

Introduction

MY MOST BASIC CONCERN in this work is with exploring ways of understanding and advancing human freedom, or liberty; to advance freedom not indiscriminately but according to rational humanist priorities.

My commitment to political inquiry in a social science context is based on the conviction that human emancipation requires two kinds of resources: adequate knowledge, and a disciplined will to struggle for universal human emancipation. Disciplined in the sense that the strategies of action must be guided by rational priorities among objectives and by realistic appraisals of historical and empirical contexts.

"Freedom," or "liberty," will in this work refer to self-expression: to any person's optimal capacity, opportunity, and incentive to express his or her own self, and to further develop one's self through authentic processes of feeling, thinking, and acting with others.[1] "Oppression" will refer to every kind of denial, limitation, obstruction, or destruction of freedom, in this wide sense. "Emancipation" will refer to every kind of process aiming at or tending to reduce oppression, or to expand freedom.

So much by way of a preliminary introduction of the three most central concepts in this work. Each of them will, of course, be subjected to closer examination in the chapters that follow. The course of my inquiry in this work will be as follows:

First, in chapter 1, I shall examine critically our conventional liberal understanding of liberty. My contention will be that it is much too narrow a concept; its chief defect is that it does not relate to the whole range of basic human needs. Liberalism's liberty is in effect incompatible with the value perspectives required to advance human emancipation ac-

1

cording to rational humanist priorities, for it is an ideological concept in the service of defending an established political system.

Chapter 2 will develop the basic concepts for an alternate approach to the study of freedom, oppression, and human emancipation. I propose to analyze three principal modes of oppression, to be called, respectively, domination, coercive oppression, and alienation.

Chapters 3 through 5 will in turn examine each of these categories of oppression, both conceptually and empirically, and develop proposals for appropriate strategies of emancipation in each context.

In conclusion, chapter 6 will, apart from summing up the results of my inquiry so far, take up the transnational and the transtemporal aspects of the problem of human emancipation. The struggle for freedom must be a global one, with priorities determined by the relative magnitudes and severities of violence and oppression in the various parts of today's world; it must be determined also by a decent concern for those least able to defend their own rights and vital interests—those, of course, who are not yet born.

My ambition in this work is not to be radically innovative. Much that will be said has been said before. My most ambitious hope is to contribute to developing a more adequate (and yet not implausible) conceptual framework than is currently available for emancipatory thought and action capable of transcending the most familiar ideological, let alone sectarian, constraints. I want to help prepare the conceptual terrain and to assemble some empirical knowledge to aid and facilitate emancipatory struggles, guided by an explicit commitment to the protection of human lives as the highest value.

As I hope to show, a consistent commitment to protect lives, each human life as an end in itself, requires a kind of politics that is designed to meet human needs according to realistic priorities. It requires a human rights approach to politics, which must be sharply distinguished from a liberal-democratic approach.

While I lack a firm sense of optimism regarding how much good can be accomplished with exercises in political philosophy, even at their best, I am an outright pessimist about what can be achieved politically in the absence of philosophy, or in the presence of dogmatic or conventional philosophies only. I hold with Marx that the objective of interpreting the world must be to improve the prospects for changing it. Moreover, as a critical empiricist I hold that we will never begin to understand the power structures of political reality until we go to work trying to change them, even in our immediate environments.

Power is the substance of politics, but it is only one side of the coin. The other side is freedom, or justice, or any kind of vision of a better society.

Power oppresses, and yet some power is required to establish order; in the complete absence of order there can be no freedom. The vision of a better society can emancipate, and yet can also deepen the sense of oppression; it offers hope but can also, in the absence of serious thought about feasible strategies, lead to deepening despair. This is particularly the case with the vision of liberty, or of the free society, or of human rights, for slogans about freedom are so easily fabricated and manipulated by those who want to monopolize the benefits of liberty for their own class.

Properly conceived, Politics* is the tension between ideals and realities, insofar as human collaborative action conceivably can make a difference. A responsible political science studies realities as well as ideals, with equal care; it seeks to bring philosophy and social action to bear on realities that ought to be changed, and that perhaps eventually can be changed once they are understood.

The task of Politics is to make oppressive realities *problematic*.[2] Alternative visions when taken seriously introduce tensions between what is and what ought to be; *problems* establish specific hypotheses to the effect that what ought to be, *can* be, perhaps, and provide incentives to try to find out—in thought, in experimental action, conceivably even in acts of revolution.

---

*I shall capitalize this word at times, to distinguish this classical concept of Politics from the modern behavioral concept of politics in the sense of competition for power and use of power.

In this work, then, "Politics" is taken to refer to thoughtful cooperative action toward *resolving* political problems. "Problem" refers to any and all discrepancies between what exists, or will probably come to pass (unless effective action intervenes), and what ought to exist, or ought to be made to happen. "Political" are all problems arising because human lives, health, social solidarity, or freedom are damaged or diminished needlessly, i.e., for economic, social, or psychological reasons, not on account of existential necessity.

Now, "resolve" is not quite the same as "solve," as I understand these terms. In Heaven or in Utopia all political problems may be solvable, and the solutions may be to everyone's satisfaction. In our own reality a *re*solution of problems is often the most that can be accomplished: an analysis of a particular problem's causes, parameters, and implications, for the purpose of determining what strategies, if any, can reduce the problem or make its costs easier to endure for everyone concerned.

Political problems differ from existential predicaments in that the former have historical roots and are in principle susceptible to political remedies. Predicaments like natural death following old age, or our dependence on oxygen or clean water, do not themselves constitute political problems, although they are among the most political-problem-relevant facts of human life, especially in a time when a runaway technology and too liberal liberties for the mighty are threatening to destroy our oxygen and clean water, and to make premature death a possible outcome for everybody. The force of gravity that keeps us on this earth and the forbidding distances to other inhabitable planets elsewhere in the universe, if any, are among our existential predicaments, but they are nevertheless politically relevant. For one thing, they make more urgent the task of making progress in improving the health, safety, and freedom of the existing human communities in our corner of the universe.

To repeat: "political" are problems arising from needless damage to or thwarting of human lives, health, solidarity, or freedom. While this is a statement of definition, it is also intended as a normative and an ontological statement. "Needless" indicates not only that it is possible to distinguish man-made or society-made (i.e., historical) problems from existential predicaments, but also that damage to human lives, etc., should in principle always be treated as political problems, insofar as we are not talking about existential necessities. If human suffering is caused or aggravated by historical events or circumstances, then political remedies must be sought; this, as I assume already in my definition, is what politics legitimately is about.

As a practical matter it is nevertheless conceded that it is not always a simple or obvious matter to distinguish political problems from existential predicaments. For example, conservatives may tend to believe that not only death but also taxes, as well as poverty, are inescapable evils in any kind of society, while most radicals will see poverty as an eminently political problem, and some will question, too, the eternal necessity of taxes.

"Political" as here defined assumes a commitment to the supreme value of human life, and health and freedom are the essential qualities of social life that Politics *must* protect, ahead of any and all other possible objectives. As a shorthand term let me call this a *rational humanist* conception of Politics: rational because it insists on careful study of realities and possibilities; humanist because, by definition, the purpose of Politics is to preserve and enhance human life, all human lives. By implication it is also a socialist conception of Politics; even if this is a term laden with heavy ideological baggage in our common language, the conception is socialist in its assumption that all human lives are of equal worth, equally entitled to protection and enhancement.

Given this rational humanist perspective, it follows that national governments and political parties* ought to be given loyalty and support only to the extent that they endeavor to meet the most basic needs of all human beings under their jurisdiction, and to meet them more adequately than alternate governments and parties would do. Priorities among

---

*I lump governments with parties because I am talking about willing support; I recognize that governments, unlike most parties, have wide powers, both symbolic and coercive, with which it is frequently prudent to comply, even in spite of our political hopes and chosen loyalties.

genuine human needs become the contentious issues of Politics, once this basic premise has been accepted. It rules out serious attention to claims for unconditional protection of social privileges unrelated to genuine human needs. I hope it will not remain intellectually respectable much longer to legitimize, in the spirit of liberal democracy, a system that allows the survival needs of marginal minorities to be subjected to the vicissitudes of the fickle "marketplace" of public opinion as expressed in elections, or of employment markets determined by corporate calculations of when and where to maximize profits. Neither the corporate marketplace of money and profits nor the liberal-democratic marketplace of ideas and votes is well suited for settling issues of priorities among human needs, or among human rights. There is a radical difference between upholding the prior right of majorities and upholding the prior right of those classes of human beings who are most in need, a difference that few liberals have cared to explore. It will be examined at some length in this work.

1

Liberalism's Liberty: Ideology and Myopia

THIS WORK TAKES ISSUE with liberalism as a philosophy of liberty. Most of my argument will be constructive rather than polemical; I propose to contribute to an alternative theory of liberty and, in particular, to the development of alternative strategies of political emancipation. But it is well to begin with a critique of some widely accepted themes in liberal political thought.

I want to focus on one crucial conception in what I take to be the mainstream liberal outlook: the liberal conception of liberty. First of all I want to explain the heading I have chosen for this chapter, and in this context I will discuss briefly the concept of ideology and the nature of ideologies. Then I consider some representative liberal philosophical and ideological exercises in defense of what is called "liberty," or "freedom." I shall claim that these conceptions of freedom are ideologically slanted and shortsighted. In conclusion I shall attempt a broader and even more damning, I think, indictment of liberalism as a political creed: I shall argue that the conventional liberal outlook, both on account of its premises of individualism and contractualism, and on account of its promotion of the myth of democracy achieved, not only is incompatible with a rational humanist outlook, but also has become a main pillar of support for a system that produces poverty in our country and destitution in much of the Third World.

1. FROM MANNHEIM TO THE "END OF IDEOLOGY" IDEOLOGY

The heading of this chapter alludes to Karl Mannheim's *Ideology and Utopia*,[1] the pioneering work that founded the modern sociology of knowledge on the basis of an essentially Marxist outlook, yet which was devoid of economic class analysis and of the Marxist utopian vision. Mannheim saw social thought as generally constricted by the perspectives of the class with which each writer was identified, and he believed that the validity of ideas generally speaking was "relational" to specific historical situations. Writers identified with traditionally privileged classes would tend to think in organic metaphors, warning against substantial changes; oppressed classes would favor chiliastic utopias; and ascendant classes would support liberal spokesmen who argued for abstract reason and progress, in opposition to authorities and constrictions of the past.

Mannheim feared the polarization between the ideological views of privileged classes and the utopian demands of the oppressed. Instead of looking to the working class for a promise of revolutionary liberation, as Marx did, Mannheim looked to the intelligentsia, the intellectuals, as a relatively free-floating social stratum potentially capable of moving beyond the relational perspectives, ideological and utopian, and thus of approximating the "total" perspective of a realistic sociology of knowledge with which to plan for a gradual expansion of liberal freedoms. Mannheim was a *liberal* who anticipated, at a deeper level of epistemological insight, the "end of ideology" perspective that was to emerge in the United States in the late 1950s,[2] only a few years before the New Left exploded that complacent perspective on American politics. In fairness to Mannheim it should be said that he wrote at the height of the turmoil of the Weimar Republic, and in his own terms, which were more ideological than he acknowledged, his liberalism may have been a valid response in that historical context. It must also be acknowledged that Mannheim in important ways anticipated post–World War II North American liberalism; a Manchester liberal he was emphatically not. In fact, his liberalism was clearly to the left of Franklin Delano Roosevelt's, his contemporary; Mannheim believed in planning for freedom and he believed in the welfare state, not just in so-called New Deals that would help keep the old systems going.

Both Mannheim's liberalism and the later end-of-ideology

liberalism represent, as I shall argue, a premature abandonment of the idea of a rational politics in the service of realistic, empirically supportable human need priorities; that is, a needless resignation regarding the possibilities of a radical expansion of freedom in the modern world, freedom for the underdogs, even at the expense, when necessary, of some of the privileges now enjoyed by other classes. Underneath that resignation there is a nearsightedness, a myopia that is, in Marx's and Mannheim's terms, surely ideological.

The end-of-ideology literature of the early 1960s represented a more retrograde position, compared to Mannheim's, in that these writers (Daniel Bell, Seymour Martin Lipset, and many others) in a sense were laissez faire pluralists who looked at their own country, the United States, and decided that all was well, or so close to being well that things would work themselves out by way of pluralist bargaining processes. In a much-quoted passage, which I suspect that today an older and wiser Lipset might wish he had never published, S. M. Lipset wrote in an "Epilogue" to his influential book from 1960, *Political Man*: "the basic premise of this book is that democracy [i.e., as practiced in the U.S.] is not only or even primarily a means through which different groups can attain their ends or seek the good society, it is the good society itself in operation."[3]

Lipset was, with Daniel Bell, among the foremost champions of what I would call the end-of-ideology *ideology*, a position that really amounted to a belief in the end of Politics in the classical sense of that term.[4] Why continue to search for the good society if one first makes believe that the good society has arrived already? If so, not only ideology, but politics, can be replaced by sociology, and political theory can be replaced by studies of behavior, on the consumer-research model.

Some years after Lipset's pronouncement that the good society had arrived, poverty was discovered in America and President Johnson even started a war against poverty, another war that the United States lost. After that, and after Vietnam and Watergate, not to mention such recalcitrant problems as unemployment, inflation, pollution, urban blight, etc., few writers today would be quite as oblivious as Lipset once was to the shortcomings of our so-called democratic social system. It must be said, in fairness to Lipset, that he had overreacted to ideological views and activities of a different kind, championed by movements that supported the other side, the Soviet Union, in the cold war.

Let us now see what are some of the major concepts of ideology. Following Mannheim, Lasswell and Kaplan define ideology succinctly as "the political myth functioning to preserve the social structure"; again like Mannheim, they reserve "utopia" for myths striving to supplant the established system.[5] "Ideology" and "utopia" both refer, then, to unsupportable belief systems. "Ideology" is the other person's belief system, if you take exception to it. Some writers further require that beliefs must be shared within a party or group to be called ideological. Others again claim that belief systems must be fairly simple for mass consumption, to be called ideological.

Increasingly, however, social scientists have taken to using "ideology" as a neutral term referring to any ordered belief system of some persistency, not necessarily logically consistent but psychologically integrated. And in Philip Converse's influential paper "The Nature of Belief Systems in Mass Publics"[6] the term "ideological" is reserved for those relatively few American citizens who have political opinions that are at all coherent, beyond repeating newspaper headlines or simplistic slogans. If a citizenry given to ideological zealotry may be a hazard, the more immediate problem in North America would seem to be that most citizens have no persistent political belief systems at all.

And, furthermore, most of those who do will sooner have views about what government policies benefit their own group than about what the American or the world's public interest requires. Labor wants higher wages, business wants higher profits, Alberta wants higher oil prices, and so on. Our political system does not practice deliberation so much as "pressure politics"; not "Come let us reason together," but at best, in Joseph Tussman's phrase, "Come let us bargain together."[7]

As I shall show in concluding this chapter, this is in the nature of liberal society, in part because it is founded on perverse priorities of liberty. I shall come to these priorities in a moment; let me first finish with the issue of how to define ideology.

I go along with Converse and many others in preferring a descriptively neutral and simple concept: any system of beliefs about social or political issues I shall call ideological, without prejudging the truth or falsity of these beliefs. At the same time I am sensitive to the fact that all belief systems, all ideologies, tend to be either justificatory of or critical of the established order, and that every political regime has an extensive control over the common usage of terms and symbols, and ideological resources.

The point in studying ideologies and belief systems, then, apart from the ontological problem of determining what is true and false, is to find out what functions they serve in upholding or challenging a system of power; I see my inquiry in this chapter as a small contribution to this enterprise: just how do the ideological conceptions of "liberty" that are shared by some or most liberals serve to uphold or challenge *our* system of government? As we shall see, these liberal perspectives on liberty turn out to be serving quite well in the defense of our regime against the critical spirit and against a more meaningful emancipation of our lives and spirits.

2. LIBERALISM'S LIBERTY:
FROM LOCKE TO HAYEK AND BERLIN

Etymologically speaking, to state that one is a liberal is to state a commitment to liberty. But everybody is, of course, in favor of freedom in one sense or another, at least for oneself and one's own reference group, class, or nationality. The questions that too seldom are asked, and almost never answered with any degree of precision, are the following: Liberty or liberties for whom? What priorities of liberty, or among liberties, under what circumstances?

I shall try to answer these questions in the next chapter, and my ambition is to reach a position that, while still ideo-

logical, will serve emancipatory rather than justificatory purposes. For the moment let us consider some leading liberal
constructions of liberty and see what side they are on.

Let us begin with a relatively extreme case of liberal nearsightedness regarding the real nature of freedom and oppression in our kind of society: that of F. A. Hayek. Hayek
published an influential liberal tract in 1944, entitled *The
Road to Serfdom*[8], in which he warned against democratic
socialism as well as against more limited experiments in economic planning, which he viewed as threats against liberty.
In 1960 he published a much larger, more systematic and
scholarly work, *The Constitution of Liberty*,[9] in which he
articulated his political outlook in much more detail. In both
works, the freedom or liberty that Hayek champions is
curiously restricted: either of the two terms (which he, too,
uses interchangeably) refers "solely to a relation of men to
other men, and the only infringement on it is coercion by
men. This means, in particular, that the range of physical
possibilities from which a person can choose at a given moment has no relevance to freedom."[10] Liberty or the lack of
liberty has, according to this definition, no clear relevance to
human need priorities; it is solely a question of the absence
or presence of *coercion*, a concept that Hayek gives an even
more eccentric definition: Coercion occurs "when one man's
actions are made to serve another man's needs, not for his
own but for the other man's sake."[11] You are being coerced,
then, if the state tells you how to invest some of your money,
or when it takes some of it away to keep another person
from starving to death.

On the other hand, according to Hayek's terminology you
are still free even when you are about to starve to death, or
when you cannot afford the medicine that could save the
life of your child. "Justice," to Hayek, has nothing to do
with economics; this concept "ought to be confined to the
deliberate treatment of men by other men."[12] By definition
be it resolved, then, that poverty next to plenty is by no
means unjust; moreover, Hayek argues that it would be
coercive, and thus in violation of liberty, if a government,
by taxation or other means, sought to limit the wealth of the
rich in order to mitigate the sufferings of the poor.[13] Hayek's
so-called constitution of liberty turns out to be a constitu-

tion that in perpetuity would protect the continuing exploitation of the poor by the wealthy against governmental interference.[14]

Few other liberal writers in our own century have been as blatant as Hayek in their defense of the liberties of the privileged classes, or as lacking in apparent concern for the human needs of those who are needy. Almost three centuries ago, to be sure, John Locke was almost equally uncompromising in his defense of the rights of property and of acquiring more property, in the name of liberty; specifically including some men's right, contractually established, to command other men's labor. Locke, moreover, like most of his contemporaries, saw people without significant property as being less than full members of the body politic.[15]

James Mill, Jeremy Bentham, and the utilitarians were the first liberals to commit themselves to democracy, and also to a mathematically equal claim to happiness for all persons; otherwise the utilitarian felicity calculus would not work. But their notions of pleasure and pain were curiously abstract and difficult to relate to need priorities bearing on long-term human well-being. It is possible, however, that this difficulty could be overcome within the framework of the felicity calculus. The crucial flaw in the utilitarian scheme of priorities is that the *sum* of happiness ratios was to be maximized, without any perceived necessity of meeting the most pressing human needs first. The neediest were in principle expendable, if relatively few in number and if the sacrifice of their needs or lives would make the large majority prosper. Moreover, like Locke, the Benthamites took for granted a private enterprise system with a free market, and human beings who were selfish individualists. There was no vision of a mankind capable of desiring social justice or well-being for all, in addition to personal liberties and opportunities for individual enrichment.

John Stuart Mill broke loose from the constrictions of the utilitarian felicity calculus, conceding that some values, like liberty, or individuality, or moral courage, are qualitatively superior to other values, regardless of comparative pleasure for the moment. A part of Mill's concern in his *On Liberty* was to point out that many constraints on freedom are social rather than legal, and he formulated a principle that would condemn the old moralistic custom of censuring and coercing others for their own alleged benefit: "the sole end for which mankind are warranted, individually or collectively, in interfering with the liberty of any of their number is self-protection."[16] This is a simple maxim, but its practicality is limited in a world of constant interference and of mutual as well as one-sided dependencies of many kinds. The rule is about as impractical as it would be to insist, in a crowded and busy marketplace, that the only justification for interfering with the freedom to trade is to make sure that every transaction benefits both the buyer and the seller.

The argument for which *On Liberty* is most famous is its spirited defense of the freedom of discussion, as necessary "to the mental well-being of mankind (on which all their other well-being depends)."[17] Mill hedges on whether this mental well-being is mainly the immediate result of the enjoyment of the liberty of discussion, or mainly a matter of improved prospects that truth, justice, and progress will result from free as opposed to restricted discussion. On both grounds his argument is not only eloquent but weighty. What is missing, however, is a cognizance of the extent to which, already in Mill's society, the overall system was programmed to bolster bourgeois priorities among human needs, notably the needs of professionals, businessmen, and entrepreneurs; free speech and free enterprise were seen as the crucial liberties. As the right of free advocacy was defended, the right to own and invest capital funds was taken for granted, while a right to be protected from starving to death was not yet even contemplated.

In our own time Isaiah Berlin is widely considered one of the most representative spokespersons for liberalism; certainly he is one of the most articulate liberal theorists on the nature of liberty. In his 1958 inaugural lecture at Oxford he chose to speak on "Two Concepts of Liberty"[18] and his argument has been widely referred to and quoted. More philosophically sophisticated than Hayek, Berlin is well aware of a large range of possible definitions of liberty, and he by no means rules out of discussion concepts of liberty that place human needs above property claims.

Where Berlin's lack of vision is most apparent, in my view,

is in his failure to see that his blanket rejection of every "absolute" in the realm of freedom, or indeed in the realm of human purpose, leads him to a virtual abandonment of reason as an instrument of liberty, or of political progress of any kind. Along with Hayek, Berlin becomes wedded to a conception of politics as free-for-all bargaining between unequals, and to a political system that merely reflects rather than attempts to regulate and direct the perpetual struggle between social classes and interest coalitions:

> Pluralism, with the measure of 'negative' liberty that it entails, seems to me a truer and more humane ideal than the goals of those who seek in the great, disciplined, authoritarian structures the ideal of 'positive' self-mastery by classes or people, or the whole of mankind. It is truer, because it does, at least, recognize the fact that human goals are many, not all of them commensurable, and in perpetual rivalry with one another.[19]

Berlin concedes, to be sure, that the choices that men keep on making among "ultimate values" are determined by "fundamental moral categories and concepts that are . . . a part of their being and thought and sense of their own identity";[20] what he apparently cannot see is that these choices and categories and concepts, *and* the very sense of identity of most individuals, are shaped in large measure by the political forces that dominate their lives, for elite-serving purposes. This articulate liberal specialist on liberty is remarkably oblivious to the difference between authentic liberties whose exercise reflects and facilitates autonomous self-expression, and ideologically manufactured feelings and perceptions of being free, which reflect and encourage programmed and predictable behavior patterns that service social stability and elite interests.

Against Berlin's and Hayek's concept of negative freedom must be posed the insistence of that maverick liberal, Thomas Hill Green, that we cannot by "freedom" mean

> . . . merely freedom to do as we like irrespectively of what it is that we like. . . . When we speak of freedom as something to be so highly prized, we mean a positive

power or capacity of doing or enjoying something
worth doing or enjoying, and that, too, something that
we do or enjoy in common with others.[21]

Progress in freedom for a society, Green continues, is measured by "the greater power of the citizens as a body to
make the most and best of themselves." A wandering savage
to be sure appears to be free, but he is "the slave of nature."[22]

In a critique of Green's position, Berlin, in my view, lays
bare the essentials of the liberal ideology and myopia regarding liberty: the ideology of special pleading for priorities of
liberty of special concern to already privileged social classes,
and the myopia of discounting humankind's possibilities of
eventually outgrowing the possessive individualism spawned
by the capitalist order and its liberal protagonists. Of all
things, Berlin charges Green with confusing freedom and
equality;[23] a charge that is all too common even today in
liberal arguments against socialist or other positions to the
left. In the absence of specifying *whose* liberties and *what*
liberties are alleged to be confused with equality (in what
sense), writers who press this charge make it embarrassingly
clear that they had the freedom of the relatively privileged
in mind all along, when they spoke of freedom in general.
For if their primary concern had been with the liberties or
rights of the least free, there could have been no conflict
between the two goal values, freedom and equality.

More basically, Berlin takes Green to task for defining
freedom positively, as a "positive power or capacity of doing or enjoying something worth doing or enjoying." Berlin
asks, who is to decide what is worth doing or enjoying? He
is so afraid of associating the concept of freedom with any
notion of absolute truth or justice that the only kind of
liberty he will champion is to be negatively defined, as freedom *from* coercion, dictation, superimposed ideals, and, he
would seem to imply, from any firmly held convictions at
all!

Berlin's heaviest charge against Green's ideal of a positively defined "true freedom" is that "many a tyrant could
use this formula to justify his worst acts of oppression."[24]
I suppose a tyrant could use almost any formula, including
Berlin's own formula of negative freedom, to justify almost

anything, especially in our own time, when modern technologies of communication, owned or controlled by members of a corporate elite, allow great possibilities for programming the majority's inclinations and preferences. But
Berlin is right in saying, in effect, that you add insult to
injury when you institute compulsion and then will have the
compelled subjects believe this compulsion actually consti-
tutes or manifests their freedom; even though it can be
argued that some kinds of specific coercive measures may
be of benefit to many people, and that most coercive measures by restraining some kinds of behavior automatically
will enhance some people's freedom, in the sense of not
having to put up with such behavior by others. As an example of coercion that may in fact benefit the compelled
subjects, in some cases at least, take obligatory schooling,
or schooling forced by parents. While I might coerce my
child to go to school, I would not have the gall, however, to
tell that child that such coercion leaves his or her present
freedom unimpaired.

But Berlin goes much further than this. In effect his flat
rejection of positive liberty rules out the possibility, for example, that education could enhance a person's freedom by
facilitating a deeper self-insight. As some liberal pluralists
are prone to, he takes an absurdly dogmatic antidogmatist
stand: there *cannot be a true self*, nor any objective criteria
for making the best of oneself.

In a trenchant critique of Berlin's essay, C. B. Macpherson
observes that Berlin actually fuses three notions in his conception of positive liberty; Macpherson refers to them as
PL^1, PL^2, and PL^3. PL^1 is the idea of self-mastery, or "the
ability to live in accordance with one's own conscious purposes." PL^2 is the Idealist or metaphysical perversion of PL^1
into the notion that only the Truth, meaning those who
allegedly represent the Truth, can make us free; freedom
then becomes a matter of being coerced by the right people.
PL^3, finally, is "the democratic concept of liberty as a share
in the controlling authority."[25] Meanwhile, Berlin's "negative liberty" is found to be too vague to be of much use to
comparative political analysis. And Macpherson argues quite
persuasively that it ought to be replaced by "counter-
extractive liberty," on the assumption that the freedom

froms that matter are remedies against people or organizations that are out to extract services (like labor) or possessions or decision power from the individual, for the benefit
of those others or third parties.

With Macpherson's conceptual approach the choice between a vacuous negative liberty and a dangerous positive
liberty, a concept or an ideal that in Berlin's treatment is
made to seem tailor-made for tyrants, becomes superfluous.
Instead, we are talking about a counter-extractive liberty in
a sense of a minimum of exploitation (or of an adequate
individual or collective power to resist exploitation), which
facilitates and in turn is strengthened by a developmental
liberty (PL[1]), a liberty to develop and grow according to
inner propensities and self-chosen purposes. The less exploitation in a society, surely the more emancipation of
most people's potentialities to achieve their full humanity—
to reach their "true selves," to speak in a language that Berlin and many liberals flatly reject.

3. LIBERALISM'S MYOPIA:
NO LONGER A VISION OF EMANCIPATION

It has been shown that liberals like Berlin, Hayek, or
Locke or Bentham are curiously rigid and unrealistic in
their assumptions about human nature, and accordingly unimaginative about possibilities for human development and
change under better social circumstances. They are interested in expanding human liberty, all right, but their concern is entirely with the liberties dear to the heart of their
contemporary professionals and business people: free speech,
equal legal protection, and protection of private property.
Taking it for granted that almost all people will continue to
be possessive individualists, always out for private advantage, these writers rule out as impossible any degree of
aggregate growth in human solidarity, or even in compassion for the most oppressed classes, within the nation's borders or beyond.

This rejection of a social vision of humanity's future has
important psychological and political consequences. It tends

to justify antisocial behavior, which makes sense if human nature is held to be necessarily indifferent to other people's needs and interests. For example, it tends to justify a social system that leaves people with property and power free to exploit and coerce the powerless. What else would they be supposed to do? If there is no shared vision of a human capability of leaving the ethics of the jungle behind and of developing an active and compelling social conscience, then ethical issues become academic. Society comes to be seen as based on bargaining between interests, not on human communities struggling to evolve according to objective conceptions of justice.

In the absence of active and visible commitments to social justice in our own social order, economic power has increasingly tended to dictate the politics of the major parties; might has tended to constitute what is pronounced to be right, as long as the formally democratic rules of our electoral system are adhered to. And it has been up to our liberal pluralist writers, including Hayek and Berlin, to impress on our disadvantaged classes that they are free and democratically sovereign, in this best of all possible worlds.

But it must now be asked: Where should the philosophy of John Rawls be placed in this picture? Of all contemporary liberal writers of influence, he surely is most radical in his opposition to social inequality and most compassionate in his principled defense of equal life opportunities, to the fullest possible extent, for society's underdogs. His seminal *A Theory of Justice* is, moreover, the most influential work of liberal social theory in North America in recent years; for this reason, too, it cannot be ignored here.

At first glance Rawls might well seem to have transcended conventional liberal positions and to point the way toward a more viable future for liberal thought about liberty and, more generally, toward turning a branch of fresh liberal theory into a new emancipatory project. In the just society, according to Rawls, each person "is to have an equal right to the most extensive system of equal basic liberties compatible with a similar system of liberty for all."[26]

This is called the First Principle in his theory of justice, with a definite lexical-order[27] priority over the second of

his two principles. The latter stipulates that social and eco-
nomical inequalities are justifiable only to the extent that
they are "to the greatest benefit of the least advantaged"
and are "consistent with the just savings principle" (unlike
most liberal-democratic writers, Rawls has the great merit
of not overlooking the needs and interests of the unborn
generations); also, there must be equality of opportunity in
the competition for public office, as well as in the struggle
for private power and status.[28]

In the context just cited, by way of elaboration of the
import of the two principles in combination, it is his "general conception" that: "All social primary goods—liberty
and opportunity, income and wealth, and the bases of self-
respect—are to be distributed equally unless an unequal distribution of any or all of these goods is to the advantage of
the least favored."[29]

This is, to be sure, an admirably humanist position, in the
abstract, but what, more precisely, is Rawls's conception of
liberty, and what are his actual priorities among liberties?

It turns out that Rawls, too, operates with a peculiarly
narrow conception of liberty, one that bears more closely
on the likely preoccupations of comfortably-off academics
than on the most basic needs of human beings in general, in
the vast, unsheltered expanses of the real world around us.
If a person is too poor or too ignorant to make use of supposedly available liberty, this, to Rawls, does not make him
or her less free. Instead, it affects negatively the *worth* of
liberty to such persons.[30] Now, his first-priority principle
of justice is to maximize liberty, not the worth of liberty,
although Rawls makes it clear that, with the two basic principles taken together, the end of social justice requires that
"the basic structure is to be arranged to maximize the worth
to the least advantaged of the complete system of liberty
shared by all."[31]

But first things come first; to Rawls, the optimal expansion of the *system* of liberties cannot be held back for the
sake of mitigating inequalities of access or, as he puts it, for
the sake of promoting equality in the worth of liberty for
different social classes.

Robert Paul Wolff has pointed to another difficulty with
the construction of liberty in Rawls: he is less than clear

about what, more specifically, "the most extensive liberty" should *mean*.[32] In the abstract, liberty to Rawls is the end value to be optimized in a just society; yet in more low-flying contexts he subsumes liberty under a category that he calls "primary goods": all those things "which it is supposed that a rational man wants whatever else he wants"—"things" like "rights and liberties, opportunities and powers, income and wealth" and "a sense of one's own worth."[33] Rawls leaves it wide open, and dependent on each person's "life plan," how priorities among primary goods are to be ordered. Suppose, says Wolff, that according to some people's life plans, "political liberty is merely a means to private ends, not one of the principal ends itself";[34] suppose that most people in our kind of social order would prefer high incomes and wealth to political liberty?

There is a rather crucial ambiguity left unresolved in a philosophical perspective that first makes optimal liberty for all the ultimate criterion of a just social order, and then neglects to lay down rules of priority among liberties. There is no systematic attempt to discriminate between liberties according to their relative bearing on the most basic human needs, quite apart from the flaw, already pointed out, that equality of actual access to liberty is made secondary to the principle of equality of hypothetical access, or "the most extensive liberty" in the abstract. There is in Rawls's theory no attempt, either, to discriminate between liberties that serve to accommodate authentic human needs and those that would cater to manufactured wants and desires or to interests associated with individual or class privileges (see chapter 4 §2).

Rawls's obliviousness to the problem of classes in liberal-corporate societies has been noted by C. B. Macpherson, who objects to the narrowness of some liberal premises in what purports to be a general theory of justice.[35] It bears equal emphasis in an extended critique of Rawls that he tends to take for granted, as most liberals will, that large social inequalities can be justified by the alleged stake of all, including the poor, in continuing increases in production. Surely this is an obsolescent premise in an age that now must face up to the necessity of conserving energy and resources, protecting nature, and promoting simpler life styles in our part of the world so that at least the basic health needs of all of humanity can be met as soon as possible.

But the most crucial philosophical problem with liberalism's liberty, which returns to haunt even the relatively humane and sophisticated liberalism of Rawls, runs deeper than this. It has been well articulated in a recent work by Donald J. C. Carmichael. John Plamenatz many years ago hinted at the same problem when he exclaimed, in a critique of the individualist premises of the utilitarian conception of the good society: "What, indeed, could be less scientific than to construct the notion of man, in abstraction from society, and then to explain society in terms of his desires?"[36]

With greater depth and more precise formulations, to which I cannot do justice in this brief treatment, Carmichael refers to the premise of *agent-individualism* which is deeply embedded in what he calls the logic of the liberal political understanding.[37] In briefest outline, the agent-individualist premise assumes—and it is a false assumption, as Carmichael demonstrates in a review of some of the evidence, and by his own argument—that most human beings are and must continue to be individualist maximizers-of-advantage, basically indifferent to the welfare of others, rather than being capable of living and acting as social beings whose very sense of self can, and even in our society often does, incorporate the good of others or of the community.

This ontological fixation on agent-individualism, as Carmichael documents in relation to several fields of political science literature, dooms liberal political thought to a sterile and unimaginative vindication of a social order that institutionalizes competitiveness and market mentality, and pits the strong against the weak; it rules out otherwise realistic possibilities of new kinds of institutions that could make it easier for most people to be in tune with their own solidarity instincts and to exert themselves in the service of community well-being, the public good, or the high-priority needs of others as well as their own.

In a chapter specifically dealing with Rawls, Carmichael shows how this admirably humane philosopher, too, is a prisoner of his agent-individualist premises. Rawls is committed to the "indifference principle," in his assumption that the metaphoric parties to the "original position" would "take no interest in one another's interests."[38] This premise impoverishes the range of primary goods to be associated with Rawls's liberty: "It implicitly restricts the range of primary social goods to those which would be of value as much in isolation as in any social relations. Conversely, it excludes from the class of primary *social* goods any values which are peculiar to social existence." (His emphasis.)[39]

With respect to liberty specifically, Carmichael argues that in fact we tend to desire, and admire, human freedom in the context of pursuing excellence in worthwhile activities—in activities that are intrinsically rewarding and not exploitive of others' needs or interests, or in activities that benefit others as well, or serve the common good. However, the postulated agent-individualism of Rawls narrows liberty to the sense of freedom from interference with whatever a person happens to be doing;[40] and thus we find Rawls, for all his commitment to humanist values in the abstract, back in the same box with Isaiah Berlin: only negative freedom is upheld as a worthy ideal; the possibility of a positive freedom for most people to develop and thrive as socially committed beings is ruled out *a priori*.

In the middle of the last century John Stuart Mill warned, in the last lines of *On Liberty*, that "a State which dwarfs its men, in order that they may be more docile instruments in its hands even for beneficial purposes—will find that with small men no great thing can really be accomplished."[41] Drawing on Carmichael's critique of Rawls, and on his implicit censure of most liberal theorizing on liberty, I think a similar point can be stated as follows, less elegantly but equally worthy of being reflected on: to the extent that the liberal premise of agent-individualism prevails, our own time's political imagination will remain confined within the narrow boundaries of social systems in pursuit of competitive, private, possessive-individualist goals only.

It must be stressed again that Rawls is the most humanist of the liberal theorists whose views on liberty have been considered, with the exception, once again, of Thomas Hill Green, the champion of a positive liberty to make the best of ourselves in cooperation with others. Agent-individualism is a basic if sometimes hidden theme, an ontological premise, that remains ubiquitous not only in mainstream liberal-democratic thought, but also in contemporary positivist social science, as Carmichael's work illuminates in other chapters.[42]

There was a time when liberalism was a liberating philosophy for a relatively disadvantaged class. The most privileged classes of feudal society were safely barricaded, ideologically speaking, behind their supernaturally based claims to superiority and God-given preeminence, until modern rationalism grew strong enough to challenge the ruling political interpretations of God's will. Strong weapons of critical reason came into the hands of the new breed of liberal philosophers that followed in the wake of Hobbes's powerful and challenging contract theory. Liberal contractarians and utilitarians became an ideological force of emancipation from ancient God-given privileges and control over lands and common peoples.

For better and for worse the new liberal creed brought immense changes to our world. Greed and envy were set free in new and broader social classes, as were thoughts of rebellion, moral idealism and political imagination. The removal of the ancient standards was enormously liberating, but only for some social classes. In the many battles between greed and idealism within the rising classes, greed most often came out the winner. But as the bourgeoisie became powerful enough to take control of states, it learned to camouflage greed and exploitation under the banners of patriotism and of a new, initially Protestant, God, and eventually the new order became more firmly legitimated by the symbols and pretenses of democracy and political freedom articulated by the modern liberal ideologists.

Most liberal theorists, except for a few mavericks like T. H. Green, have tended to overlook how much has been lost to humanity under the liberal-capitalist regimes, especially to the well-being of the so-called lower classes, above all the world's peasants and landless workers. For practical purposes they have become reduced to being at best mere means of production, and at worst expendable means. The working classes in the industrializing societies were given the liberal symbols of liberty and, eventually, when this seemed safe, even the power to vote. But to make a daily living they had been forced away from their earlier homes on the land and into the jungle of merciless competition for scarce jobs and inadequate supplies of food and shelter. Their new rulers no longer recognized, even in principle, any objective standards of morality to which the most miserable could appeal, for Darwinism as a descriptive account of the evolution of animal species had been transformed into a moral justification for sacrificing, by the millions, and on the altar of liberty and progress, the losers in the struggle for social survival.

In North America the winners, the most successful entrepreneurs, those who came to be called the robber barons, eventually became anointed as this country's culture heroes, to take the place of royalty in this most liberal-democratic among liberal-democratic civilizations. Subsequently the flamboyant robber barons have been replaced by more publicity-shy executives and boards of giant corporations, who are now busily practicing their social Darwinism chiefly in Third World countries; in some places, such as the Amazon valley, this extends to pushing for a continuous genocide against indigenous peoples said to be in the way of "development" (see 6 §3). Within North America, welfarism and the symbols of affirmative action have mitigated the industrial strife of the 1930s and the racial strife of the 1960s, and a temporary stability appears to have been achieved as of now (1980), with public feelings running high against governmental inefficiencies and high public taxes and with little awareness of private corporate profiteering and enormous private taxes through inflated prices and interest rates. This apparent stability is in my view bound to terminate and give way to new social upheavals when the corporate waste of ecological and human resources, even in North America, comes close enough to endangering heavily populated areas. By the end of this century, I am convinced, the liberal ideology of continuous growth will have lost the remainder of its dwindling credibility.

To conclude: two kinds of myopia remain at the core of the prevailing liberal ideology. First, the liberties of main concern to the privileged classes, including us academics, liberties like free speech and free enterprise and the protection of all property rights, have come to be seen as the crucial rights that the state has an obligation to protect, unconditionally. On the other hand, liberties having to do with meeting the basic needs of the less privileged, like free access to quality health care, to guaranteed sustenance, and to the basic dignities of a comfortable life, are simply not seen at all as requirements of liberalism's liberty, even though liberal-democratic regimes at times may deem it expedient, or even morally right, to expand public health and welfare services. Second, it has come to be widely assumed that "human nature can't be changed": that most people are always going to remain selfish individualists, concerned *only* with the narrowly perceived best interests of themselves and their immediate kin, with time perspectives limited to a few years or, at most, one or two decades ahead. This narrow privatism, mind you, is seen not as a possibly necessary response to conditions of life under liberal-corporate capitalism, but as proof of permanent infirmities of human nature.

I assume in this work that it is premature to write off humanity as a lost cause. My most basic working hypothesis is that commonly observed defects in human behavior most probably reflect the conditions of life that so many people have to endure and have had to grow up with, rather than defects in the human gene pool. In the second chapter I shall attempt a realistic analysis of some of the major parameters of freedom and oppression in our society at this time. Realistic strategies of emancipation require first of all, I think, a critical analysis of where we are at this time; in this light we must weigh the adequacy of available resources of political thought in our search for viable strategies in the struggle toward freedom.

Modes of Oppression in
Liberal-Corporate Societies

1. AN OVERVIEW OF BASIC ASSUMPTIONS

MOST OF THE ANALYSIS and argument in this book deals with the relatively rich, highly industrialized, capitalist societies which in our time are often referred to as the countries of the First World. Alternatively I shall call them liberal-corporate systems, to distinguish them from the state-corporate systems of the so-called Second World. Most regimes of liberal-corporate countries claim to be democratic, and most of their state-corporate counterparts claim to be socialist. As I shall argue, "democracy" and "socialism" are terms that should be taken to refer to worthy aspirations, constructive utopias, but all claims that either of these two age-old aspirations have been achieved in specific countries, West or East, are at best innocently naive and at worst deliberate mystifications in the service of domination (see 3 §2).

I have argued in the first chapter that liberalism's conception of liberty, as exemplified in the writings of Locke and Bentham and, in our time, in those of Hayek, Berlin, and Rawls, is too narrow a concept, and too slanted to rights of ownership and other liberties most salient to the professional and business classes. The alternative approach to be introduced here, and elaborated on in the subsequent chapters, is to relate the concept of freedom to the whole range of the most basic human needs, so that every violation of a basic need by definition becomes an impairment of someone's (or many people's) freedom, or, as the other side of the coin, a manifestation of oppression.

As I shall argue in chapter 4, underneath cultural diversities and historical developments there remains a core of basic characteristics of the human species, including an objectively given hierarchy of the most basic human needs. On the rational humanist assumption that acceptable political institutions and public policies must meet human needs in the order of their importance to preserve life, health, and freedom, in that order, it now becomes in principle possible to establish objective, "naturally" given *priorities* among liberties. But this argument will have to wait its turn (see 4 §2).

This chapter will mainly be an exercise in conceptual clarification: I shall define "freedom" as a much broader concept than liberalism's liberty,* and spell out some general assumptions associated with this concept, before I proceed to define three component subconcepts of freedom and the three corresponding modes of oppression. Each subconcept of freedom and of oppression will be the topic of a subsequent chapter.

If freedom is an ever-present ideal, so is oppression a permanent reality. More strictly speaking, oppression is the historical human condition, but it has been and is tempered, according to time and place and historical situation, by varying kinds and amounts of freedom: more for some social classes, less for others.

My assumption is not that every human being aspires to freedom, or to a fuller freedom. It is well known that extreme oppression can cause apathy, and that "bread and circuses," or ideological mystification, can make even slaves feel free and contented. "Slavery is freedom" is one of the regime-legitimating slogans in George Orwell's *1984*,[1] a work that captures and magnifies some present political techniques of domination.

For this writer, however, as for Orwell, and surely for most readers of books like this one, freedom remains an ever-present ideal, in that we attribute to every human being *qua* human at least a potential desire for being free, or for achieving a fuller freedom. It is axiomatic in my argument that a fuller self-realization, insofar as it does not take a

---

*But let me remind the reader here that "freedom" and "liberty" will be used interchangeably in this work, to refer to the broad concept to be developed here.

course destructive of the rights of others, should be desired and struggled for, *with* all of mankind when possible, but also *in behalf* of those parts of mankind whose depth of oppression may have incapacitated them and placed them on the sidelines of the struggle for liberty.

I take it to be a fact of social life, then, that every human being's freedom is impaired to some extent; it is less than complete. In this trivial sense, at least, oppression is everywhere; but more about this shortly. What is practically important is to distinguish between different modes of oppression and between degrees of oppression: some kinds of oppression are more destructive, more crippling than others, depending on (a) mode of oppression, (b) degree of severity (e.g., how relentless, how long-lasting, how extreme the means of punishment, etc.), and (c) on how basic are the human needs that are suppressed or violated.

2. THE UBIQUITY OF OPPRESSION IN LIBERAL-CORPORATE SOCIETIES

On the theme of the ever-presence of oppression, it is worth observing at the outset that even the members of the most privileged classes in liberal-corporate societies are in a real sense oppressed. Let me recall a memorable session we had at the University of Alberta with the late and lamented Saul Alinsky,[2] in the fall of 1971, I believe, less than a year before his death.

After his lecture and his replies to questions from a large audience, he was asked, in a small group, over a glass of beer, whether it was true that he could organize rich people as well as poor people. I cannot, alas, give a rendering in the colorful language in which he couched his reply, but he gave a vivid report on a then recent session at Dartmouth College where he had been invited to meet with the high brass of the I.T.T. (a company so large, he said, that General Motors by comparison is like a corner grocery store), who wanted to know what could make a radical like Alinsky tick.

Alinsky said that in their first session, when that question was put to him, he decided to turn the table on his hosts—

an all-male cast, of course: "I want first to know what makes *you* people put up with *your* oppression";—I am not quoting Alinsky, just paraphrasing—"you belong to the jet set all right, but when you're off to Paris you stick to your corn flakes on account of your ulcers, and you stay away from the night spots because you worry about your high blood pressure. And you wake up in the morning next to an old battle-axe whom you know you should have divorced twenty years ago. I suspect that the only thing that keeps you people going is regular doses of double scotch." There was a long silence after this, said Alinsky, until finally some-one at the table burst out: "I kind of feel like having a dou-ble scotch right now!"

Capitalists, too, are oppressed, at least in the sense that as individuals they are of course subjected to pressures of many kinds, pressures dictated by the exigencies of the system, pressures that force them to engage in activities that intrin-sically are far from rewarding and are sometimes revolting. Tycoons, too, engage in alienated labor. While they tend to be handsomely compensated, financially speaking, their loss in freedom may be quite heavy, and virtually inescapable; not many will have the strength of mind to escape, as did one Swedish heir to a wood products fortune whom I met many years ago, from a life of plush servitude to wealth to the relative freedom and poverty of a life of making pots in France.

Bertell Ollman, in his book on Marx's concept of aliena-tion, devotes a chapter to the alienation of the capitalist class, in which he points out that the forces of the all-powerful market, the so-called free market that dictates terms to all buyers and sellers, establishes dependencies and stunts human relationships within the capitalist class, too. Ollman suggests that we "compare how capitalists treat their fellow men with human relations in communist society to see the degree to which capitalists are socially alienated."[3] In an empirical sense such a comparison is not a simple matter, as the kind of communist society Ollman has in mind exists only in our imagination, or at any rate in Marx's and Ollman's. But few would quarrel, I suspect, with the basic contention that cap-italists, too, live in a world that is short on basic trust, brotherly love, and freedom to live beautiful, intrinsically rewarding lives.

I would like to make two points on the possible psychological impact of an understanding that capitalists, too, are lacking in freedom, before I return to the general discussion of freedom and oppression in our kind of society. First, among corporate executives themselves there might possibly arise a yearning to cast off their chains to job and social status and respectability, as apparently Alinsky in his more optimistic moments had hoped; perhaps deep down they might really want to get away from it all, either by opting out or by becoming rebels. At latest report, though, the I.T.T. is still going strong, and is as busy as ever turning Third World poverty into private wealth and working with the CIA to rescue backward, unreliable countries from incipient socialism and communism.

My second point pertains to the impression it makes on everybody else when they come to think that capitalists, too, are just folks, who are in a bind and often find their hands tied, like most of us. In North America, in particular, where many of the rich mingle with lesser breeds, a downright empathy with their plight is something that can serve further to stabilize the system; once people see that the rich, too, are caught within the system, they are left with a lack of visible villains of the sort found in the perennial *Daily Worker*-type cartoons of top-hatted, enormously fat Wall Street tycoons. "Our own capitalism's demise seems slated for yet another postponement," as Andrew Hacker wrote not long ago, "until its attackers find ways of rousing mass anger against an edifice whose power depends neither on the personal qualities of those who hold it nor on their membership in a ruling class."[4]

The fact remains that the concentration of wealth at the top of our social system is associated with a concentration of poverty at the bottom, while the middle layers are economically oppressed in the sense of constantly having to struggle to compete for scarce employment and career opportunities and to pay for scarce consumer goods and status symbols. As Joe Conason and Jack Newfield recently put it in a heartwarming Christmastime series on New York's "One

Hundred Greediest" in the *Village Voice*, "generally it is
often the greediest who make the neediest possible."[5] However, most middle-class Americans, daily struggling to cope
with high prices, high rents or mortgage payments, and high
taxes, have been taught that *their* economic oppression has
nothing to do with exploitation or with private oligopoly
ownership of capital, for supposedly it is "the private sector" that generates the nation's wealth and pays most of the
wages and taxes. Instead, their anger is directed against the
poor, the "welfare cheaters," the supposedly lazy and undeserving whose "free rides" are enjoyed at the expense of
all hard-working taxpayers. Edgar Z. Friedenberg has with
his inimitable grace and wit demonstrated how a well or-
chestrated, yet profoundly righteous moral indignation
against our society's underdogs has left the top dogs virtually invulnerable to political criticism, and indeed to fair
taxation and regulation policies as well.[6]

I trust I have made it clear that in my own commitment
to freedom I am a universalist. Nobody should be left out in
the good society to come, the free society, not even those
who are now very rich. And with today's less than free
society, our empathy should extend to their oppression, too,
philosophically speaking, even if the need for emergency relief from stark oppression is more immediate in other classes.
Before I attempt to formulate more precisely my concepts
of oppression and of freedom, which will serve as baselines
for my analysis of prevailing modes of oppression and of
possible strategies of political emancipation in the remaining
chapters, let me explicate the sense in which our kind of
liberal-corporate society is indeed an oppressive system,
when measured against our human possibilities.

First of all, which concrete societies are we talking about?
It need not be specified exactly how many societies should
be called liberal-corporate for present purposes, other than
the United States and Canada. Other predominantly white
Commonwealth countries, surely; most West and South
European countries also, possibly all; and Japan. "First
World" countries is a convenient shorthand phrase, which
will be used. This phrase, too, is appropriately nonspecific in
the periphery of its field of reference; countries like Portugal

or Mexico, for example, are in many respects more like Third World countries than they are, or were, like North American and other First World societies.

What do all liberal-corporate or First World countries have in common? An industrial base, first of all, with much less than one third of the population engaged in agriculture. Also, there are incentives for most of the population to acquire literacy and other elementary skills required of industrial as well as clerical hired workers. And most important of all, at least for my purposes, production is largely for sale and for profit: it is a market economy, in which large corporations predominate, and keep growing and consolidating their power. This kind of society provides "a high-intensity market setting" in William Leiss's phrase, with "a very large number of commodities available to large numbers of people, and . . . many commodities are the result of highly complex industrial production processes involving sophisticated scientific and technological knowledge."[7] In fact, not only does the job market require fairly advanced literacy skills; so does the modern consumer market, too, in our kind of society.

As Alan Wolfe stresses in a recent work,[8] this kind of social order keeps accumulating expanding capital for most of the larger corporations, so that the distribution of wealth becomes more and more lopsided, and this creates problems of legitimation: how can most people be kept loyal to a system that manifestly keeps rewarding mainly the wealthiest class? That is where the welfare state and the illusion of democracy come in.

As Murray Edelman has taught us, when conflicts of interest arise, or seem imminent, between well organized elites and poorly organized masses, the usual kind of grand "democratic" compromise is that the economic interests and the power claims of elites are satisfied while for the mass of unorganized people there is a generous treat of symbolic satisfaction, like flattering rhetoric, nice-looking legislation embodying high principles, and even, perhaps, new Federal agencies to look after the public interest. But such agencies, in fairness to private financial interests, tend to be staffed with *their* representatives, or else with people eager for lucrative private interest careers after their public service, people who will be anxious to make friends within the industries they are charged with trying to regulate. Edelman discusses at length the Federal Communications Commission as a case in point, where a public that had become outraged over offensive commercialism over the air waves was given symbolic satisfaction while at the same time the private interests were left free to continue exploiting the air waves commercially, with very few restrictions.[9]

To come back to Wolfe's concern with how an increasingly unequal distribution of wealth is being legitimated to the dispossessed majority, the basic processes are the same as those just described, on a grander scale. The public in our kind of society are given two kinds of satisfaction: welfare state–type programs, just enough to prevent riot-prone anger among those who would have the strength to riot, which incidentally explains why most old age pensioners live in conditions of bleak poverty; and ostensibly democratic election procedures, serving to foster the illusion that the People is King, in the United States as in other liberal-corporate societies.

That illusion, to be called the democratic makebelieve, and the functions it serves today will be discussed in the next chapter. In this immediate context belongs only a brief account of the origins of electoral institutions in this country. The United States Constitution was hammered out by good leaders who wanted only the best for their own class *and* country, and who did their best to achieve a liberal society without running the risk of having it deteriorate into a democracy; therefore the emphasis on checks and balances, to emasculate potential factionalism, potential tyranny, *and* potential popular power.

As for the subsequent advances toward more democratic electoral institutions, they were promoted by a variety of political leaders, some of whom were idealistic believers in populist democracy, while others were mainly trying to look good to new voters and achieve party advantage. One thing that all the pioneers for the cause of a nearly universal suffrage had in common was a conviction that thereby the whole American people would develop a real sense of a stake in our political system, and be disposed to preserving it—checks, balances, and all—thus removing or weakening any possible incentives toward revolution or other drastic changes in property relationships. When the income tax was first introduced in 1861, and much later the progressive income tax, there were those who saw these newfangled attempts at confiscation of private property as proof that democracy had gone too far in this country. But times have been changing, and even most right-wing Republicans today realize that a considerable welfare apparatus, which has to be paid for somehow, is as necessary as democratic electoral institutions to keep the balance of the population politically quiescent and pliable. Their argument with the liberals is mainly over political symbolism: people like Barry Goldwater and Ronald Reagan still want the media to promote an image of America as a land of rugged individualists, while at the other end of the spectrum of political power the liberal Democrats favor the image of America as a land of compassion, where the poor should not be starving; they should be given food, housing, and color TV sets, so long as they don't demand political power, too.

To put an end to poverty, in the sense of dependency and relative deprivation, is out of the question in practical American politics. For in our kind of society there must be competition for scarce goods, or else people would not exert themselves, according to profoundly held liberal convictions from the early days of capitalist development, when scarcity was an all-important fact. If we run out of objective scarcity, as has happened in this country, then artificial scarcity is required; the manufacture of artificial scarcity is being taken care of in two principal ways: (1) by limiting most people's incomes below what is required to secure good health and free time for education and (other) meaningful leisure activities, and (2) by inducing most people to want far more commodities than they need or can pay for.

The corporations that dominate our market system have been very successful on both counts: they have maintained huge wage differentials between their highest and their lowest paid employees, and their investments in advertising their products, thus making them seem scarce in relation to potential demand, are sometimes larger than the actual production costs. As C. Wright Mills observed, a good ad campaign not only sells a product, but promotes a general pre-

disposition to irrational impulse buying, thus smoothing the
path for future ads for other products that few people rationally would desire to buy.[10]

The further benefit gained for the corporate interests from
this two-pronged promotion of perceptions of scarcity is
that most people become too preoccupied with consumption
gadgetry and too enamored of their possessions to have
much of an attention span left for ethical and political concern for the good of their communities, and less still for the
good of all the less-favored communities, those on the other
side of the tracks and those beyond the oceans.

In fact, the ethics of possessive individualism, to use C. B.
Macpherson's indispensable term,[11] becomes so taken for
granted that a learned British economist recently could conclude a paper on poverty in the First World with the flat
assertion that it cannot be abolished *because* there are too
few among us who are really poor: "for the first time in
history the poor have no political power. And it is not obvious that there is any force at work to ensure that they will
acquire any. In that case the poor will always be with us."[12]
Wilfred Beckerman, whom we shall meet again in a later
chapter (see 6 § 1), evidently takes it for granted that reasonably affluent people will never be capable of acting from a
sense of political justice: they will always be too busy consuming and earning to inconvenience themselves even very
slightly in order to abolish abject poverty in their own society. Beckerman estimates (it is irrelevant that I would
want to dispute the figures he uses) that it would take less
than 1 percent of the GNP in the most advanced countries
to abolish poverty, if anybody else but the poor themselves
could ever take an interest in such a purpose.

This lack of political consciousness, in the sense of inabil-
ity to perceive one's stake in bringing about better communities and better societies, is a fact; while Beckerman clearly
exaggerates the extent and depth of the apolitical privatism
in our society, or in his, the British, *he* obviously exists, and
there are probably millions of liberals and conservatives who
share his myopia regarding human possibilities. Empirically
speaking, in the shallow sense, they are right: large numbers
and perhaps majorities of North Americans today cannot
see beyond their own immediate group's short-term, private

interests. If so, then to me this represents a *problem*; to Beckerman it seems to represent an immutable social fact.

I think this apparent unwillingness of many people to be inconvenienced, even ever so mildly, in order that the most basic needs of other persons can be met, illustrates as clearly as any one observation can the two-sided nature of oppression inherent to modern liberal-capitalist social systems: first, they tend to allocate wealth so as to continue to increase the fortunes and the power of a few, while deepening the dependency and the relative or absolute deprivation of the many. Second, they continually promote the ideology that the system is truly competitive and truly fair; that wealth depends on effort; and that the losers in the struggle consequently have only themselves to blame.

On top of the objective victimization of the disadvantaged classes, therefore, comes the flattening out of perhaps most people's ethical and political consciousness. This severely limits the possibilities of political solidarity among the have-nots and makes their plight either invisible to or seemingly irrelevant to most members of the privileged classes. Thus, the cries of the victims are muffled in our kind of social order; to make matters worse, the hearing of those who are on top is seriously impaired.

3. THE MODES OF OPPRESSION: INTRODUCTORY

After this brief account of what I take to be some basic features of oppression in our kind of society, it is time for a more careful analytical approach. The remainder of this chapter will be given to an introductory presentation of my conceptions of levels of freedom and modes of oppression, with their rationale and some of their most general political implications.

It is true but, I have conceded, trivial, to state that everybody in our society, or in every society, is oppressed. If "oppression" is the negative of "freedom," that is the same as saying that everybody is less than fully free, which is hardly news to anyone. In no kind of social order in the real world can any one individual be fully free. Even the dictator in a near-totalitarian society will be constrained in many ways by the historical situation and by each new policy decision, as well as by his or her subjects' actual and possible action propensities. The questions of oppression that are of concern to political theorists and practitioners of politics are questions of *kinds* and *degrees* of oppression, or of freedom (see above, 2 §1).

How to define freedom? Most fundamentally, I think, "freedom" should refer to self-expression, the expression of the self. But what is the self? What if there is no self to express?

a. Locus of Freedom: the Human Self

I think there is a self in every human being, even in a psychotic, or in a severely mentally disabled person, or in a newborn infant. The self is associated with the will to stay alive, or even with the will to die (or with the ultimate decision to give up the struggle to stay alive). The self is, in Solomon Asch's phrase, the conscious representation of the ego,[13] or one's perception of what kind of human being one is, whether that perception be dim or clear. The self may be embryonic, or crippled, but it is always there, or so we must assume, even as an act of faith if necessary, unless we are prepared to write off some categories of individuals as less than human.

That perception of one's own self is determined in part by one's inner processes and in part by external appraisals.[14] Within the unconscious, there are instinctual drives and there are inhibitions and conditioning due to experience; and individuals differ widely in the stability of the unconscious compromises that have been achieved between, on the one hand, the id, or the instincts associated with infantile hedonism, the pleasure principle in Freud's language, and on the other hand the superego, or the inhibitions and promptings from the superego, or the reality principle. A "healthy ego" is associated with the stability of such a balance, whether it is slightly tilted in favor of impulsiveness or in favor of control and responsibility. I said "slightly" tilted, for the task of the ego is to mediate between the two powers, as it were, for neither of them can be entirely suppressed. Without a

functioning id there would be no individual life, only a programmed automaton; without a functioning superego there
would be no human life, only inhuman psychopaths, persons
disconnected from social and even physical reality. Both
extremes are psychologically impossible; approximations exist
and require psychiatric treatment.

One cannot speak with exactitude in these matters. There
is no way of defining how broad are the limits within which
the balance between the id and the superego can tilt before
we confront not a healthy person but one that borders on
being either an automaton or a psychopath. But for practical purposes we are aided by the fact that socialization processes within each community and culture determine the
norms for self-appraisal as well as for the appraisal of others.
Unusually large imbalances are difficult to live with both
consciously and unconsciously; both reflected appraisals and
self-appraisals will push the ego to battle with either the id
or the superego, depending on which appears to have been
favored, in relation to the culturally determined proper mid-
point.

But the battling ego is not necessarily victorious, either
in the struggle to readjust the tilt or in the initial struggle to
achieve a stable and socially acceptable id/superego balance in
the first place.When self-expression founders on the weakness
or underdevelopment of the self, it is generally due to the
weakness of the ego; the ego has succeeded in establishing
only precarious and short-lived truces in the continuing contest between the pleasure principle and the reality principle.
This is a scary way to live. Where the ego is weak and un-
steady, it tends to "look the other way"—block out unpleas-
ant memories, develop distorted views of reality and of the
self, and gradually build up a makebelieve system of beliefs
that permit and also require the person's partial abdication
from reality. This is a depth-psychological parallel to Marx's
observation that people who neglect the study of history
are doomed to repeat it. Neurotics, too, are likely to repeat
their own maladaptive behaviors, as their access to certain
kinds of new experience is blocked and as their capacity for
processing new experience is impaired.

Let us go back to the fundamental conception of freedom
as self-expression. The self is the perception of what kind of

a person one is, I have said; this self-perception depends on internal as well as external circumstances: it depends on an ego in reasonably firm control over a stable id/superego balance, not too badly tilted in either direction, and on reasonably positive external appraisals. These appraisals will be favorably influenced by a firm and acceptable ego control, although in times of change and in situations of cultural diversity, appraisals may be negatively influenced by differences between ideologies or cultural norms. In a sense all education and all social change depend on the power of external appraisals to influence patterns of ego control and the *selves* that go with them. But the point of immediate concern, in the process of defining "self" and "self-expression," is the observation that a healthy ego will not be threatened by moderately negative appraisals from all but a few of the most significant others, these few possibly including a spouse, other family members, a few close friends. Negative appraisals from more distant persons will be treated as input of limited importance that may or may not call for gradual modifications in one's established id/superego balance. Precariously functioning egos, on the other hand, may become quite badly affected even by mildly negative appraisals, and even from total strangers, and the person may respond with hostility or aggression, thus further increasing the likelihood of future negative appraisals.

The self, then, is shaped by internal as well as external factors and reflects the person's individuality as well as his or her humanity, and it reflects one's conception of pleasure as well as one's conception of reality. Let me now proceed to observe that freedom in the sense of self-expression requires (1) the capacity to express one's self, (2) the opportunity to do so, and also (3) the "good reason" or incentive to express and further develop one's self. The capacity for self-expression is ultimately a question of what goes on inside the person; the question of opportunity is about whether other persons or circumstances will allow or restrict one's self-expression; and the question of incentive, finally, is about whether one's culture or knowledge encourages or discourages self-expression.[15]

Freedom, then, is a question of relationships (1) within

the person; (2) between persons, or persons and organizations, or persons and collectivities; and (3) between persons and their own culture. So is oppression: (1) Within the person, the conscious self can be *alienated* (a) from awareness of basic needs, impulses, wishes, or (b) from objective potentialities for growth toward optimal humanity—optimal competency and optimal moral stature. (2) Between persons, or within organizations, communities, or society, persons can be physically *coerced,* or *deprived,* or victimized by *violence.* (3) Within the confines of a given culture, ideology, or socialization process, persons can be *dominated* so that they willingly come to serve other people's perceived interests at the expense of their own; or they come to take their own exploitation, serfdom, or other kind of accustomed oppression for granted.

b. Alienation, or Impaired Psychological Freedom

Consider first alienation, or impaired intrapersonal freedom. "Know Thyself" was the ancient Greek admonition. "An unexamined life is not worth living," Socrates is supposed to have said. Animals don't examine their own lives, but free human beings do. Even slaves are in this sense free; they can formulate questions to themselves about what kinds of life they want to live, or ought to live, within available options. It is a kind of freedom that no unsophisticated tyrant can take away.[16] Socrates was in this sense a free man as a prisoner, even as he drank his hemlock.

I call freedom in this sense *psychological freedom*, and I define this term as "degree of harmony between basic motives and overt behavior."[17] Optimal capacity for self-expression means free access to the whole range of basic motivations, and optimal self-knowledge, *and* self-acceptance or self-esteem. Not all one's basic motives need to be acted on, for the healthy ego is the rational judge of what acts are appropriate in each kind of situation, external and internal. And not every basic motive needs to be positively esteemed, of course. The empirical point to be made is that the self as a whole needs to feel worthwhile. What happens when self-knowledge is incompatible with positive self-esteem is that the offending aspect of self-knowledge is blocked from consciousness; it is *repressed*, along with the memories that would remind one of the repressed self-insight.

There is no space, or necessity, for undertaking a discussion of the Freudian theories of repression and neurosis here, and I shall use Freudian terms without elaborating on their context. The point to be made is that repression by definition negates psychological freedom and leads to neurosis or, in more extreme cases, to psychosis, which amounts to a broader-gauged and more irrevocable departure from reality.

Much of Freud's life was devoted to the treatment of individual neuroses of many kinds, aiming at "making conscious the unconscious, removing the repressions, filling in the gaps in memory."[18] Marx used a different term though a related concept; in his "Philosophical Manuscripts of 1844" he was concerned with *alienation*: "*The alienation of self-consciousness* establishes *thinghood*."[19] Marx's concern with alienation, or *self-estrangement* as he also called it, was historically specific and focused on man as a producer, as a worker, in a capitalist system that reduced the worker to a thing, a commodity, an object with a price. The worker in capitalist society is, according to Marx, deprived of his opportunity to become a creative producer, a priceless human being, someone who can create values through his or her own freely chosen work efforts.[20]

Let me attempt to extrapolate from Marx's concept of estranged labor under capitalism, to formulate a Marxist concept of alienation that could apply to the human condition generally, thus making it subject to empirical examination whether or how far there is alienation beyond the capitalist system and beyond the processes of hired labor and work. In the spirit of Marx as well as Freud, I think, the term alienation may be used to refer to all neuroses that are quite generally induced in a given society, indicating tensions and conflicts between people's consciousness and some of their basic needs and motives. These tensions and conflicts may either lead to acute suffering (and to psychoses, when the neuroses become agonizing beyond endurance) when the repressed needs and motives are central and persistent, with the required mechanisms of defense precarious and heavy with anxieties. Alternatively, the neuroses or the alienation may become chronic and stable in individuals whose growth and self-development needs are repressed while the more basic physical, health, and affiliation needs are being met (priorities among categories of basic needs will be discussed in chapter 4).

In *The Structure of Freedom* I attempted a deeper-going analysis of the conceptual relationship between psychological freedom and other levels of freedom, as well as levels of security (avoidance of anxiety, fear, and objective danger); also, I attempted an empirical assessment of determinants of major kinds of impairment of psychological freedom, with special emphasis on *authoritarianism* as a syndrome of neurotic predispositions to avoid recognizing basic motives of aggression against authority figures within one's own unconscious.[21] This emphasis was chosen both because neurotic authoritarianism is a common behavior tendency that creates serious obstacles to prospects for democratic citizenship and other democratic human relationships, and because a massive research literature has produced a fair amount of knowledge about manifestations of authoritarian syndromes as well as, more speculatively, about their likely origin and development.

The emphasis in this work, relative to psychological freedom, is on the problem of understanding and overcoming alienation. That will be the main theme in chapter 5. Only one further point about the nature of psychological freedom must be made right here: I shall argue that man is by nature a social as well as an individual human being, and that a society such as ours, which tends to magnify our consciousness of being individuals and to make us forget, or even repress, our social solidarity impulses, not only makes us in an objective sense complicit in the continuing oppression of the least privileged in the modern world; it also profoundly impairs our individual psychological freedom, which must be assessed in comparison to the levels of psychological freedom attainable under hypothetical conditions following the abolition of alienation. The surpassing of alienation-producing social institutions, therefore, must be the overriding aim to dictate our choice of strategies in the struggle for optimal psychological freedom, a crucial part of which, at least for our kind of society, must be the struggle to overcome alienation. And alienation must today be understood as a mode of oppression that is not limited to the working class, or to the work roles of exploited industrial laborers; nor is alienation to be found only in capitalist or liberal-corporate societies, as we shall see.

c. Coercion, Deprivation, Violence:
Impaired Social Freedom

Now let us consider the most visible and obvious varieties of oppression: those involving coercion, deprivation, and/or violence. These are impairments of *social* freedom, or freedom in the conventionally most common sense: freedom in relations between people or between people and groups or organizations. Liberal writers, including Hayek, Berlin, and Rawls, as I related in the first chapter, have regarded this as the only justifiable conception of freedom, while my position is that we require a conception of freedom that combines three levels, or three dimensions, corresponding to the three basic modes of oppression that keep us repressed, oppressed, and underdeveloped as human beings, or less fully human than we could become. In *The Structure of Freedom* I defined social freedom as "the relative absence of external restraints on individual behavior."[22] Today I would have to say "on individual action or behavior," as I take "action" to refer to intentional activity and "behavior" to refer to whatever we do that is merely reactive, habitual, more or less automatic, and utterly predictable and therefore favored by measurement-minded social scientists, who for a time even liked to call themselves behavioral scientists; thus we flaunted the grievous limitations of our work. I shall use "activity" as the broader term to include both action and behavior. Whatever imposes unwanted restraints on a person's desired activity, then, restricts his or her social freedom, unless or until the person comes to take the restraints for granted, or even to crave them. From then on there is a problem of cultural freedom instead.

Restraints above a certain degree of severity, which prove effective in keeping the individual from doing what he or she would want to do, will be called *coercion*. Coercion may be deliberate, like incarceration or involuntary military service, or be a matter of circumstance, like starvation or lack of adequate shelter. Restraints that inflict suffering will be called *deprivation*, whether or not they actually coerce—that is, bend the will of the victims. Coercion or deprivation that either threaten or bring about serious physical harm will be called *violence*, which I shall consider, along with writers as different as Hobbes, Gandhi, and Camus, the most grievous political evil, which legitimate politics must make it a top priority to combat, reduce, and do away with.

You will understand that our freedom in the social sense is restricted in many ways that amount to neither coercion, deprivation, or violence. Living together in any society imposes innumerable do's and don'ts, after all. Most of these come to be taken for granted by most people, and so are removed from the realm of "perceived restraints." But, as John Stuart Mill argued so eloquently in *On Liberty*, conventions that most people take for granted can impose severe deprivation on certain individuals, oftentimes imposing social sanctions that hurt worse than legal punishment would.[23] My point here is that there is a large gray area between being coerced or deprived, on the one hand, and on the other hand taking various everyday constraints totally for granted. Our daily lives limit our social freedom in many relatively trivial ways, too, of which we are fully or dimly aware from time to time. Many perceived external restraints on our daily activities are either benign or too trivial to worry about.

Of political concern, then, are losses of social freedom by way of violence, deprivation, and coercion, in that order, if the overriding principle that human lives must not be harmed needlessly is to be maintained.

A particularly urgent aspect of the problem of social freedom in our time is the problem of deprivation and violence that we may be inflicting on future generations, now that we have become aware of how recklessly our generation, or our political-economic system, is going about depleting and poisoning our planet's nonrenewable resources, now nearing the point of endangering even its life-sustaining biosphere. But a further consideration of the problems of social freedom, and of the strategies of emancipation relevant to social freedom, must wait till chapter 4; a fuller consideration of the problem of protecting the life chances of future generations will be attempted in chapter 6.

d. Domination: Impaired Cultural Freedom

"*Domination*" will refer to the mode of oppression that leaves the victims oblivious to their oppression.[24] What is impaired is their *cultural* freedom, their freedom to outgrow culturally prescribed, conventional, or ideological restraints. Symbolic freedom, or autonomy, or potential freedom, are alternate terms that could serve the same concept. In *The Structure of Freedom* I preferred the term "potential freedom," defined as "the relative absence of unperceived external restraints on individual behavior."[25] In the same context, by way of illustration, I quoted the famous lament of that great French aristocrat Alexis de Tocqueville about tendencies in America toward majority tyranny. Royal tyrannies, he pointed out, make people obey but do not subdue their will, "but the majority possesses a power that is physical and moral at the same time, which acts upon the will as much as upon the actions and represses not only all contest, but all controversy."[26]

While chieftains and kings through the ages have ruled by visible force of arms in addition to varying resources of authority and charisma, our contemporary ruling classes and power elites are in a position to hide their stick, as it were, in the same closet where the paraphernalia for "states of emergency" are being kept. Traditional techniques of visible intimidation and punishment have increasingly been replaced by the far more sophisticated and unobtrusive modern instrumentalities of domination. As I will show in the next chapter, in our parts of the modern world the fine arts of domination have become perfected to the point where the dominated tend to be taught, and to believe, that they are the masters and that their rulers are really their servants; this is what the myth of democracy achieved is all about (and the myth of socialism achieved serves a corresponding function in state-corporate societies today).

Only a few additional conceptual points need to be made

in this context. "Cultural freedom" is a much trickier concept than the other two sub-concepts of freedom, in that it would be absurd to state, without qualifying limits, that the more cultural freedom we can achieve the better off we are. In our daily lives, and even for sustaining our individual selves, we all need a lot of "unperceived external restraints" on our activities, even on our thoughts. We all need our bearings, our cultural contexts; we need friends and associates and communities to help us direct and run our lives; we are social beings, and every healthy person needs to live in close, and in a broad sense restraining, association with at least a few other persons. In *this* sense like atoms, if I may exaggerate a little, individual human beings cannot make it on their own, divorced from all restraining norms and other persons.

e. Exploitive, Paternalistic, and Fraternal Restraints on Cultural Freedom

On this level of analysis of freedom it is necessary, first of all, to distinguish exploitive from nonexploitive restraints on cultural freedom (compare Macpherson's concept of "counter-extractive liberty" above, 1 §2, but keep in mind that in this context we are talking about freedom from ideologically or traditionally "accepted" oppression, not of freedom from blatantly coercive and visible oppression). Every traditional culture imposes restraints on human activities that most people take for granted (and for those who don't take them for granted, problems of social freedom, not of cultural freedom, arise). Some of these are surely in the common interest of all, while others just as surely are in the interest of preserving various kinds of prerogatives for the privileged classes or castes at the expense of the freedom or well-being of most others, who are aware of no option but to obey and comply.

A critical social theory is needed, therefore, to distinguish traditions that ought to be honored from those that, at least from a rational humanist perspective, should be questioned and perhaps be resisted or done away with.

Having distinguished exploitive from nonexploitive restraints on cultural freedom we must proceed to distinguish, among nonexploitive categories of restraint, between those that are paternalistic and those that are fraternal, in intent or in effect. Unlike exploitive manipulation, paternalistic manipulation is ostensibly, and perhaps even in fact, serving or intending to serve the other person's or persons' best interests. When for example we relate to our children, most of us rarely are conscious of any exploitive intent. Much of John Stuart Mill's argument in *On Liberty* is that all paternalistic pressures that coercively limit the actual or perceived options of adults, unlike those of children, are to be condemned, at least when the adults are "civilized" Europeans or Americans. I want to make the same point, and in relation to all adults, about unobtrusive paternalistic manipulation: it should with few exceptions be condemned. In principle that should apply in relation to children as well, I think, except where their safety or health or that of others is at stake. What is wrong with apparently nonexploitive, paternalistic influencing, even if we are to assume that it is in fact nonexploitive rather than a form of disguised exploitation? Paternalistic influencing still involves one person choosing priorities for another, attempting to program him or her without bringing all the available options out in the open, and without attempting to assist the other person, through frank dialogue, in reaching his or her own decisions.

That is what fraternal influencing processes seek to accomplish: an optimal articulation of issues followed by an optimal freedom of choice for each individual in matters affecting mainly his or her own life, subject only to such friendly urgings as others may attempt, others who care for that individual's welfare, yet who also care for the individual's ultimate right to reach his or her own decisions. Fraternal influencing processes may or may not be effective in reaching their intended goals in each case, but in general they are certainly a desirable category of impediments to untrammeled cultural freedom.

In the modern state's repertoire of domination, exploitive and paternalistic ideological manipulation intersect all the time. While in rhetoric and even, perhaps, in the consciousness of many power holders and influentials, every major policy decision is made "in the best interest of the public," less presentable exploitive motivations, less likely to be admitted to, are frequently in the picture as well; perhaps most of the time. For my present purpose, though, which is to clarify the various modes of oppression conceptually, it is enough to point out in principle the distinction between exploitive and paternalistic domination; in political practice the two tend to merge. For the development of strategies for the struggle to overcome domination it makes very little difference whether the people in charge are, or merely pretend to be, motivated by commonweal priorities, such as they choose to order them.

When we seek ways to struggle more effectively for a fuller freedom from domination, the ideal cannot be an untrammeled New Left–type vision of enabling everybody to "do their own thing," however. As we shall see, our most basic human needs are social even before they are individual; while the ideal of a more complete emancipation must include a more advanced capacity to perceive, to question, and to resist many now accepted aspects of our socialization, ideology, and culture, even an optimal emancipation from domination does require some firm human community bonds with fraternal restraining influences. Solipsism bears only a superficial, psychologically and historically untenable relationship to individual autonomy, or cultural freedom as here understood.[27]

What makes the problems of cultural freedom (or, more precisely, freedom from exploitive as well as paternalistic domination) such a major problem particularly in our own time is that science and technology have accelerated the development of new techniques of manipulation, until it now, to paraphrase but also to update Lincoln, is becoming not only possible, but disturbingly easy for strategically placed power elites to launch projects designed to "fool all of the people all of the time."

In chapter 3 I will attempt an analysis of domination in our liberal-corporate kind of society, and discuss strategies for exposing and transcending domination. It will be seen that in the chapters following the present one I shall reverse the order in which I have here introduced the three modes of oppression, along with the three component concepts of freedom: I shall deal with cultural freedom and domination first; then with social freedom versus violence, deprivation, and coercion; and last with psychological freedom and the problem of overcoming or moving beyond alienation.

3

To Expose and Transcend Domination

IN THIS CHAPTER I propose to begin just below the surface of tangible, visible oppression, and to move toward only a moderate-depth level of analysis. On the surface, as visible phenomena, are the issues to be dealt with in the next chapter: coercion, deprivation, and violence, the flagrant impairments of social freedom. Impairments of cultural freedom are by definition going unnoticed by the victims of oppression. That is why domination, as suggested by the chapter heading, must be exposed and understood before it can be resisted and transcended.

Paradoxically, in a successful struggle against domination the amounts of coercive oppression are bound to increase, at least temporarily; as cultural freedom expands with the victim's increasing awareness of his or her own oppression, so the same person's social freedom is reduced, for coercive oppression by definition involves *perceived* restraints. (Social freedom means freedom not only from coercion but from deprivation and violence as well, and with respect to the latter two this is regardless of whether the victim is aware of being oppressed; with a new awareness of the coercive element involved in enforcing conditions of deprivation and/or violence, it is strictly speaking only the coercion that becomes magnified, not the deprivation or the violence; but the relationship between these concepts cannot be explored until the next chapter.)

I shall not attempt to move to great depths, in this brief work, with respect to the problematics of ideally complete emancipation from domination or of the highest attainable levels of cultural freedom. I believe there is great promise in Jürgen Habermas's strategy of exploring distorted communication.[1] The point is not to attribute a superhuman power of intellectual sophistication and cunning to some hidden conspiracy in behalf of the ruling class; rather, it is to

51

remind ourselves that semantical practices and even the linguistic structures belong to the cultural superstructure that,
regardless of subjectivities and human intentions, reflects the
stable power relations in any given social order. This is an
extension of Marx's point that the social class which controls the material production in a given social order "has control at the same time over the means of mental production,
so that thereby, generally speaking, the ideas of those who
lack the means of mental production are subject to it."[2]
Everyday language is, of course, the most important means
of mental production.

It would take us too far afield to explore these complex-
ities here. This chapter will end with a brief discussion of
Paulo Freire's strategy of political emancipation through a
radically language-critical dialogue. Freire's position approximates and intelligently applies a similar perspective, in embryo as it were, but does not appropriate or examine Habermas's theory of emancipatory communication. My interest
here is primarily pedagogical, like Freire's, and I shall not
attempt to make a contribution toward the theory of emancipatory communication.

My inquiry will begin near the surface with the problem
of political domination in the name of democracy. There
will be no discussion in this context of Ralph Miliband's important work, *The State in Capitalist Society*,[3] because this
work moves *on* the surface, as here understood: Miliband
treats systematically a number of tangible, by now readily
visible, forces that invariably defeat every social-democratic
regime's initial hopes and ambitions of transcending or radically changing the established capitalist system. In the present chapter Miliband's findings will only be kept in mind as
additional evidence that it is false to claim that *democracy*
has been achieved in any country as yet, unless the word is
taken to refer to electoral procedures only and not to popular sovereignty in any defensible sense of that term.

This chapter's first section, then, will discuss the "democratic makebelieve"[4] as a major obstacle to freedom from
domination, taking off from a formulation by Herbert Marcuse on how to determine, or who shall determine, the difference between what he calls true and false needs. Second, I
shall briefly discuss some essential insights of organizational

sociologists and of Marxists to the effect that social organizations as such, and class-divided societies as such, give rise to,
and require, ideologies of domination, whose function is to
mystify and pacify the oppressed.

Third, I discuss the role of modern professions as agencies
of domination, focusing on Ivan Illich's powerful indictment
of the medical profession while extrapolating to professions
and professionalism in general. The doctors may be skating
on thin ice these days, particularly in the United States; they
may be dangerously close now to the limits of intelligent
people's tolerance of being used; they are becoming the most
convenient targets in an impending struggle that is likely to
yield much emancipatory insight. That new awareness is
likely to pay off, I think, in a wider awareness of and resistance to professional domination in general; in time it may
also lead more people to become sensitive to and resentful of
well established rationalizations for political and legal domination as well.[5]

Fourth, as a special case of professional domination, one
that suggests greater depths of significance than I can do
justice to in this brief account, I shall touch on scientists and
scientism as an increasingly important and all-pervasive
source of domination in the modern world, and I will point
to the importance of the perspectives of critical theory and
of dialectical inquiry as supplements and correctives to modern empirical science, and above all to modern scientism.
Positivist research has an important role to play, but so does
serious dialectical investigation, within the world of higher
learning, and also in the many pedagogical encounters and
should-be pedagogical encounters of everyday life.

This will lead up to the concluding discussion of, and a
follow up to, Paulo Freire's approach to the pedagogy of
political emancipation.

1. THE DEMOCRATIC MAKEBELIEVE

Herbert Marcuse was deeply aware of the dilemma to
democratic theory that is caused by his distinction between
"true" and "false" needs: between authentic human needs

originating within each person, reflecting his or her nature and individuality, and artificial counterfeits of needs, attributable to manipulative programming in behalf of other people's interests by way of advertising or other exploitive or paternalistic influencing processes.

Marcuse takes off from the point at which Isaiah Berlin finishes (see 1 §2): who is to decide what needs are true and what are false? Berlin, as we saw, throws up his hands and says that nobody could ever decide that for others, or we would have tyranny; therefore, negative liberty is the only tenable ideal of freedom: there can be no guidance from psychology or philosophy with respect to laying down any priorities among categories of needs. In other words, what follows from Berlin's perspective on freedom is that the marketplace must decide. As we have seen, but as Berlin himself hasn't, this leads to sanctioning, behind the facade of liberal-democratic institutions, Might becoming Right. In the marketplace the trivial needs or wants of people with clout easily outweigh the dire necessities of those who have no wealth or power.

Marcuse, unlike Berlin, is prepared to accommodate the distinction he sees between high-priority and low-priority needs (or between true and false needs, as he calls them; about these terms I shall take issue with Marcuse, see below 4 §2), by questioning the unconditional legitimacy of the democratic majority principle as it is understood by most liberals; that is, with the principle of majority votes as the authoritative basis for legitimate political decisions. In effect Marcuse, who here follows in the footsteps of Plato, reasserts Philosophy, or Reason, as a higher authority than Democracy; or, at any rate, as a badly needed corrective to so-called democratic processes that in fact reflect manipulated opinions rather than dialectically well considered and knowledgeable beliefs held by autonomous citizens.

"In the last analysis," Marcuse replies to his own query, "the question of what are true and false needs must be answered by the individuals themselves, but only in the last analysis; that is, if and when they are free to give their own answer. As long as they are kept incapable of being autonomous, as long as they are indoctrinated and manipulated (down to their very instincts), their answer to this question cannot be taken as their own."[6] While this situation lasts, democracy can be no more than a pretense. "Man was born free, and everywhere he is in chains," lamented Rousseau. Like Marcuse, Rousseau did not see how democratic institutions could be made to work as long as the minds of men continued to be in chains, and, at least in the large nation-states, he saw very little hope for an end to domination. "Were there a people of gods, their government would be democratic. So perfect a government is not for men."[7]

In the *Republic* and the *Gorgias*[8] Plato long ago had argued forcefully that the achievement of justice and the common good depends on bringing philosophical dialectics of truth-seeking into the councils of government; an approach that is antithetical to so-called democratic processes of government. In democracies, Plato believed, self-seeking rhetoricians will exploit the mass of citizens with their superior training in the arts (or knacks) of persuading the ignorant, flattering those who are vain, and convincing those who are gullible.

The case against democracy is strong in the writings of Plato, Rousseau, and Marcuse, and I think the modern liberal case for democracy is grievously deficient in its failure to meet these ancient and modern arguments which, in effect, assert that democracy presupposes an autonomous citizenry, men and women who are not themselves dominated and programmed to behave according to the interests of a power elite.

It so happens that I am in favor of democratic institutions and share with most liberals the ideal of a democratically governed society. Where I most emphatically part company with most liberals is in my insistence that democratic governments have as yet been achieved nowhere, and that our own electoral institutions, though democratic in form and potentially compatible with democratic processes, today are serving mainly to make the privileges of power look legitimate, while in substance falling far short of being democratic in the sense of enabling the majority to determine autonomously the course of public policies.

Not only do I disagree with liberal descriptions of our political order as democratic; I insist that they are patently false, for there are mountains of evidence, for all to see, that small groups in corporate boardrooms and other secluded areas (they used to be called "smoke-filled room," but times have changed to the extent that there probably are fewer cigars now) go about determining which issues are to be paraded before the public and which are to be decided in private. In our saner moments we are all aware that American presidential campaigns, in particular, are competitive rituals of personality cult with a minimum of reasoned discourse, and that a phrase offensive to certain ethnic loyalties or a slip of the tongue can do more to swing an election than any number of thoughtful arguments or imaginative proposals. The voters' fears and antipathies are mobilized in election campaigns, and sometimes their hopes and sympathies, too, but rarely if ever are the voters encouraged to a reasoned debate within their own communities by candidates running for public office. "Bread and circuses" was what the Roman Emperors thought that the people required to remain quiet and obedient. Their modern American equivalents—Mark Roelofs calls them our barons of finance and industry—give the people welfare programs for bread and electoral campaigns and contests for circuses.[9]

Those who use the term "democracy" as a term to refer to our liberal-corporate political system are in effect, though not necessarily intentionally, helping to distort most people's perceptions of the political facts of life. In a subjective sense I suppose this may be innocent enough; it is a plausible individual excuse that "everybody's doing it." But it is at this point that I level my gravest charge against the collectivity of mainstream liberals, or against what I take to be the conventional liberal wisdom: acquiescence in the language of democracy achieved, the language of the democratic makebelieve, amounts to support and promotion of perhaps the single most potent ideological obstacle to political emancipation. A continuing use of this language of "democracy achieved" helps to destroy our chances of ever achieving something like democratic self-government in fact.

In the first place, the struggle for any kind of ideal tends to terminate, if, or to the extent that it comes to be believed that, these ideals already have been realized. Second, even outrageous government policies, from wars of aggression in Asia to soaking-the-poor and placating-the-rich tax policies at home, are made to seem acceptable by the liberal-democratic illusion of a popular mandate to the person and/or party that won the last election. Third, it comes to be widely believed that every people gets the government that it deserves, and that the ballot box is the only possible remedy against political injustice. Instead of feeling free, even obligated, to break any patently unjust privilege-serving law, most people under the sway of the democratic makebelieve become resigned to seeking remedies through the ballot box—precisely the arena where poor people and other underprivileged are most severely handicapped (see Beckerman's remark cited above, 2 §2). In practice, that amounts to a resignation to the feeling that nothing can be done; in other words, to political passivity and apathy.

But the democratic makebelieve is only one special case of the universal sociological principle that every regime seeks legitimation—that is, seeks willing rather than forced obedience on the part of subjects or citizens, by way of proper programming, including myths or beliefs that will not stand up to critical scrutiny. Even in his utopian *Republic* Plato faced up to this necessity and prescribed a public double standard regarding truth and lies: "Then, it's appropriate for rulers, if for anyone at all, to lie for the benefit of the city in cases involving enemies or citizens, while all the rest must not put their hands to anything of the sort."[10]

In ancient and medieval times, most regimes sought legitimacy in claims to represent the will of the Deity. It was the bold Thomas Hobbes who inaugurated modern secular political philosophy with his claim that the legitimacy of a state must be based on an empirical assessment of human propensities and on principles of right reason. He developed the first science of politics designed to work out the best way of preserving men from their own proneness to violence, in their natural condition of fierce competition for resources in limited supply. The best way, to Hobbes, was an authoritarian state, in full control of all instruments of violence and of all political and religious opinions as well.

From Hobbes to Rawls the idea of a social contract, more often seen as metaphor rather than as historical event, has been a favorite construction for justifying particular kinds of regimes. From Locke to Rawls these regimes have always been liberal in the sense that individual liberties and rights, including the freedom of business enterprise, were supposed to be guaranteed, and in the sense that the rulers were held to be ultimately responsible to the people, both in theory and in the practice of elections at regular intervals. The utilitarians, on the other hand, rejected the notion of a social contract but argued in favor of liberal democracy on the ground that the greater happiness of the greater number would be the most likely outcome, over the long run at least, when governments and parliaments would have to seek continuing mandates in popular elections. To be sure, early liberals like Locke took a strictly limited suffrage for granted, just as Locke took the political subservience of God-fearing common laborers for granted; but over the last century a nearly universal suffrage has been fought for and achieved in all First World countries, usually with the eventual support or approval of liberals and conservatives alike. However, no appreciable reduction in the safety of private wealth or other privilege has ensued, for with expanding suffrage public education and other efforts at socialization into the appropriate sentiments of God and country have been expanded as well. As I shall come back to in the last chapter, social scientists and philosophers have made their important contributions to these processes of political socialization not only in learned books on the theory and practice of democracy and in behavioral research bearing on how our system works and on how egalitarian and emancipatory sentiments can be kept from getting out of hand. Also, a literature on political obligation has emerged, which adroitly bypasses the most basic question of whether we ought to give the state our loyalty and instead focuses on how best to justify our obligation to an allegedly democratic regime or to an allegedly just state. This literature scrupulously avoids a scrutiny of the realities of power and domination in the same states to which a duty of loyalty is simply affirmed and then interpreted in terms of specific obligations or practices.[11]

For now, let us probe a bit deeper, inquiring whether it is possible to achieve or approximate democratic regimes in modern states or in other powerful organizations.

2. THE REALITY OF ORGANIZATIONAL AND
CLASS DOMINATION

Social organizations, unless they are to be quite ineffective or have trivial purposes (like bridge clubs, for example), require some measure of domination by the leaders over the rank and file. The less trivial the purposes, or the more that seems to be at stake from the point of view of a given organization—that is, as perceived by its actual leaders—the more domination is to be expected. Also, to the extent that domination fails, or succeeds to a degree that is deemed insufficient, more coercion is to be expected, if the leaders can get away with it. No organization can work on the basis of coercion alone, however. In Kenneth Boulding's words:

> There must always be some small element of identification with the purposes of the organization if *effective* cooperation of an individual is to be obtained. Even the slave and the conscript must in some sense be willing to be enslaved or conscripted, and there is some threshold of unwillingness below which no amount of coercive power can force individuals to contribute.[12]

Robert Michels, the founder of the modern discipline of organizational sociology, formulated what he called the "iron law of oligarchy": "It is organization which gives birth to the dominion of the elected over the electors, of the mandataries over the mandators, of the delegates over the delegators. Who says organization, says oligarchy."[13]

Yet Michels was mistaken in his assumption that social democratic and socialist organizations, on account of their democratic aims, should be expected to be less oligarchical in structure than other, less democratically or humanistically motivated organizations. Rather, we should assume degrees of oligarchy to depend on, as suggested above, how much appears to be at stake, both to the leadership *and* to the followership (who must to a considerable extent share these perceptions with their leaders, if they are to be dominated rather than coerced). For example:

(1) Moderate political parties in liberal-corporate societies may be quite democratic internally if electoral defeat makes

little difference to the system's stability, or even to the leaders' personal careers (for example, if they may return to secure law practices, if there would be no great temptations or opportunities to make a lot of extra money on account of remaining in office, and if there had been no past misdeeds while in office that would have to remain covered up). (2) Labor unions in liberal-corporate societies may tend to be more oligarchical than moderate political parties, *to the extent that*, for example, (a) much money can be made by union officers on account of inefficient accounting practices, or (b) union officers are paid far more than and have far more pleasant working conditions than rank-and-file workers. (3) Militant radical as well as reactionary parties, respectively at the extreme Left and the extreme Right on the political spectrum, although the aims of the former are egalitarian and those of the latter are not, both tend to be highly oligarchical internally, because they tend to see themselves at war, certainly with each other and generally with the mainstream political tendencies, "the system," as well. Their propaganda, more persuasive internally then externally, always emphasizes that much is at stake, and that what separates their own Party (with a capital P) from all other organizations (excepting "front" organizations) vastly outweighs the common bonds. Consequently such parties tend to require and to obtain a tight internal discipline.

How much appears to be at stake, from the point of view of a given political organization, is not only a matter of kinds of aims and commitments, nor is it only a matter of whether actual suppression and violence or police harassment has been suffered or is anticipated.[14] It is also a matter of sheer size of the organization, both in terms of numbers of members and in terms of how much wealth and power an organization's leadership, when united, is in a position to control. The larger and more powerful an organization, the stronger the incentives for any entrenched leadership group to protect its prerogatives and to perpetuate them, by fair means or foul.

If this is accepted, then we must reflect on the fact that most modern states tend to be among the most powerful social organizations the world has ever seen. Consequently we must expect that most states will be highly oligarchically structured in fact, regardless of whether they claim to be democratically governed, or even base their own legality and legitimacy on such claims. When such is the main basis for a regime's claim to legitimacy, as is the case for virtually every liberal-corporate regime, the importance to the regime of mystifications like the democratic makebelieve is easily understood.

It should be mentioned here that some private multinational corporations control far more wealth than do many states, and that their power appears to be growing fast. According to one authority, the "average growth rate of many of the largest multinational corporations is two to three times that of the most advanced industrial countries."[15] Multinationals differ from states in that (a) they do not pretend to be working in pursuit of the common good, for their primary task is always to make profits, which is readily admitted; and (b) they do pretend that nobody has to join them or work for them, even where people in fact can see no other alternatives that will keep them alive; for multinationals are voluntary organizations, unlike states, which claim the right to rule over and even to coerce and do violence, when necessary, to their citizens. I shall postpone a further discussion of multinational corporations till the last chapter (see 6 §2).

Let us conclude this brief excursion into organizational sociology by observing, first, that social organizations tend to be, other things being equal, more oppressive and more dominating the larger and more resource rich they are; and second, that modern states tend to be, compared to most (although not all) other organizations, very large and very resource rich, and consequently must be expected to be more oppressive than most other organizations. Since states claim the right to rule, even by violence when necessary, their opportunities to oppress are wide and, moreover, widely accepted, in the spirit of legitimacy, democracy, and patriotism (or, in state-corporate societies, in the spirit of revolutionary legitimacy, socialism, and patriotism). Through our school systems, churches, and (other) media of communication, our liberal-corporate regimes seek to dominate us ideologically, "liberal-democratically," rather than by way of coercion. As well trained, well socialized, loyal citizens, who are ready to work or even die or kill for our country, we are not being coerced but dominated by the state, most of the time; it is our cultural freedom, not our social freedom that remains impaired, unless or until we develop a politically critical consciousness.

Robert Michels was skeptical, of course, about prospects for a socialist revolution: "The socialists might conquer, but not socialism, which would perish in the moment of its adherents' triumph."[16] But his critique of bourgeois society's false pretensions to democracy was compatible with the critique by Marx and Engels. To Michels, the nature of all social organizations as such was the main obstacle to democracy, while Marx and Engels instead stressed the nature of class rule in capitalist society as the crucial obstacle to democracy and freedom. Unlike Michels, therefore, the Marxists were optimistic: class oppression belongs to a particular historical stage; it can and will be abolished, and a society free from political oppression will emerge after the revolution—though not necessarily right after.

Under feudalism, those who controlled the land were in a position to exert a vast and varied influence over how the rest of humanity lived out their lives. Most often, in times of peace, the feudal classes controlled not only the land but the armed forces as well (usually peasant armies, employed by their local feudal lords), and they were allied with the clergy, who controlled access to Salvation and Eternal Life. The Mother Church, headed by the Pope in Rome, was in a position to dominate the minds of men and women to an extent that in a more secular age is difficult to comprehend. Against this background the rise of the bourgeoisie, of liberal individualism, and of private capitalism amounted to a vast emancipatory achievement for mankind. A new, vigorous social class emerged and eventually gained control of the industrializing process; their access to power inaugurated an unprecedented growth in production, in education, in scientific knowledge, and in the emancipation of countless human minds. An era of relative freedom dawned; it emerged with different force and speed in different countries, sometimes quietly and sometimes with dramatic, even revolutionary force. The most important political watersheds were

Cromwell's revolution in England, the American War of Independence, and the French Revolution.

But, to use the language of Rawls (see 1 §3), while a new liberty emerged, the worth of the new liberty to the impoverished peasantries or to the new industrial working class was minimal, or perhaps mainly negative: their former roots, their sense of belonging in local communities and in the Church was to a considerable extent destroyed, and their struggle for sheer physical survival often became even more anguished and hazardous than it had been under the feudal system.

The capitalists, those in control of private and corporate wealth, are, in our social order, in a position to exert a vast and varied influence over how the rest of us live out our lives. As Marx observed more than a century ago, under capitalism both the machines and their accumulating products represent "dead labor," while living labor, and living laborers, become reduced to mere appendages to capital. "Labor power, therefore, is a commodity, neither more nor less than sugar. The former is measured by the clock, the latter by the scales."[17] Perversely, "dead" capital reduces living workers to expendable *things*; with the continuing accumulation of capital in private or corporate hands, this process accelerates. As it is said in the *Manifesto*: "In bourgeois society . . . the past dominates the present . . . capital is independent and has individuality, while the living person is dependent and has no individuality."[18]

The *Manifesto* nevertheless offers an optimistic prognosis, anticipating that the capitalists will produce their own gravediggers in the shape of a fast-growing proletariat that will confront a dwindling number of capitalists, in large factories, under conditions miserable enough to ensure a fertile ground for revolutionary agitation and organizing. These prospects must have been plausible at the time when Marx and Engels wrote their *Streitschrift*.[19] But today this prognosis seems valid, even in part, only on a global scale: internationally, the Third World proletariats have indeed been expanding in our own time, and so has their immiseration. However, in much of today's Third World it appears that the industrial and rural proletariats and peasantry have been too divided geographically and psychologically and have been too miserable to challenge the imperialist superpowers effectively.

In First World countries the proletariats have dwindled in size and strength, while growing proportions of blue-collar workers have become property owners and have aspired to join, or have their children join, the bourgeoisie. Most trade unions in North America now tend to support the corporate system, provided it assures to their members an acceptable level of prosperity, and many unionists now take it in their stride that others are left out in the cold and that large Third World populations seem destined to continue to subsist or perish on fractions of what their own members earn.

One crucial motivational force in the wide acceptance in advanced societies today of the corporate system appears to be embedded in what Marx termed "commodity fetishism": that is, in the attribution of inherent value to commodities, with the practical result that people become utterly dependent on their access to and control of commodities, or of the money that can buy commodities.

In this way possessive individualism has become a nearly universal ambition and way of life in the First World countries: people increasingly have come to base not only their personal sense of security but their very sense of identity and worth as human beings on their relative "success" in acquiring access to commodities. No revolutionary struggle, no yearning for a just society is likely within a working class, or a middle class, whose members are constantly struggling to maintain or expand their relative affluence as owners and consumers of commodities. William Leiss in a recent book well analyzes how commodity fetishism in our own society not only impoverishes our human sensitivities and our social relationships, as I shall come back to in chapter 5, but also, at an accelerating pace, is exhausting the resources of the natural environment on which our collective human survival depends.[20]

Paradoxically, these very hazards of modern commodity fetishism may well offer some hopes toward eventual liberation from liberal-capitalist domination. Popular awareness of ecological hazards and limits is unmistakably growing, and scientific and professional awareness, more important in the short run, appears to be growing fast, especially in the First World.[21] If this continues, hopes for human survival into the twenty-first century and beyond will be improved; in addition, and contributing to these hopes, the legitimation of the liberal-corporate system will be grievously undermined, for private capitalism's principal claim to legitimacy has always been the assumption that the system could expand the production of commodities, and of fresh capital for still more commodities, more effectively than any other system. Nobody could claim that liberal capitalism is a good system for purposes of equitable *distribution* of commodities or for purposes of responsible *scaling down* of commodity production.

One does not require much of a crystal ball to conclude from the impending ecological crisis, or even from the food crises and energy crises that are with us right now, that the wasteful ways of liberal capitalism in the First World cannot continue much longer without catastrophic consequences all over the world. I conclude that it is necessary to seek to free ourselves from our present dependency (even in our own lifestyles—"if we are not part of the solution, we are part of the problem") on the many commodities that serve social status rather than sustenance purposes. As the New Left students showed so dramatically in the heyday of their influence (which declined, at least temporarily, for quite different reasons): all that is required to expand our cultural freedom to this extent is a healthy common sense; a personal determination to resist the slick appeals of modern advertising and to limit our commodity acquisitions to those that are essential to our well-being; and a stubborn will to be independent in our choice of commitments, of value priorities, and of how to plan and to live our own lives.

3. PROFESSIONALISM AND DOMINATION

In our struggle for cultural freedom there are two heavy hands, as it were, that hold us back. One is the heavy hand of traditions, customs, established conventions. Not all traditions are oppressive—that is, mainly in the interests of the ruling class at the expense of other people's best interests—but many traditions are. And that certainly includes the political core tradition of every social order, the "Sir" syndrome—the expectation that ordinary folk will be uncritically deferent, without reciprocation, to all appointed or anointed authority figures. The other heavy hand has brought us emancipation as well as oppression, in ever-changing configurations, but its oppressiveness is not as widely or as well understood as its benefits. I refer to the heavy hand of Science, of Technology and Progress, and of the whole retinue of Experts and Professionals of so many kinds, all of whom are thought of as qualified specialists in knowing what is best for the rest of us.

Turning now to deal with this second heavy hand, with the problematics of scientific knowledge and domination, let me once again begin near the surface, with the problem of professional domination, in the name of up-to-date scientific knowledge. In section 4 we shall see that the problem of science itself, and especially of scientism, as a problem of domination cuts deeper. In this section let us see how the mantle of science can be used by professionals to take charge of key aspects of the lives of their fellow human beings. I shall here focus on perhaps the most articulate critic of professional domination of our time, Ivan Illich; I shall pass over his critique of schooling[22] and of transportation policies,[23] in order to consider his challenge to professionalism in the health care field.

Illich's *Limits to Medicine*[24] offers, I think, a model for the kind of critique that all our professional interest groups ought to be subjected to in the interest of the cultural liberation of professionals and nonprofessionals alike. The health field is, of all the contexts in which domination utilizes modern science and technology, the field in which most people probably are optimally educable toward a critical consciousness which, when aroused, may come to illuminate other contexts of modern professional dominance as well. Our deteriorating, profit-oriented, and far too costly health services, when illuminated by radical questioning, are likely to provoke not only a determination to take responsibility for one's own health but a determination to resist domination in other sectors as well, in our increasingly welfare-oriented, allegedly democratic social order.

Our personal health and that of persons dear to us are matters of great interest to all of us. Until recently, the professional mystique of doctordom had made most people more than willing to accept as the whole truth, and nothing but the truth, not only the medical diagnoses administered to them, but the implicit psychological diagnosis of themselves as incompetent to choose their personal health strategies or to treat their own common ailments intelligently. In the United States a wealthy and politically still powerful medical profession has not yet (as of late 1980) been dislodged from its virtual private monopoly over a system that explicitly denies to the poor an equal access to highest-quality medical care as a human right; there have been few public restraints on the size of the fees, and of course no antitrust prosecutions, with the result that the medical profession (as distinct from other health service personnel) has become very wealthy even compared to lawyers and other most influential and most privileged professions.

No doubt even the United States is now headed for a national health service system which will ensure certain basic rights of access to medical help for everyone, probably at a heavy cost to the taxpayers, so that the medical doctors can maintain their high incomes. Yet, as Illich argues, this development will not by itself facilitate our liberation from the health-professional domination over our lives; in fact, more equality of access may mean that all of us will become more deeply stuck in the mire of dependency, on account of our own health needs and our well-learned incapacity to understand them and to seek to remedy them. This easier access may well deepen our dependency without over the long run improving our health.

Illich focuses on the concept of *iatrogenesis*, that is, illnesses caused by physicians, and he makes the range of problems of iatrogenesis paradigmatic for modern men's and women's general condition of induced helplessness. First, there are the relatively limited problems of *clinical* iatrogenesis: the damage done to patients by inappropriate diagnosis and treatment, or bad or poorly communicated medical advice.

Second, *social* iatrogenesis amounts to a more pervasive source of ill health: "medical practice sponsors sickness by reinforcing a morbid society that encourages people to become consumers of curative, preventive, industrial, and environmental medicine."[25] Modern social and preventive medicine is in the process of turning majorities of reasonably healthy people into lifelong patients: "Previously modern medicine controlled only a limited market; now this market has lost all boundaries. Unsick people have come to depend on professional care for the sake of their future health. The result is a morbid society that demands universal medicalization and a medical establishment that certifies universal morbidity."[26]

Third, and with still wider implications, there is *structural* iatrogenesis: "Professionally organized medicine has come to function as a domineering moral enterprise that advertises industrial expansion as a war against all suffering. It has thereby undermined the ability of individuals to face their reality, to express their own values, and to accept inevitable and often irremediable pain and impairment, decline, and death."[27]

Traditionally, as Illich points out, medicine has served to console, care for, and comfort afflicted people as a vital part in trying to heal them, when possible, as well as to strengthen them in any adversity due to failing health. The modern medicalization ideology, quite to the contrary, has produced "a prolific bureaucratic program based on the denial of each man's need to deal with pain . . . and to abolish the need for an art of suffering and dying."[28] Most people's ability to respond to challenges and to cope with their own maturation and aging processes, or with changes in their environments, is being drastically reduced.[29]

The medical killing of pain as a rule has no bearing on prospects for recovery, although I think that in all fairness it must be stressed more than Illich does that to ease intense suffering is a highly worthy objective. But medication against pain on the grand scale desired by the pharmaceutical companies and abetted by physicians is something else: "Increasingly, pain-killing turns people into unfeeling spectators of their own decaying selves."[30] This suggests to Illich a parallel with dependency on alcohol and a variety of licit and illicit drugs; *their* function, it should be added, at times may be to dull political pain and rebellious indignation. "Society has become a clinic," Illich writes, "and all citizens have become patients whose blood pressure is constantly being watched and regulated to fall 'within' normal limits."[31] Recent developments in Soviet psychiatry suggest that medical establishments may be helpful to nervous governments in checking political blood pressures as well, and even in prescribing compulsory therapies for the regime's critics and dissidents,[32] perhaps to the detriment of a nation's prospects for political recovery.

Even the right to die in one's home, as a last assertion of the individual's will and worth, is being taken away, writes Illich; the "epoch of natural death" has ended: "Society, acting through the medical system, decides when and after what indignities and mutilations [the sick person in critical condition] shall die.... Western man has lost the right to preside at his act of dying."[33] The machines will keep you going, even as a pathetic vegetable, for the greater glory of medical technology, at your relatives' or your health plan's or the taxpayers' expense.

In the first edition of Illich's book, entitled *Medical Nemesis*, the author calls medicine a sacred cow and suggests that its slaughter could have a "vibration effect": "people who can face suffering and death without the need for magicians and mystagogues are free to rebel against other forms of expropriation now practiced by teachers, engineers, lawyers, priests and party officials."[34] In the definitive edition, Illich greatly expands the first edition's concluding section on the politics of health, and he calls for legislation that would "recognize each man's right to define his own health—subject only to limitations imposed by respect for his neighbor's rights" and that would "give the public a voice in the election of healers to tax-supported health jobs." Illich says that what is needed is neither continuing medical progress nor expanded public control over private medicine, but new levels of "willingness and competence to engage in self-care" throughout society. "The recovery of this power depends on the recognition of our present delusions."[35] This recovery of personal autonomy that Illich anticipates will be aided by a massive but decentralized political resistance to domination against self-serving professional castes and technocracies in other areas of life in addition to health care; Illich specifically refers to the school systems and the transportation systems. His measured optimism about the possibility of recovering from the delusions of technological progress arises from the very depth of the crises in the modern world and from the apparently growing apprehension throughout the First World that our fancy technologies are speeding us all on our way to oblivion.

Illich's indictment of the medical system is not only paradigmatic in suggesting how other structures of domination must be attacked; it is also of particular strategic value, for good health is in everyone's obvious interest. Even the most timid and the most apolitical among us care intensely about our own and our families' and friends' good health; here are issues around which participatory solidarity is natural. Also, a political awareness of the increasing rate of expropriation of our health is probably within everyone's reach. A recovery of our powers of indignation and autonomy in matters directly affecting our health could well spark a demand for political self-determination and resistance to domination in all aspects of our daily lives. If need is the mother of inventions, perhaps the need to be well will yet prove to be the mother of a deeper political insight and of radical innovations in the struggle against domination.

The rising status of professionals and the deepening mystique of professionalism, and not only in the medical field, have led to increasing passivity on the part of most people, accompanied by a reduced confidence in the person's own judgment and competencies. From keeping accounts to administering haircuts, from fixing a broken window to writing out a will, specialists are always on hand to convince us that we cannot do these things well enough ourselves. Many people have come to feel incapable of dealing with even a headache or a common cold.

But it could be that the pendulum is now on its way back, thanks in part to Illich and other contemporary critics of professionalism.[36] When many people begin to sense that they are more capable of handling their own health problems than they had been given to understand, perhaps their next discovery will be that they can also handle their own neighborhood and community problems a lot better than their traditional political leaders had given them to understand.

4. SCIENCE, SCIENTISM, AND DOMINATION

"Science" can be variously defined. I shall here use the term broadly, as referring to systematic knowledge of all kinds, including all the vast probabilistic (or even just hypothetical) systems of beliefs that are based on accumulated records of human observations and experience, systematically analyzed and inferred from, and subject to continuing critical inquiry and reformulations. While I believe that all scientific knowledge in principle must be considered tentative in all its particulars, science as a whole is a human project that is here to stay, if human beings are here to stay; its actual and potential benefits to the human species are vast. While many scientific discoveries and theories have been badly used, in the service of oppression and even large-scale violence, it would be absurd to come out flatly against scientific research, or to be unconditionally opposed to the role of universities in promoting and communicating scientific knowledge.

What I think we ought to be critical of are the priorities, or the lack of rational priorities, that are apparent in the general support—academic, political, and lay—that is currently being lavished on scientific research in all corners of the world. I shall limit this discussion to the social sciences. On the whole, technically and conceptually advanced work here is being promoted either indiscriminately or according to shifting paradigms that have little substantive bearing on, say, the reduction of human suffering. There is no parallel in social research to what I take to be an axiomatic emphasis in reputable medical research: that the overall aim is to seek more reliable and effective ways to prolong human lives and to reduce the incidence of ill health, physical impairments, and suffering. Peace research is one of the few exceptional endeavors: in this area, research efforts generally do seek to expand, not just academic knowledge in the abstract, but knowledge of how to reduce the risks of international violence.

Yet "scientism" is a frequently occurring phenomenon event in such fields of research,[37] and in my view it is a prevailing phenomenon in countless academic departments and institutes, to judge by most academic journals and textbooks. "Scientism" will here refer to the belief that all kinds of research and research-based (therefore "scientific") knowledge are valuable in themselves and need no other justification. The term is similarly defined by Abraham Kaplan as "the pernicious exaggeration of both the status and function of science in relation to our values"; he urges his readers to believe in the potential benefits of science and yet to "recognize how little we know" and above all to understand that scientific knowledge is to be prized only in the service of wisely chosen values.[38] Many public and private funding agencies despite good initial intentions about serving "humanity" tend to slide backwards into scientism, on account of the timidity of their administrators and boards. These agencies tend to be timid, not about spending funds on technologically advanced and politically neutral, therefore "safe" projects, though they may be of dubious benefit to mankind, or to any portions thereof not academically or otherwise privileged; the timidity relates to research that could be construed as "political," meaning projects that could stimulate a critical questioning of existing patterns of oppression.

Many social scientists are not themselves scientistic-minded, especially at the outset of their careers, just as many artists don't really believe in *l'art pour l'art* as a decent attitude in an oppressive society. But in the highly competitive field of grantsmanship—how to compete successfully in the struggle for research grants with which to advance careers and individual fame—most social scientists who wish to succeed must take on a scientistic coloring: they must promise to make contributions to scientific knowledge in the abstract, not to the kinds of specific knowledge that can be used in the political struggle to reduce oppression and suffering, or to expose establishment-serving myths and frauds. C. Wright Mills has shown with particular clarity that leading social scientists have tended to shy away from politically dangerous terrain, seeking safe refuge either in "grand theory" or in "abstracted empiricism."[39] Hans J. Morgenthau said with particular reference to his own field, political science:

> A political science that is mistreated and persecuted is likely to have earned that enmity because it has put its moral commitment to the truth above social convenience and ambition. . . . A political science that is respected is likely to have earned that respect because it performs useful functions for society. It helps to cover political relations with the veil of ideologies which mollify the conscience of society; by justifying the existing power relations, it reassures the powers-that-be in their possession of power; it illuminates certain aspects of the existing power relations; and it contributes to the improvement of the technical operations of government. The relevance of this political science does not lie primarily in the discovery of the truth about politics, but in its contribution to the stability of society.[40]

In short, schools and universities ordinarily do not encourage radical innovators with bold visions of a better future for mankind. Neither Karl Marx nor Sigmund Freud could win acceptance as teachers in the academic institutions to which each of them initially aspired. While the First World has seen a considerable expansion of academic freedom in recent decades, especially for senior, tenured professors, on the whole it remains true that most universities and colleges are engaged not so much in the disinterested search for truth or social justice as they are engaged in the training and molding of able but meek future employees. They are state- and corporate-supported institutions; they are not in the business of educating independent-thinking, critically-minded intellectuals (see 3 §5).

The business of America, President Calvin Coolidge is reported to have said, is business. Harold J. Laski observed three decades ago:

> It is no exaggeration to say that in no previous civilization has the business man enjoyed either the power or the prestige that he possesses in the United States. . . . Certainly in modern times, the only men who have rivalled them in power have been either political despots,

like Napoleon or Hitler, or great aristocrats who exercise the main functions of the state.[41]

To the extent that there is no well articulated critical political purpose in the minds of social scientists, their business, also, is business. In their search for knowledge they will be tacitly guided by the priorities of the liberal-corporate ruling class, or power elite. Their political and scientific imagination will be confined within the limits of formal rationality, attempting to achieve optimally rational thought and inquiry about means but not about ends. In theory, society's ends are to be decided on democratically. "It is the function of science to understand and interpret the world, not to change it," wrote Heinz Eulau, one of the most respected and influential American political scientists, and he concluded that "political science, as all science, should be put in the service of whatever goals men pursue in politics."[42] Who are the people who decide what these goals are to be? Not democratic majorities, surely, but whichever corporate elites or coalitions have the power to pick the political candidates, to finance the campaigns, and to formulate the issues that the campaigns will be about.

In this context a value-neutral scientism fits well with the requirements of the liberal ideology and of the corporate system that it serves to legitimate. If a nation's most advanced brainpower can be brought to service Science and Technology, asking no fundamental questions about what purposes they are to serve, what could be better for business prosperity and for the continuing accumulation of private corporate capital?

Let us return for a moment to the concept of commodity fetishism. Every shining new gadget, every new convenience, is widely felt to be an added tribute to modern science and technology and to the social order that sets science and technology free. But the price we are all paying, not only in money but in impoverished individual and social lives, and in the reckless destruction of nonrenewable resources for the future of our children, is very heavy. And the most insidious part of it is that our commodity fetishism is gradually depriving us more and more of our capacity to choose how to order our own lives, individually and collectively. The rich supply of products for the favored minorities in the First World is doing something to our political eyesight: we become blind to alternative possibilities, blind above all to the possibility of trying to build a social order that does not exploit and victimize other peoples so that large corporations and their First World beneficiaries, the relatively affluent classes, may prosper.

Critical theorists like Max Horkheimer and Theodor Adorno are particularly clear on this point. They acknowledge that the growth of productivity under capitalism has furnished all the material prerequisites for a just social order; *but*, "on the other hand it allows the technical apparatus and the social groups which administer it a disproportionate superiority to the rest of the population. The individual is wholly devalued in relation to the economic powers. . . . In an unjust state of life, the impotence and pliability of the masses grow with the quantitative increase in commodities allowed them."[43]

The task of the human spirit, they add, is to achieve liberation from commodity fetishism, which has become a principal instrument of perpetuating domination. Rousseau, too, had seen that the inflation of human wants, or felt needs, is an effective way of establishing authoritarian domination over most people's minds.[44]

Marcuse in his 1960 introduction to a new edition of his *Reason and Revolution* points out how the modern capitalist society has appropriated science and technology for the purpose of "stream-lining rather than abolishing the domination of man, both by man and by the products of his labor. Progress becomes quantitative and tends tc delay indefinitely the turn from quantity to quality—that is, the emergence of new modes of existence with new forms of reason and freedom."[45]

Yet it is in *One-Dimensional Man* that Marcuse develops more systematically his theme that empirical scientism and the technology that it has spawned have become very powerful instruments of domination. Scientism fosters one-dimensional thought, preoccupied with extrapolating from superficial facts, oblivious of the dialectical tension between "facticity" and possibility, between what (superficially) exists and what ought to be or even (fundamentally) is in the making, with or perhaps even without purposive human intervention. And technology fosters the instrumental and quantitative view of man, collectively and individually: in the same process as nature is made subservient, so do most men and women become subservient to, or dominated by, the technological-rational designs of other men and women.[46]

5. THE STRATEGY OF PROBLEM-POSING EDUCATION

Political education is an important strategy in the struggle against oppression on all levels, as we shall see in the subsequent chapters, but the role of political education is particularly crucial in the struggle against domination, for domination first must be discovered and exposed; unlike coercion, it must be understood before it can be resisted. Domination amounts to ideological distortions of perceptions and cognitions, so that words are used and realities interpreted in ways that tend to assure the continuing predominance of the powers that be; indoctrination, mystifications, and actual fraud are common techniques in the repertoire of domination.

By "political education" I do not mean to refer to what usually passes for education in civics, political history, and political institutions in the schools, colleges, and universities of this country or any other country that I know anything about. The main purpose of nearly all schooling of this kind is to nurture patriotism and expand knowledge about our political system's past and present as well as to improve currently useful skills; it is not to encourage radical questioning of the merits of the system, nor to make students sensitive to the falseness of many claims in the patriotic, democratic, or other system-supporting ideologies.

By "education" in the present context I mean the liberation of the intellect, to the point where the individual is prepared to question even the most basic assumptions about the meanings and purposes of life and of society. The educated person in this sense requires certain minimum powers of articulation as well as independence, in order to ask searching fundamental questions, and enough linguistic and logical skills to develop over time a basic rationality and consistency in his or her own outlook. And there must be a sense of trust in one's own strength of mind, built up through experience in discussion, in dialogue, and in dialectical encounter, sufficient to enable the person to choose his or her own answers to all the searching questions, answers most satisfactory to the self, regardless of the pressures of conventional wisdom.

Education in my sense of liberating and strengthening (making articulate and uncompromising) the intellect is of course antithetical to much of what is going on in our schools and universities, which I would rather refer to by such terms as training, molding, socialization, mystification, memorizing of facts, obfuscation of meaning—all processes designed to produce intelligent citizens who are ready to execute jobs faithfully and not ask any questions about their meaning or purpose or value to fellow human beings.

By "political" education I mean liberating education that focuses on political *problems* and on posing new political problems; in Paulo Freire's sense, education aiming at questioning the conventionally accepted limit situations by posing questions about justice and about the possibility of transcending traditionally accepted patterns of domination and deprivation.

Paulo Freire, the exiled Brazilian educator, is the most important current innovator, I think, in the field of political education.[67] Paradoxically, Freire himself claims knowledge about the appropriateness of his educational approach only in Latin American peasant populations, in which he has shown that spectacular advances in literacy skills are possible in the context of continual political-educational dialogue. As a matter of fact, the political gains made as a result of his educational project have more often than not been wiped out by brutal oppression, as these and most other Third World regimes today have no dependable commitment even to the appearance or pretense of liberal constitutional processes or individual liberties.

In the First World, on the other hand, where such commitments exist and indeed appear crucial in maintaining a continuing legitimation and popular acceptance of our kinds of state, I think a Freire-type approach to political education is highly feasible. I think massive results can be achieved, at a minimal risk or cost, when many more educators catch on to the promise of work of this kind.

I have earlier (pp. 64-65) pointed to an expanding ecological consciousness and to an increasing realization of liberal capitalism's incompatibility with a realistic planning for the future as sources of hope that the legitimation problems of this system of domination are outgrowing the system's capacity for keeping itself credible. It takes something more than even an advanced liberal imagination to explain just how a profit-centered system of private corporate power is going to focus on the necessary objectives of reducing waste, of scaling down needless production and superfluous consumption, and of finding ways to an equitable sharing of the earth's remaining resources, within and beyond national boundaries and within and beyond the present century. Liberal capitalism may be a good system for expanding production, I have said, but it is by its nature ill suited for the most necessary task confronting our world today: how to learn to live in a reduced-growth society, within our ecological means, in a just world order (sufficiently just, at any rate, to save us from wars to determine which nations will survive).

A dialogue on these issues will be given added potency within the framework of Paulo Freire's approach, which assumes that all education proceeds by way of dialogues between political equals (all men and women must treat one another as political equals, regardless of age, class, or book learning vs. practical learning experience) about the problems that affect each person's freedom. Each of us has unique personal experience and insight to share, and the task of fruitful mutual sharing is aided by close critical attention to the most basic political terms that we use, terms like freedom, power, domination, politics, justice, equality. Every society has a privileged class with a vested interest in obfuscating the realities of oppression by discouraging informed dialogues about power and domination (domination is, after all, camouflaged coercion and/or deprivation) and also by making the oppressed used to and inclined to take for granted a basic *terminology* that discourage intelligent questions about domination. The first objective of political education by Freirean dialogue is, therefore, to achieve mastery of key words and of one's own perception of one's political situation as it bears on issues of power and justice.

The conquest of key words has consequences. Using the oppressor's words uncritically leads to passive, thoughtless political behavior on the part of the oppressed. Learning to use words with meanings that are valid for the oppressed, thereby challenging conventional usage, can initiate political consciousness and provide incentives to act in harmony with one's new understanding. As Freire himself puts it in a memorable phrase: "There is no true word that is not at the same time a praxis. Thus, to speak a true word is to transform the world."[48]

I shall have more to say about Freire's approach to political education, as I judge its relevance in our kind of society, in the remaining chapters. In this chapter I conclude on one of Freire's themes as I think it ought to be applied in our own institutions of higher learning—an environment rather different from Freire's peasant villages of South America.

That theme is the notion that hierarchy and educational achievement are antithetical. What Freire calls the banking approach to education, which I would refer to as training in memory and other skills, in the context of authoritarian socialization, does indeed require a teacher who talks and students who are passive listeners except when asked to regurgitate. What he calls problem-posing education, on the other hand, requires political equality between teachers and learners and a breaking down of their separate roles: the teacher is there also as a learner, and the learner must teach the teacher, as well as learn from him or her. Every acknowledged status differential is dysfunctional, for it interferes with the student's incentives to think out loud and to express himself or herself with complete candor, and it reduces the teacher's care and attention in listening.

For this reason, there is at least one of the demands of many of the student rebels of the 1960s that I hope will come back with renewed force: the demand that universities should be ruled by students and professors on the basis of the parity principle—not on the principle of "one man one vote," which could reduce the faculty to a position of menial servitude to a possibly arrogant student majority, but on the principle of a system of parity in a joint student-faculty elected assembly, which would make university administrators accountable to policies laid down by the entire academic community in each university, as the outcome of serious and continuing academic and political dialogues. Such a system should amount to a clean break with the notion that universities are here to serve a variety of special interests with money or power, the service-station concept, or the multiversity;[49] a self-governing academic community would give priority to responsible planning for the future, ahead of placating vested interests. And the current almost exclusive emphasis on positivist fact-gathering, on discovering "truth" in a narrow positivist sense, would be augmented by the cultivation of dialectical truth, of truth associated with issues of relevance to justice and long-term political responsibility, for the continuing dialogue on which the governance of a democratically constituted university community will be based is bound to become searching and lead to increasingly deeper insights.

The last point I want to make about a parity-based system of academic self-government is that, for the first time, the intelligence of teachers as well as that of students will become fully free to contribute the best that each generation has to offer. More often than not, teachers have more book learning and worldly experience to contribute while students can offer fresher intuitive insights, more openness to cues from a changing reality, and a keener feeling of future possibilities, being less stuck within patterns of established thinking and perhaps also more innocent of the subtly corrupting impact of a longer life in a capitalist society. Every kind of social order may be corrupting; what is particularly debilitating in our social order is the systematic camouflaging under a liberal ideology of grievous social injustice as well as callous indifference to the needs of the unborn, the children of the future.

Perhaps a vigorous radical-liberal dialogue about priorities in academic education would be one of the first results of a change toward student-faculty government of a university; in the spirit of Paulo Freire, I think, I would welcome this.

This brings me back to the passage of Marcuse cited above (see pp. 54-55), to the effect that people can decide democratically what their needs are only when they are no longer so victimized by domination that they are incapable of giving answers that are truly their own. University communities, supposedly centers leading the nations in the achievement of learning and independence of thought, can do much for political education throughout society by exposing and exploring the problems of domination under which we have been laboring. If experiments in real democracy are possible anywhere in our social order, they are possible in our academic communities, for in most of these communities the levels of articulation are relatively high and the levels of desperation relatively low.

I think it is up to our academic communities to demonstrate that political education and democracy are possible, if only we are determined to expose and transcend the conventional frauds of the democratic makebelieve, while at the same time we insist on engaging in a praxis that approximates fully democratic participation. Such a contrast between conventional liberal-democratic ideology and truthful democratic praxis in communities of teachers and learners could do much to show up the fraud of the democratic make-believe on the large political arena of the state. And it could help to expose to public scrutiny other essential ideological supports for domination as well, including conventional patriotism, empiricist fixation on purely factual knowledge in the name of science, and the equation of "progress" with expanding consumerism and professionalism. Once effective exposure is achieved, a free dialogue and the association of words with praxis, i.e., social experimentation, could make inroads on domination, or even make transcendence of domination a real possibility in many communities, in many parts of the world. In a real sense, institutions of higher learning could become resource centers in the ongoing struggle for human emancipation, not only with what they teach but with how they live, work, and govern themselves.

4

Resistance against Coercion, Deprivation, and Violence

HERE WE TURN to the topic of oppression in the most common understanding of that term: people pushing other people around, with varying degrees of deliberate intent or of grievousness of consequences—consequences in terms of subjugation or resistance, or in terms of seriousness of physical or spiritual harm suffered by the victims of coercive oppression (I shall use "coercive oppression" as a shorthand term for coercion, deprivation, and violence).

Coercive oppression is a big topic to be discussed within the small space available in this chapter. I want not only to clarify the central concepts but to use them to generalize about what is going on in our modern world, and to formulate some rational judgments about how urgently the various modes of coercive oppression need to be stopped, or at least resisted; I also want to contribute some general recommendations toward viable and rational strategies of resistance to coercive oppression.

That part of my task was easier in chapter 3, on the theme of domination, where it seems so clear that critique, articulated understanding, exposure, ultimately a radical political education, are the essential emancipatory strategies; for with a large-scale and effective consciousness-raising and critical forcefulness, developed and activated within participatory communities, the myths and frauds at the root of domination are bound to lose some of their force and become less serviceable as legitimators of authority. Some of the domination may wither away, as has happened in a lot of locations in which there used to be clerical domination over ordinary people's private lives, or domination by males over the females in their proximity; but the more normal outcome of resistance to domination is that it becomes transformed into starkly visible, coercive oppression. Most victories over domination, then, will lead to coercive oppression, the topic of this chapter.

I shall begin by defining again the key terms and the modes of coercive oppression and by clarifying the basic differences between utilitarian or liberal-democratic priorities of emancipation and the human right strategy that I shall be advocating. Next I will discuss the problem of determining the right priorities among rights, and in the same context I will discuss what I take to be a basic dilemma in every kind of social order: while rights priorities *ought* to be ordered according to objective human need priorities, privileged classes and governments always develop vested interests in pursuing priorities that bolster their own power and privileges. Governments will therefore tend to be inhospitable to serious dialogues about human rights priorities, as distinct from advocacy of the general idea of human rights or from indulging in highminded but vague slogans in support of *the* human rights cause.

How to overcome such weighty and persistent obstacles to the struggle for the emancipation of those, first of all, who are most badly oppressed? In the third part of this chapter I shall discuss various basic issues of organizational strategies; I shall emphasize the need for horizontal organizations and for strategies that are planned out in the open and are consistently nonviolent, while at the same time militant and wary of cooptation tendencies: confrontations must press for settlements that weaken the antagonists' power in future contests, as integral parts of longterm strategies, and avoid settlements that merely resolve immediate economic grievances. In the last part I shall briefly argue for a strategy that demands a guaranteed annual income as a human right. This is a liberal-type remedy for oppression, in that it is in line with the welfare-state approach to political legitimation, but it is in my view a kind of remedy that can open radically new possibilities for political education, consciousness raising, and nonviolent revolutionary action in the struggle against deprivation and other coercive oppression as well as domination. Even advancing the demand seriously can bring about healthy political repercussions, I shall argue.

1. KEY CONCEPTS AND ASSUMPTIONS:
COERCIVE OPPRESSION AND HUMAN RIGHTS

The evils of violence, deprivation, and coercion—in that order—are in principle contested by hardly anyone, even if in their political practices people keep on inflicting such evils on one another. In the jungle of the animal world, as in Thomas Hobbes's state of nature, animals and men would seem perpetually doomed to hurt and kill, or else *be* hurt or killed—"Do unto others before they do unto you!" Hobbes saw it as the crucial task of the political enterprise, the state, to put an end to the state of nature for the human species. In recent years some remarkably imaginative optimists have toyed with the idea, at least, of liberating even the animal world itself, at least the "sentient" animal world, from the laws of the jungle, to make it possible for the lion and the lamb to lie down together, in carefully sheltered parkland environments.[1] Compassionate explorers like the Adamsons[2] have indeed shown that a lioness and her cubs can be socialized to become trustworthy friends of some humans, and there is much experience on record with the "taming" of animals of many species. However, I have seen no evidence as yet that lions or other predators can be induced to prefer a vegetarian diet; *homo sapiens* appears to be the only species of predator whose members sometimes acquire this capacity.

While, personally speaking, I abhor the violence of the jungle as it affects animals, as a social scientist and even as a political theorist I must in this book, at least, limit my emancipatory zeal to the task of *human* emancipation from violence and other modes of oppression. To define my key terms again, "violence" here will refer to coercion or deprivation that causes or amounts to serious physical or mental harm to one or more human beings. All existentially needless suffering will be referred to as "deprivation"; all inducements which by threatened punishment (violence or deprivation) or promised reward (escape from violence or deprivation) make the individual abandon strongly desired courses of action (or inaction) will here be called "coercion." Inevitably, the three concepts overlap; to me the more

important distinctions are not between these three but between coercive oppression and domination, and between
either of these two and the third basic mode of oppression,
alienation, the topic of the next chapter. Note, however, that
"coercion" presupposes actors intending to coerce, unlike
violence and deprivation, which may be caused by deliberate
political/economic action but which may also be, exclusively
or in part, *structural*, i.e., not intended, perhaps not even
acknowledged, by those who uphold and perhaps benefit
from a particular political system. For the hundreds of millions in today's world who are trapped in health-destroying,
hopeless poverty, it would be of little comfort to be told
that they are victimized by the liberal-corporate system, not
by individual persons who wish them ill.

Emancipation from coercive oppression is, conceptually
speaking, a clearer objective than emancipation from either
domination or alienation, for what is at stake is out in the
open, visible to oppressors and victims alike, and to outside
observers as well. Empirical inquiry can in principle obtain
measurements of absolute and relative deprivation and of
the incidence and severity of violence suffered; on the latter
score the size of medical bills is one kind of indicator, even
though this magnitude to be sure is influenced by the status
of the doctor as well as by the graveness of the injury. To
assess in comparative terms the costs of or degrees of mental
anguish and suffering inflicted on victims of coercion is admittedly a lot more difficult, in that it is hard to measure
directly the importance to one or more victims of coercion
of the various plans or activities that had to be abandoned
or altered. But possibilities for indirect measurement are
there for resourceful researchers; over time, indicators of
trends toward harsher or less severe coercion in a given
society are in principle attainable, at least in ordinal-
comparative terms, which are what matters: are coercion,
deprivation, and violence (their incidence tends to inter-
correlate) on the increase, or is freedom from coercive oppression increasing?

The legitimacy of a regime, I submit, should depend on
whether it promotes expanding freedom or expanding oppression; in principle, I would entertain a sense of political
obligation only to the extent that I am persuaded that a

regime or a government is working to expand freedom from coercive oppression, and with better results than I would expect from an alternate regime or an alternate government. But whose freedom are we talking about: the freedom of my own reference group (ethnic? religious? occupational?) or class? the freedom of the majority? the freedom of the least privileged in society? The first alternative is in practice widely taken for granted in our kind of society, I dare say, but as it cannot be justified in philosophical terms, I shall ignore it in this context. The second represents the liberal-democratic and more particularly the utilitarian outlook, while the third represents the human rights outlook that I shall adopt.

The utilitarian perspective judges the merits of a regime by the impact over time of its policies on the extent or degree of happiness of the greatest number. How can research be of help in establishing baselines and trends in happiness? Ordinary survey research techniques can lead to profoundly misleading results in the assessment of public happiness: in a society of domination and alienation we are all programmed, even if the programming doesn't always stick, to give happy answers. In recent years considerable efforts have been invested in developing better social indicators of the quality of life, yet the subjective dimensions of the various aspects of qualities in each life are as elusive to researchers as they are dimly articulated by most people. Take tranquillity of mind, for example, or the meaningfulness of life, or the quality of love-relationships, in a broad sense of "love." How to assess the depth of intention in each respondent's reply? How to weigh each reply in assessing a respondent's relative happiness or freedom? To take an example from a recent compilation of social indicator–based data on well-being in the United States, what are we to make of this tidbit of information, based on formally impeccable data: "The percentage of [the American] people saying they were 'very happy' has gradually declined between 1957 and 1972"?[3]

The value of research on social indicators should not be discounted, however; the measures have been improved upon over the years and are becoming more meaningful and more comprehensive.[4] We must grant to the utilitarians the point that trends in the public's happiness are not in principle beyond rational assessment. Yet some of Bentham's ontological shortcuts, which John Stuart Mill rebelled against, will continue to vex the researcher in this area, and more so the policy theorist who wants to interpret research data on social indicators: How do we assess modes of happiness unrelated to scarcity issues in comparison to zero-sum–oriented modes of happiness, where pleasure is associated with rankings in status or competitive good fortune? What do we do with *Schadenfreude*, the cheerful contemplation of the misery of others? How do we assess the happiness derived from a sense of accomplishments in virtue, in the classical sense of this term, compared to happiness derived from private acquisitions or from physical feats? As the younger Mill discovered, there certainly are qualitative as well as quantitative differences among modes of happiness.

Yet it is on ethical, not ontological, grounds, and not on account of heavier obstacles to research on comparative oppression, that I reject the utilitarian and, more generally, the liberal-democratic approach to political priority-setting and choose to adopt the human rights approach instead. While there are important research advantages in this choice,[5] my crucial concern is to uphold the Kantian commitment that each human being must be valued equally, and infinitely, as an end in himself or herself; no human being's basic happiness or freedom must be sacrificed to benefit the majority. This orientation is also deeply rooted, of course, in Christian theology. Only less basic freedoms, liberties that I shall call *privileges* rather than human rights, can and indeed when necessary *should* be sacrificed so that other people's, or even one other person's, basic rights can be secured.

"Privilege" shall here refer to any freedom that by its nature is competitive or scarce, in the sense that its enjoyment by one person means that there is less of the same freedom left to enjoy for others, or less of other freedoms that are equally basic or more basic in terms of their relevance to human health and well-being. Examples of privileges are the ownership of sizable tracts of land, fishing rights when fish are scarce, enjoyment of larger-than-average income, positions of power in a corporation. As an empirical generalization I think it is probably true to say that no privileged freedom, in this sense, is necessary for a person's health, nor for his or her basic well-being, unless he or she has been programmed to think otherwise (admittedly a big *if!*). My ethical/political premise is that the freedoms that *are* essential to individual health and basic well-being *must always take precedence over privileged freedoms*, to the fullest *possible* extent: that is, to the extent that they can in fact be made available to all by the powers that be, should they be so inclined; existentially speaking, these are the freedoms that without logical contradiction and without depletion of nonrenewable resources can be made available to all human beings, with proper political arrangements and policies. These preferred freedoms, the freedoms that in principle *can* be made universally available, constitute the range of empirically possible human rights.

I shall not dwell on issues of ontology here. As I shall be using the term, a right is a claim, not a revealed entitlement. When I speak of human rights I refer to all the basic political claims that *ought* to be made, and supported, in behalf of every human being, *qua* human being.[6] When I say that I adopt the human rights approach to politics, this may be a statement with ontological implications, but my intention is to make a fundamental political choice: I mean to support the claim, to the extent of calling it a human right, for all human beings to have their essential needs met, and to make the connecting assertion that it is the primary and indeed the legitimating purpose of any government to enforce, make universal, and expand all human rights, within the limits of ecological responsibility. Moreover, I mean to affirm that human rights must be enforced and expanded according to just priorities, and, finally, that just priorities are to be determined, not by the conventional wisdom or other pragmatic considerations nor by democratic contests, but by the best available knowledge of biological and psychological priorities among basic human *needs*. I shall come back to this issue of needs priorities shortly; let me at this point only state what to me seems a self-evident point of departure: the need for life itself must come first; next, the need to be spared from violence or deprivation destructive of one's health.

H. L. A. Hart argues that *if* there are any moral rights at all, then there must be at least one basic right, which he chooses to call *natural*: "the equal right of all men to be free."[7] Hart's argument is that the acts of promising, consenting, etc., which are widely recognized as a principal basis for moral rights and duties, could not be so construed without the prior assumption that a person has the right to choose freely whether to promise or consent or not, etc. My own construction of human rights objectives as a just hierarchy of aims asserts in a somewhat parallel fashion that if particular political and legal rights and duties are to be judged as legitimate (i.e., recognized as morally binding), then we must first be satisfied that the *system* of legislation and of government is committed to securing equal and optimal legal protection of the freedoms of all persons, according to the priorities among needs. As rights must be prior to privileges, so must more basic rights (those that protect more basic needs) take precedence over less basic rights.

While one might choose to call this political claim natural, or naturally based, in that the hierarchy of needs is determined by the most pressing requirements of man's biological and psychological nature, I repeat that I prefer to steer clear of ontological arguments about human nature, at least for now, and rest my case on the rationality of the argument that no government can merit loyalty and a sense of political obligation on the part of rational citizens except to the extent that it—within the limits of ecological responsibility—consistently works to protect and expand human rights equally for all, according to the priorities established by the best available knowledge of human need priorities.

In substance I think Herbert Marcuse's distinction between "true" and "false" needs (see 3 §1) dramatizes a most important insight, which has been lost on liberal theorists, although Plato had placed this insight at the center of his political theorizing: there is a radical difference, Plato taught, between reality and appearance in human affairs, and in political affairs there is a constant temptation for establishment ideologists (or, in Plato's language, for rhetoricians who are not critical, truth-seeking philosophers with a Socratic kind of integrity) to hoodwink ordinary people into thinking that their welfare is being served when all they get is an appearance of being benefited.

Having been the real founder of so many modern fields of academic inquiry, Plato may also be considered the first organizational and political sociologist: he saw with astounding clarity that ambitious politicians will find their easiest way to fame and fortune through flattering the public, taking advantage of most people's vanity and gullibility. Flatterers will become popular while critics like Socrates, who are morally compelled to seek to benefit the people by identifying and serving their real needs, are likely to lose out against the glib-talking careerists and may well come to a bad end, if that is how we will characterize the sentencing and death of Socrates.

Yet I differ with Marcuse on how to conceptualize this core political issue. I think the concepts of "true" and "false" needs are misleadingly facile, for they suggest a clear empirical distinction, even an easy classification. Moreover, this suggestion makes it all too easy for liberal writers like Berlin (see 1 §2) to establish the plausibility of refusing to make any distinction between a positive freedom of self-expression, worthwhile in terms of individual needs and aspirations, and an externally imposed, ideologically or commercially programmed *appearance* of self-expression. A critical biographer of Marcuse plausibly infers "inescapable elitist consequences of his viewpoint"[8] on the basis of this unfortunate terminology.

My preferred alternative is to make an empirically far more feasible distinction between (genuine) *needs* and (genuine or artificially stimulated) *wants*.[9]

Wants are readily ascertainable facts. What assets people try to obtain, or say they need or want, are by definition to be classified among these people's wants. The extent and distribution of wants, their relative intensity, and how given individuals rank their wants, or how all individuals in a given society rank some of their wants relative to others, are readily ascertainable by various well known methods of behavioral research. Economists and market researchers have their own ways of studying some, though perhaps not all, kinds of wants, in terms of what people are prepared to pay (or would pay, if they had the means), or barter, or otherwise sacrifice to obtain desired assets.

With respect to *needs*, however, there is no easy way of empirical ranking, let alone measurement. Needs are hypothetical constructs. The concept is empirically based, but almost as elusive to the researcher as "human nature." "Human need" will in this work refer to any and all minimum requirements for every individual's health and well-being, as distinct from the needs of specific categories of individuals, or needs that are shared by all or most people within a given social order and/or culture. By definition, when a person becomes psychosomatically sick, or commits suicide, or becomes dependent on health-destructive drugs, some of his or her individual needs are not being met; if such things happen to many in a given class or culture, then class-shared or culturally imprinted needs are not being met; if in the study of sickness in this broad sense we begin to find regularities across cultures and across generations, then we may develop tentative empirical generalizations about human need priorities in general. We can also study conditions under which, in various societies, high levels of public health are achieved.

For practical purposes, though, we make our assumptions about human need priorities in given societies, rightly or wrongly implying that the most basic human needs are probably the same everywhere, beneath their varieties of cultural and class manifestations. To determine what people in difficulties *need* is the practical task of the health professions and other helping professions in the "social sector" of our kind of society, but it is also the task of caring families, neighbors, friends, and acquaintances. Most often it is a complex task to establish with sufficient exactitude the relevant range of needs of individuals in trouble; not an insoluble task but yet a taxing, perhaps a never-ending task.

To determine what *many* people need, or *most* people need, is the task of caring, critical philosophers like Socrates, and it is the task of all critical humanists. Liberal philosophers, by contrast, tend to set themselves easier tasks: they tend to be either utilitarians or contractually oriented democrats, who assume that their day's work is done if they can do their utmost to attempt to give people what they say they want. If people were not living in an alienating society, and could be assumed to be free to develop conscious wants that really reflected their basic need priorities, then straightforward liberal democracy might well give all the required answers. But in a social order such as ours—or such as Plato's, for that matter—such simplemindedness will not work.

But neither will it do to take an opposite course, so easily suggested by Marcuse's terminology, and simply hold that our politicians must choose to serve, when this is within their power, the people's "true" needs while ignoring or suppressing or explaining away their "false" needs. This course could indeed come to vindicate Plato's Republic, or Stalin's Politburo.

The resolution of this dilemma must be sought in dialectics as well as in positivist social research. We must begin with a healthy dose of respect for people's actual wants, whatever their origin, or "genuine"-ness; in other words, with a determination to champion negative liberty, in Berlin's sense: freedom from coercion. To do people good against their own will is to serve people badly.

Next, however, we must acknowledge that many people may be artificially *and precariously* programmed, on the surface of their consciousness, to prefer certain policies or values, but we may yet suspect that slightly below the surface they may (or, of course, they may not) strongly prefer other policies, or other values.[10] The task is not to make decisions about what most people need at variance with what they say they need, but to activate public discussion about what is needed; the task is to activate ourselves and one another in continuing discussions of our values and their policy implications. Plato saw the need for a continuing dialogue clearly, and so did Hegel and Marx: ideas develop, in history as in the minds of individuals, through rational confrontations, through challenges and counterchallenges.

In our time we know much about how to facilitate confrontations between ideas, in the kinds of situations in which people are free to consider ideas on their merits, after weighing all the arguments. In our better universities we do this most of the time in the natural or consensually supported sciences.[11] There are many possibilities, too, for achieving this in the dissensual, "controversial" sciences, in which establishment resistance (in *our* social order, ideological liberal resistance) at the present time limits the range of rational discussion.

Paulo Freire (see 3 §5) has demonstrated how it is possible to move out of our relatively sheltered academic arenas for intellectual confrontations and assist people in all walks of life in the task of finding their own voices and learning to articulate with more confidence wants that are in line with their own enduring needs.

It is a mistake, I think, for Marxists to dissociate themselves from Marcuse's true-needs/false-needs distinction by way of historicizing all needs, as some critical Marxists are prone to do. William Leiss does this, in his important work *Limits to Satisfaction*.[12] His approach loses sight of the basic biological-psychological unity of the human species, which I think we must assume to be there. While universal basic needs and propensities to be sure are hard to establish empirically, let alone with any degree of exactitude, I think we must reject the notion that, of all species, mankind is the one that is entirely without instinctual equipment or species-wide psychological characteristics of any kind.

My position is, as will be amplified in section 2, that all human beings have at least three broad classes of basic needs, only the first of which is shared by all animal species: basic physical needs, community needs, and subjectivity needs. Moreover, I shall assume that there is a universal hierarchy among these need categories, in the sense that the basic physical needs precede the other two, followed by community or social-belongingness needs. I shall try to make a case that human rights priorities must be based on these elementary assumptions, and that a legitimate government, whether liberal-democratic or otherwise-democratic,[13] must honor and promote human rights as effectively as possible, in the order of these priorities. Such, in my view, is the rational humanist agenda in the macropolitical struggle against political coercion.

2. RIGHT AND WRONG PRIORITIES AMONG HUMAN RIGHTS

If it is granted that social privileges must yield to human rights and that less basic human rights must yield to more basic ones, on the basis of priorities among human needs, it follows that the most oppressed persons in any social order must have prior claims on protection, support, and redress of grievances from any government that claims political legitimacy.

Who are the most oppressed? We must seek a way to determine objectively, or at least rationally, what are the worst categories of oppression. If many kinds of human need are badly met in a given society, which kinds of neglect of need, or of which kinds of need, should be considered the worst outrage?

It would seem that common sense can take us the first few steps without risk of challenge, and I think the very first observation must be that there are some basic collective requirements for human life, now and in the future, which must be met prior to any and all individual needs: any clear or probable menace to the biosphere or to the ecosystem on which all human, animal, and plant life depends, must be faced up to and remedied, at all costs. Second, short of omnicide and short of humanicide, genocide must be considered the ultimate crime against humanity, closely followed by other varieties of mass murder, whether with the state's active complicity or, only slightly less damnable, with the state's passive, perhaps conniving, tolerance. For example, a state that allows its defenseless indigenous peoples to be decimated, whether by tolerating privately financed hunting parties out to clear Amazonian real estate of so-called squatters, or by failing to provide life-saving medicines against our expansive civilization's diseases; governments guilty of allowing genocide within the state's borders deserve the most extreme acts of resistance, even punishment when possible, from its citizenry, and from all the rest of mankind (my point of view on what such a government *deserves* is of course a subjective position, but I maintain that the *principle* that genocide is the gravest of all crimes against humanity, short of humanicide, is self-evident if one starts out assuming that human life, every human life, is the highest value).

Common sense can carry us beyond genocide, I believe, to stipulate that murder and homicide represent the most extreme violation of individual human need: when a life is destroyed, every need of that person is irreparably violated. Thus, the right to life must be the ultimate individual human right, taking precedence over all others.

And we can move one more step before we leave the comfortable realm of common sense: next to murder and homicide comes other grievous violence against the person, grievous enough to harm that person's health, resulting in long-lasting infirmities and scars. Physical and mental torture and brutal assault come first to mind, but let us stress that "violence" should refer to actual harm suffered by human beings; therefore, degrees of violence must be measured by degrees of harm or damage suffered. This is where we need to go beyond the conventional common sense that associates violence only with deliberate acts, and especially with the acts of criminals and revolutionaries. As I argued in a paper some years ago, every state has its semantical defense system which involves slanting the uses of key terms so that so-called hurrah words become associated with the established order (words like democracy, patriotism, freedom), while so-called boo words become associated with anti–established-order activities (like violence, disloyalty, subversion). I tried in that paper to "liberate" the word violence from its subservience to the established order by way of defining it broadly as referring to all kinds of existentially unnecessary harm done to a person's health or freedom; if we stick to this broad definition of violence, it becomes a researchable question how the amounts and degrees of violence inflicted on persons by the state, or with the connivance of the state, compare to the amounts and degrees of violence inflicted by, or contemplated by, revolutionaries.[14] As John Stuart Mill was deeply aware of coerciveness relative to his and Harriet's salient subjectivity needs, like privacy, we ought to recognize that the same holds for more basic needs as well: in different social orders there are varying levels of *structural violence* (see 4 §1); poverty and unemployment, for example, can in many cases destroy lives, and so can the ostracism suffered by many kinds of minorities with deviant attitudes or behavior tendencies. The general point I am making with regard to rights priorities is that violations of rights should be considered equally grievous, whether the damage is done by structural violence or by deliberate acts of violence; the amount of harm suffered should be the crucial consideration. One application of this principle is that I think a position of strict pacifism cannot be deduced from the basic political premise that I have adopted, that violence against human beings, especially lethal violence, is the supreme evil that government and politics exist to prevent; for structural violence may at times and in places be so destructive that counterviolence, *if* it will work, may be justifiable, and could conceivably even become a humanist's moral obligation.[15]

If we cannot claim the backing of conventional common sense in handling the issue of how human need priorities are affected by violence, we can even less claim that a further extension of the need hierarchy follows from common sense. Nevertheless I think a strong case can be made for arguing, in substantial agreement with Abraham H. Maslow, that sustenance needs come next; Maslow actually places them ahead of safety needs; I shall from here on group both categories of need together and call them *basic physical needs*.[16] For sustenance needs, too, a reasoning parallel to that pertaining to the issue of violence must hold: the causing of death, for example by starvation, must be the extreme violation of human need, followed by deprivation grievous enough to damage the person's health, leaving lasting infirmities and scars.

Next, Maslow proposes a need for belongingness, affection, being loved; followed by a need for self-esteem, dignity, social recognition. I shall group these two clusters together as *community solidarity needs*. Since Plato and Aristotle, through Hegel and Marx in modern times, the mainstream of political philosophy has held that man is a social animal; even if in our part of the world the liberal aberration that Hobbes and Locke inaugurated has been programming several generations to think of ourselves as largely self-sufficient, atomized, competitive individualists. Yet the need for social acceptance and certainly the need not to be banished or ostracized from our own communities have remained obviously powerful needs also in liberal-thinking societies. Anthropologists have noted that evildoers who are banished from their own tribes often die very quickly without other apparent cause; in our own civilization the results of banishment are as a rule not equally dramatic, perhaps, but surely the severing of all social ties is destructive of mental health unless new ties can be established without much delay.

In practical terms I conclude that many isolated individuals in our urbanized society badly need assistance to find new communities to belong to, or to find the way back to their old ones; also, that underprivileged communities need protection against continuing invasion by the symbols of the affluent individualist commodity-cult and its inherent tendency to pit man against man in competition for resources under conditions of scarcity (real or perceived, natural or contrived). The plight of so many North American natives, communities as well as displaced persons, can best be seen in terms of the destruction of their customary ways of meeting their community needs, a result of the continuing cultural invasion by the dominant liberal/capitalist culture. With respect to our own culture, Philip Slater has argued persuasively in his *The Pursuit of Loneliness* that our official ethos of rugged individualism rests precariously on a barely adequate suppression of deep-going communitarian needs of our own; he subtitles his book *American Culture at the Breaking Point.*[17]

The next need in the basic hierarchy, Maslow proposes, is the need for self-actualization, growth, development of the person; in his later works he calls these needs Being-needs, or B-needs, as distinct from Deficiency-needs, or D-needs.[18] I shall prefer the term *subjectivity needs*, following the usage of David J. Baugh.[19] "The use and fulfillment of our humanity—its powers and wants—to the outer limits fixed by the material conditions and capacity of the time," this is how Richard N. Goodwin defines freedom.[20] We may conceive of a tree capable of an optimal height, straightness, and strength, under ideal conditions of soil, moisture, sunlight, etc.; figuratively speaking, we may think of every person being capable of reaching optimal powers of intellect, sensitivity, responsibility to self and others under ideal social and cultural circumstances. The concept of self-actualization, while in its application it poses issues of degrees of development, envisages the ideal of human beings eventually coming into their own and realizing their full potentialities. This is a conceptual bridge to Utopia, but also a conception that suggests, as we shall see, that it is possible to struggle for a fuller self-assertion and growth even while our social order remains such as it is today.

I shall venture only one or two steps onto that bridge, and leave it to more adventurous spirits to assess Maslow's claims regarding such alleged universal Being-needs as creativity, or the need for beauty. Perhaps, as we become progressively emancipated from deficiencies in sustenance and safety, and succeed in building more adequately caring communities, we will universally develop such subjectivity needs, and several others as well. I suspect this may well be the case, but will not take a position here, except to say that I do not believe that Maslow in his later works succeeded in making an adequate empirical case for the existence of invariant relationships between stages of self-actualization and factors like concern for others, creativity, or other developmental achievements. While stopping short of *The Farther Reaches of Human Nature*,[21] let me state as my own belief, supported by some converging evidence, that among subjectivity needs these three, at least, are basic and potentially[22] universal: the need for a sense of personal freedom, or power to make decisions affecting one's life;[23] the need for a sense of worth as a moral person, a sense of having a self worthy of being loved and capable of loving;[24] and the need for a sense of competency or growth toward increasing competency.[25]

Do subjectivity needs, too, justify claims to corresponding human rights? They most certainly do, I shall argue; but some qualifications must be made here, for in the name of supposedly hallowed rights or liberties one often hears claims that have no justification in the kinds of subjectivity needs that have been acknowledged here; claims, in fact, that would ride roughshod over other people's more basic rights and liberties. I am thinking particularly of the supposed individual right to acquire property without limits, a claim that Robert Nozick most recently has reaffirmed as if it were axiomatically valid.[26] (I shall also take issue, if more gingerly, with the liberal tendency to endorse the right to free speech ahead of most other rights.) Let us make a brief detour here, to consider the philosophical origins of this complication, as it affects the concept of subjectivity rights and the relationship of subjectivity rights to more basic human rights.

That great philosopher of property, John Locke, in some of his formulations does indicate some natural limits to the individual's right to accumulate property, with particular reference to property in land and in the products of the soil (and we must here bear in mind that in Locke's time, with the vast American continents opened up for European settlers so recently, there did seem to be almost limitless land resources available): one acquires personal entitlement to property by way of mixing one's labor with what previously belonged to mankind in common, assuming that (1) one leaves enough for others to acquire in the same way, (2) one only acquires a right to as much products of the land as one can make use of before it spoils, and (3) one is only entitled to as much land as oneself, with one's household, can effectively cultivate and harvest.[27]

However, for Locke this was just the beginning; "in the beginning," he wrote, "all the world was America . . . for no such thing as *Money* was ever known."[28] Far away from markets, on the American prairies, what could a man do with ten thousand, or a hundred thousand, grain-growing acres? Locke perhaps forgot that out of grains you can make liquor, which is slow to spoil and far less bulky than grains, but he made the more important point that the market and the money economy had been expanding fast in postfeudal times. To Locke, that had created a new situation, and, alas, he lets go by the board his initial moral limitations on the acquisition of property; this turnabout on his part incidentally goes a long way to explaining the good press that Locke has kept receiving in liberal societies: Due to the artificial but universally agreed upon value of gold and silver, for exchange purposes rather than for utility purposes in relation to human needs, "it is plain, that Men have agreed to disproportionate and unequal Possession of the Earth, they having by a tacit and voluntary consent found out a way, how a man may fairly possess more land than he himself can

use the product of, by receiving in exchange for the over-
plus, Gold and Silver, which may be hoarded up without injury to any one. . . ."[29]

"Gold and Silver, which may be hoarded up *without injury to any one* . . ." (my italics); there is the crunch; the
last moral leverage that remains in Locke's theory of entitlement to acquisition and possession of property. It is implicitly a more powerful lever today than most Locke-
quoting proponents of private property would care to admit.
There have been ever greater changes *since* the days of
Locke, and it is hardly possible in our days to argue that
when some people and some corporations hoard up great
amounts of gold and silver, or of capital in general, this
causes no injury to others. Vast amounts of property have
been accumulating in ever fewer hands; most of the richest
hands today are those of multinational corporations, which
in many respects are above or beyond the reach of state or
national legislation. The other side of the same process is
that most of mankind are nowadays forced to sell their labor
power for a very meagre sustenance, while an increasing
minority have no prospects of regular sustenance at all, as
there is insufficient demand for labor power due to the glut
of capital concentration. Short of revolutionary upheavals
the resources of unused or available land, too, are negligible;
the landless no longer have the ancient option of growing
their own food for a meagre sustenance. Most of the good
soil outside the Second (state-corporate) World has been
taken by the rich families or by the world's corporate
hoarders, yet the liberal ideology's commitment to private
property rights without limits persists, in our part of the
world, and often in the name of Locke. I think he is being
used, but he is no longer here to protest.[30]

As C. B. Macpherson has argued, the concept of property
badly needs to be redefined if we are to continue to respect,
or even to acknowledge, property *rights* in any morally significant sense: at least for property in land, in capital, and in
commodities, we need to think of property rights as *right of
access* to valued resources for all, rather than right of *exclusive* access by individual entitlement.[31] Moreover, we need
to distinguish property claims according to functions for
the person: some rights of access, exclusive or not, meet basic

needs for sustenance (food, shelter, etc.); some serve to affirm one's sense of identity and self-esteem; some may serve
one's need for a sense of personal growth; and some may
serve the most basic needs of new persons (like the means
to acquire homes of their own, for young couples living
together).

In the field of property rights the liberal indiscriminate
commitment to "the Rights of Man" has caused and is
causing much suffering, as well as much stunting of human
potentialities. In the next chapter I shall endorse Marx's argument that the liberal rights philosophy has elevated egoistic man at the expense of man as citizen, thus tending to
justify and perpetuate an economic system that alienates men
from their social nature and from one another. In the present
context I shall only stress the urgency of cutting loose from
that same liberal philosophy with respect to its indiscriminate
defense of all property rights and all civil liberties.

My stress here is on "indiscriminate." I do not want to be
understood as an opponent of property rights or of civil liberties, least of all as an indiscriminate opponent. I like to own
my own things. And, as the reader will suspect, I take great
pleasure in my own liberty to hold forth, for example in
these pages. Yet this is for me not the ultimate pleasure, and
still less the ultimate value. Free speech cannot be a right
above all others in importance. In principle, I feel that I
should willingly accept being silenced if, demonstrably, this
would probably contribute to saving other people's lives or
health; although I admit to being hard put to think of a
kind of demonstration that would be convincing unless there
were a climate of freedom that would allow the censor's case
to be challenged, openly.

The general point here is that there are not always enough
liberties to go around, especially when it comes to property
rights—to the free speech issue I shall return—and that we
need to become much more rational and explicit than hitherto in deciding about priorities, so that we can go to work
with articulated principles when we seek alternatives to the
present obscene maldistribution of property rights in today's
so-called Free World. I think the late E. F. Schumacher was

exactly right when he wrote as follows not long ago: "As. I see it, the main task of those who profess Christianity is to define the economic concept of 'enough.' If there is no idea of 'enough,' all problems become insoluble."[32]

As a general principle in resolving the tangled issues of what are the proper property rights, those rights must first of all be related to our knowledge of human need-priorities. Take the basic physical needs first: sustenance and safety. It should be evident that in a rational society every person has a *basic* right of access to available food resources, or to soil in which to grow them, when his or her family otherwise would face the prospect of starving. Laws and courts may decree otherwise; if so, these decrees should be null and void, seen from a rational humanist perspective.

Next, the community solidarity needs. Here, the conceptual terrain is less certain, in that it is harder in this area to conceive of conflicting individual property rights; but the native peoples in the Americas and in Australia have all been threatened with virtual extinction—many have in fact become extinct—under the onslaught of an avaricious and technologically superior civilization that unjustly took away from them natural property in their communal ways of life in their traditional environments. Today, when it is too late to rescue many of the once well adapted native peoples, there are at long last a few influential voices, that of Justice Thomas Berger for example, demanding that native land claims in Canada be recognized and respected,[33] but no equally strong, insistent, and humane voice like his has as yet been heard in Australia or in Latin America, to my knowledge. At any rate, our North American mass media have so far paid scant attention to the faint cries for help from voices of the doomed indigenous peoples, whose languages may die out with their own voices.

The subjectivity needs raise the most complex issues of property rights, for three principal reasons: (1) these needs are more difficult to conceptualize and place in a generally acceptable, rational order; (2) in this realm of need the ideological onslaught that Marx referred to as commodity fetishism makes it complicated to disentangle the authentic subjectivity needs from the consumerist *wants* that result from high-powered promotion and programming; and (3) there is also the mystification of corporations being supposedly morally entitled to property rights, as if they were human beings with human needs.

Let me proceed in reverse order and first touch on the issue of corporate rights. Legally, corporations are now treated as persons, whereas in fact they have no human needs; their entitlements should therefore according to rational humanist principles always yield to need-based entitlements. To be sure, corporations are the instrumentalities of real persons: staffs as well as shareholders do have human needs. Within the natural limits of a scheme that settles all rights priorities in terms of human need priorities, perhaps corporations *should* be entitled to operate in a predictable legal environment, so that they know what policies can be productive and what policies are legal.

But it seems to me clear that the entitlements of corporations must be limited at least in the following three ways: (1) legal protection of corporate holdings of land and capital must be limited to those that are sufficient to allow for a better servicing of public needs than could be achieved by individuals or by less job-specialized, cooperative communities; (2) all corporate books and all information about fiscal transactions and about production, marketing, and waste disposal must be made freely available to all, including potential competitors and critics—yes, especially to environmentalists, whose concern usually is with the survival rights of the least protected human beings, those not yet born;[34] and, last but not least, (3) any corporation can and should be disbanded with fair, though not necessarily full, compensation to staff and stockholders when in the view of politically responsible assessors these operations are no longer, on balance, in the public interest. If a corporation's sharp practices have inflated the value of its stocks, I can see no justification, barring the usual liberal sanctification of property rights, for paying more than a fractional compensation out of the public purse. I understand that President Allende was of the same opinion but that, alas, Dr. Henry Kissinger's contrary opinion proved to have greater force in Chile at the time.[35]

Returning now to individual property rights, a distinction must be attempted between (1) rights of acquisition of means of production; (2) rights of acquisition for hoarding or display purposes, bearing on wants and desires that are not clearly related to basic physical needs or even to the primary subjectivity needs; and (3) rights of acquisition or access for purposes basic to physical needs or community needs.

Few words need to be added to the case that Marx and other socialists have made against private ownership of the means of production: under the laws of the capitalist marketplace, this leads inevitably to the extraction of surplus value and to the accumulation of large concentrations of private capital in few hands, as the growing number of dispossessed are exploited and alienated from their own needs and nature. In today's world and in the light of a century of hindsight I would want to make three exceptions, however, from the Marxist ban on private property rights in means of production: (1) small, one-family or cooperatively organized, private service agencies, including shops, (2) modest-sized family farms (neither of these require the use of hired labor; they should be not only tolerated but encouraged), and, (3) somewhat larger productive enterprises of many kinds that are run by "horizontal communities"—communities of politically equal members, a concept I shall return to in the next chapter (see 5 §4). *Kibbutzim* that have not yet taken to using hired labor are a good example of this third category.

These proposed principles still leave us with perhaps the thorniest problem: how to distinguish personal acquisitions wanted for hoarding or display purposes from acquisitions for meeting basic individual needs or collective requirements? Underlying and implicit is the distinction between alienated wants and authentic human needs, itself a difficult distinction to make plausible as well as clear with few words.

Remember that we are now in the realm of individual subjectivity needs; I have argued before that access to property rights with which to meet basic physical needs must be prior to property rights bearing on community and subjectivity needs.

The first subjectivity need, I submit, is for a sense of a free and worthwhile self: a self with a measure of freedom, competency, and capability to make ethically good choices and to act on them. The self is by definition associated with a particular person, and has an identity, a name, along with a sense of being a (1) human (2) individual. While the former aspect of the self, the sense of being human, is at the root of his or her community needs, as we have seen, the latter, the sense of being an individual, is at the root of the need for freedom and for the other subjectivity needs.

On the subject of individual property rights bearing on subjectivity needs, a right to free choice on personal issues affecting how one lives would seem to be the first priority: the right to choose, among available alternatives, where to live; how to dress and how to groom oneself; what books and records and mementos to acquire, etc., insofar as one's proposed acquisitions do not exceed amounts or values that could be made available to all other persons with similar or overlapping subjectivity needs, and on the understanding that subjectivity-need–based rights to acquisitions in principle must yield to rights based on basic physical needs as well as community needs. These "insofar as's" merely reflect the Kantian universal moral imperative that throughout this book is assumed to follow from the rational humanist commitment to the supreme (and equal) value of each human life.[36]

That same principle of universality, also at the root of my distinction between human rights and privileges (see pp. 88-89), comes in particularly handy for the purpose of positioning civil liberties in relation to property rights: civil liberties such as free speech, freedom of association, freedom of religion. While these liberties are all in the realm that bears on either community or subjectivity needs, and therefore in principle must be secondary to rights bearing on survival needs, in practice it can rarely be shown that civil liberties–kinds of rights are incompatible with one another or with more basic human rights. One can therefore on most occasions be an uncompromising civil libertarian and yet a rational humanist, provided one maintains a sense of proportion and is ready to condemn violations of survival and community rights even more severely than violations of civil liberties, and is ready also to make some kinds of property rights yield, whenever they get in the way of more basic rights. There were times during the days of resistance against the American warfare in Vietnam when, in the hope of dramatizing atrocity issues, student war resisters clearly infringed upon the civil liberties and property rights of some academics by, for example, barring them from their offices; *if* in fact such violations did or could contribute to an earlier end to the war, such strong-arm tactics, at the time apparently repugnant to most civil libertarians, could from my own humanist perspective be justified, even commended.

The same universality axiom, when applied to ordering priorities among rights of access to or of private acquisition of property, is complicated by the ideology of scarcity in liberal-corporate societies: they vigorously manufacture an artificial sense of scarcity throughout society. We are all being programmed, through advertising and liberal journalism, to compete for commodities "in limited supply"; that is how sales are promoted and profits are made. In the last chapter I shall show that, objectively speaking, there is no necessity today for scarcity anywhere in the world, least of all with respect to protein and other crucial nutritional requirements (see 6 §3). It is all the more clear that other existing scarcities, especially in our own relatively affluent societies, are artificially produced and often perceived rather than real; they are not a matter of too many people and of a too limited capacity to produce. Eventually, if a libertarian socialist society is ever achieved, I anticipate that community life and social relationships will be so enriched that most people's want of commodities to meet subjectivity needs will be radically reduced, and result in an end not only to scarcity but to the illusion of scarcity.

In the meantime, however, and for the foreseeable future, objective shortages will persist with respect to various consumer commodities, and schemes of distributive justice will be required. Apart from making sure that survival needs are met first, in the whole world, it would seem to me that the right strategy toward limiting waste as well as consumption of not-needed commodities should include (but not be limited to) the following action programs: (1) an end to all promotional commodity advertising; (2) a reduction, by progressive taxation, of all major discrepancies in levels of income and of property accumulation; and (3) the introduction of nationwide rationing schemes. As many of us who have lived with wartime and postwar rationing schemes have found, shortages are much easier to live with when it is known that they are shared on an equitable basis. In fact, in our time there may be positive benefits, too, from national rationing schemes: they may help create a good climate for extensive collaboration for conservation and for recycling of raw materials in limited supply; such colaboration in turn may stimulate new bonds and solidarity feelings which may well do more for human happiness than our present patterns of competitive acquisitiveness in search of that elusive comfort, social status.

What makes it seem particularly appropriate to call for these and similar antiliberal strategies today, at least as issues to discuss, even if they cannot yet be implemented, is first of all the increasingly acknowledged objective need for scaling down the waste and the literally need-less misuse of natural and human resources in our liberal-capitalist societies. Something must be done to stop the present drift soon, lest there be too little left to subsist on, healthily, for future generations; moreover, something must be done soon if we are to make possible, today and tomorrow, decent standards of life for our fellow human beings who live in much poorer countries. The idea of *sharing* with others is a fundamental principle in our Judeo-Christian tradition, as it is in other religions and in the humanist traditions as well. It may come back. But our liberal ideology has for much too long diverted our attention from the joys of sharing. Now that the issue of human rights has caught much of mankind's attention, it is a challenge to keep that great aspiration from becoming a mere adjunct to liberalism, a celebration of bourgeois property rights and American-style civil liberties. The humanist task is to insist on the *universality* of human rights, in space and in time, internationally and through the generations, and on rational, need-based *priorities* among them: the only kind of world order that is good enough to struggle for is one that requires no more victims of structural violence or deprivation elsewhere so that ample liberties may prosper for privileged classes and individuals in our own "advanced" parts of the world.

3. DILEMMAS IN EMANCIPATORY ORGANIZATIONAL STRATEGIES

Strategies in the struggle against coercive oppression must in principle be worldwide; thought about strategies must be universalistic in overall conception. A century ago it could still make moral sense in this part of the world to argue that our concern should be with our own country, for it was not obvious then that the United States was doing violence to peoples in other continents. In our time it is all too clear that the destruction of lives in the Third World is to a large extent attributable to the international economic system that is enforced by and serves the perceived interests of those who have power in the First World nations. We all witness the continuing drama of economically strong multinational corporations, under banners like "private enterprise" and "free trade," dealing with weak and corrupt regimes, many of which condemn the bulk of their fellow nationals to unspeakable deprivation rather than suffer losses in national revenue, so vital to keeping their armies and bureaucracies adequately supplied. And in virtuous antagonism to communist oppression the great powers in the West have accumulated vast armaments, which have served not only to impose a heavy burden of armaments on the USSR and its allies but have also helped crush Third World uprisings in behalf of the most oppressed classes.

While coercive oppression can be brutal in the United States, too—in jails and mental institutions, in violence-prone homes and neighborhoods, in ghettos and in rural slums—for the majority of its people this country provides a relatively sheltered environment, compared to most Third World countries. The oppression that limits and confines most American lives is unobtrusive and smooth rather than brutal and violent. This is even more true in North European countries, where the pacifying influence of social democracy has made even the poor and the old a bit more comfortable, I think, than are most of their respective peers in North America.

The point to stress at the outset is that the First World nowadays is exporting most of the violence and stark deprivation that the liberal-corporate system produces. The most predatory corporations have kept moving much of their efforts into Third World environments, where there are whole armies of unemployed to supply willing labor for a pittance; where nascent labor unions can be crushed with the assistance of armies and secret police; where international credit requirements render the regimes all but impotent to interfere with private industry and trade; and where corporate taxes and concerns for the environment are so modest in scope that they amount to at most a nuisance for the multinational corporations operating there.

In this chapter I shall nevertheless limit my discussion of strategies of resisting coercive oppression to what we can do in the United States and other liberal-corporate societies. I return to the issue of worldwide strategies in chapter 6.

While the major kind of remedy in combatting domination must be sought in a more effective political pedagogy (see chapter 3), the main strategy in the struggle against coercive oppression, at least in liberal-corporate societies, must be to build more effective horizontal political organizations. By *organizations* I mean cooperative efforts of any kind that are coordinated and disciplined in order to achieve optimal results on a continuing basis. By *horizontal* organizations I mean organizations whose members work together as political equals, as partners mutually committed to a continuing dialogue as the basis for majoritarian decisions about ends, priorities, and strategies. Every organization is *coordinated* or it falls apart; most organizations today ensure coordination by being *disciplined* from the top down. The primary challenge to political activists in the struggle against coercive oppression is to raise political consciousness and the amount and quality of learning from experience to the point where *self*-discipline can ensure adequate coordination. A more effective political pedagogy can of course be of great help here, both toward keeping some new organizations horizontal, and toward gradually making many hierarchical organizations become a little less so, i.e., a little more horizontal.

In this country there have been a variety of important

movements that have struggled to put an end to violent oppression, with varying degrees of success: the antislavery movements, the trade union movement, the civil rights movement, the feminist movements, the movements to defend the rights of gays and other sexual minorities, poor people's movements, and most recently the movements in defense of our natural environment. Many other kinds of movements could be mentioned.

There is no space here for a review of what we can learn from the experience of each of these kinds of movements; only a few points will be made about the most important of them up to now, the trade union movement.

Referring to the American experience, Frances Fox Piven and Richard A. Cloward are quite right to take issue with the common belief that the economic and political advances of the working class have been mainly a result of developing strong trade unions; they call this "the organizer's credo," along with the conviction that this is the way, too, that all other powerless groups must follow, since the "experience of labor unions in the United States is the bedrock on which the organizer's credo is grounded":

> But on closer historical scrutiny, the bedrock turns out to be sand. Factory workers had their greatest influence and were able to extract their most substantial concessions from government during the early years of the Great Depression *before they were organized into unions.* Their power was not rooted in organization, but in their capacity to disrupt the economy. For the most part strikes, demonstrations, and sitdowns spread during the mid-1930s despite existing unions rather than because of them. Since these disorders occurred at a time of widespread political instability, threatened political leaders were forced to respond with placating concessions. One of these concessions was protection by the government of the right to organize. Afterwords, union membership rose, largely because government supported unionization. But once organized, the political influence of workers declined.[37]

Let us emphasize again the oligarchical tendencies in enduring organizations, which tend to accelerate when organizations grow big and strong. While the early, fledgling labor unions were clearly emancipatory organizations, fully committed to improving the lot of the whole working class as well as that of their own members, the modern large unions tend to serve narrow interests rather than broad ideals; they have come to resemble corporations in some ways, with inflated salaries at the top, a bureaucratic apparatus with career opportunities for those who develop the habit of getting along well with the top officers, and with elaborate precautions to ensure the kind of information flow that will make the membership keep on reelecting the incumbent leaders. As S. M. Lipset and others have observed, oligarchies within unions benefit not only their own retinues but the employers as well, who know with whom they deal, or with whom they can make deals.[38]

Even oligarchical union leaderships have to deliver benefits to the rank and file, however. And, with increasing productive capacity, American employers and unions have over the years reached agreements that, in some industries at least, have dispensed wages and other financial benefits that compare favorably to the levels achieved in most other economically advanced countries. However, it has been an uneven development, confined largely to the relatively strong, oligopolistic or for other reasons profitable industries. And access to membership in the unions that control the most desirable jobs has increasingly become restricted to people with connections; even though this trend has in recent years been modified as a result of Equal Opportunities statutes and court decisions, so that some blacks, Hispanic-Americans, and women have been able to enter through doors that previously were closed to all of them. But such legislation does not increase the overall employment opportunities. Many who are "called but not chosen" suffer the indignity and deprivation associated with long-term, perhaps permanent unemployment; others are underemployed (they work part time only, or they work at more menial jobs than they had been trained for); and many more work in marginal industries for substandard wages.

Although the large international unions are the outcome rather than the originators of the struggles that led to more

liveable wages in their industries, they should be compared
to political parties as a potential resource in future struggles
against deprivation and coercion. Most large unions, like
most broad-based political parties in liberal-corporate societies, today actively support the liberal myth of democracy achieved, and help to socialize obedient employees/
conformist citizens; both kinds of organizations serve to ensure their publics' submissiveness to the rules of the liberal-
corporate order.[39] Yet union locals, even more so than local
constituency parties, may at certain times become activated
and develop strong solidarity sentiments, or even develop a
stubborn and enduring political will. There are many kinds
of issues waiting in the wings for the right time—issues like
industrial health and safety; self-management or democracy
in the work-place; even the production of socially useful
rather than destructive output (fertilizers rather than na-
palm, ploughs rather than swords). Business unionism that
shuns politics still remains the prevailing orthodoxy in the
United States, but realities of objective limits to the exploitation of nature and to the worldwide maldistribution of food
and energy, now so visibly in limited supply, are slowly but
surely eroding the old liberal faith in collective bargaining as
an *alternative* to seeking political ways to achieve well-
being and freedom for the underprivileged classes.

How can we improve the prospects (1) for constructive
political activities in the workplace and (2) for breaking
down union hierarchies to the extent that the labor movement can become more horizontal, with vigorous local initiatives in the spirit of self-management and local autonomy?
This is like asking, "How can political consciousness be
raised, at every place of work, not only to achieve awareness of the deceptions, the makebelieves, and the mystifications that serve to legitimate established authority patterns
(see chapter 3), but also to develop faith in the feasibility
and indeed necessity of choosing to struggle against the
major political evils like structural violence and deprivation
and oppression of many kinds?"

In the past, the Marxist theory of the inevitable proletarian
revolution gave heart to sizable revolutionary parties and
unions, in many countries, which were prepared to employ
mass violence to overthrow the state at the ripe time. Fol-

lowing Lenin's spectacular success in leading the action that destroyed Russia's new bourgeois regime in 1917, Marxist-Leninists have believed in well disciplined cadre parties capable of making historical shortcuts, conspiring to topple discredited regimes much before a politically conscious, socialist-thinking working class had developed; and special circumstances following the defeat of the fascist powers in World War II saw a considerable number of Marxist-Leninist regimes come to power in East Europe.

Western Marxists have been less successful in their attempts to win political power, however. While most workers in France and Italy have tended to vote Communist, as other alternatives on the Left are seen as even less credible, our secular-minded age has undercut popular faith in Marxist as well as in Christian roads to salvation. The obvious bureaucratic oppression in the so-called socialist world has disenchanted so many in the West that most communist parties in Western Europe have taken to calling themselves "Eurocommunist," to dramatize the differences between their own political plans and strategies and those of the communist parties in the USSR and East Europe.[40] With more pragmatic leaderships, "less doctrinaire," as they like to call themselves,[41] the Eurocommunist parties have come to resemble social-democratic parties more and more, or so it seems to me. This metamorphosis may well be complete before any one of them is ever voted into power; if so, their prospects of being able to change the state and the economic institutions by gaining power within the system would seem less than bright.[42]

What remains to be stressed in positive rather than negative terms, about organized emancipatory strategies, is that organizations must be made to rise, but also to fall or to change. The lasting, most basic dilemma in organized struggles for freedom is, as Michels saw, that all organizations, once they become well established, tend to become ends in themselves rather than means, at least as they are portrayed to their memberships; and yet it is necessary to organize, again and again, to achieve effective coordination of industrial and political action. Organizations should be short-lived, one might want to conclude. I would put the point differently: people must be educated to be critical of their own organizations as well as of those of their supposed enemies; people must become stimulated and educated to struggle to assert control over their own lives and to make their organizational loyalties second to their loyalty to humanist or socialist principles and to persons who are victimized.

There are some critical points in time, to be sure, when disciplined combat may be required, and when open dissent within revolutionary organizations should yield to the necessity of defeating the enemy; but if such critical points in time are extended to exceed a week or a month, or at any rate a very brief period of time, chances are that what emerges, should victory come, will be a victory for a revolutionary clique, not for a revolution (to paraphrase Michels, cited above, p. 62). And such critical moments in time, that could justify a blind revolutionary obedience, are highly unlikely in our own kind of stable liberal-corporate societies; for the foreseeable future I see no rational justification for joining disciplined revolutionary conspiracies that aspire to impose their own rule on an uncomprehending society, however admirably emancipatory those goals might be.

Let me try to probe a bit deeper into our most central dilemma of how to achieve effective emancipatory organizations without imposing virtual dictatorships within the organizations. Without horizontal (democratic) decision-making practices internally, a revolutionary organization that takes power will be quick to impose strict hierarchies in the new state—and more coercive ones, the more serious the new leaders are about abolishing traditionally accepted structures of oppression. On the other hand, without a tight internal discipline at the right moment, sufficient to ensure carefully planned and well coordinated political action, no revolutionary organization is likely to be victorious at the crucial time.

Perhaps our only option within the major Western powers is to face up to the necessity of abandoning the heady revolutionary rhetoric of the last hundred years and to recognize that, on the nuclear tinderbox that our world has become, it is now an existential necessity to avoid playing with fire; as we need to avoid international wars, so we need to avoid large-scale civil wars, at almost any cost, and especially within the highly armed First World. Within our stable liberal-corporate societies (and here I am limiting my discussion to these) I think our best hope for the next decades lies in activating citizenries through limited-purpose, ad hoc organizations which are ready to challenge established policies and establishments both from inside the system (within parties, unions, lobbying pressure groups, school boards, courts, etc.) and from outside the system (through street demonstrations, confrontations of many kinds, illegal strikes, mass trespassing and other large-scale civil disobedience, illegal boycotts, etc.).

American students in the late 1960s showed how much could be accomplished to frustrate the American war effort in Indochina; President Johnson was induced to step down, as he acknowledged,[43] by the accumulating evidence of deep division about the Vietnam war within the American public, a devision that hundreds of campus confrontations had done much to bring about.

The Vietnam war has passed, but other ugly policies remain or recur, and so does the need for active citizenries, prepared to organize to disrupt and frustrate oppressive institutions that cause violence and deprivation. While the activist student movements of the 1960s have left the scene for the time being, both in North America and in Europe, their strategies of building ad hoc organizations with accent on nonviolent confrontation have been taken over and further developed by many other parts of the general public: poor people, tenants, feminists, gays, antiabortion groups and, on a wider scale than most others, organizations to protect our natural environment: animal species protection agencies, wilderness protection groups, antipollution coalitions, anti–nuclear power organizations, and many others.

Ecological consciousness promises to become the single most important kind of political consciousness, in terms of strength to influence events and legislation, as the new decade is about to begin. Feminist consciousness is also a major force which may profoundly benefit countless children as well as adults; the same may be said about the new racial and ethnic consciousness, especially within communities that have been or still are suffering from discrimination of one kind or another. All these kinds of political awakenings, and others as well, tend to lead to organized efforts and emancipatory struggles, whether to protect the lives and health of future generations, to enhance freedom and democracies within families, or to resist economic discrimination and exploitation, etc.

Many of these efforts have been and will continue to be channeled into the work of labor unions and political parties, but many new organizations have kept sprouting in all the liberal-corporate societies. At last count there were, in the German Federal Republic alone, some 50,000 "civic initiative" groups "which were able to jointly mobilize more members than all the political parties put together," according to a report in *Die Welt* cited by Udo Bermbach.[44] In Austria and in Denmark, civic initiative movements have up to this point (summer 1980) succeeded in barring nuclear power works altogether; in many other First World countries this issue has become a major one, with the antinuclear groups apparently gaining ground at this time.

Liberal-corporate regimes are relatively defenseless against open, democratic efforts at mass political pedagogy and action; their ideology of legitimation makes it very awkward for them to suppress such movements openly and, since the Freedom of Information Act in the United States, police efforts at surreptitious sabotage of such movements have become more risky, too. But every well armed state knows how to handle secret revolutionary conspiracies, let alone armed uprisings. As Germans know only too well, political terrorism can provoke more blatant oppression; so far from leading to a new public awareness of the regime's oppressive nature, terrorism and subsequent police terror feed political confusion and paranoia. Violence breeds more violence; acts of terrorist violence make it all but impossible to achieve gains in political enlightenment through the dialectics of peaceful or industrial political confrontation. Most people are scared of open violence, naturally, but most governments, certainly in the First World, are much more afraid of nonviolent campaigns, if they grow too large to be written off as eccentric or narrowly based.

What can be said in general, in a few words, about strategies that should be adopted by new, more or less ad hoc, emancipatory organizations?

For example, let us take our concern to protect our own

health, and that of generations to come, by opposing the accelerating depletion and poisoning of our natural environment caused by large corporations in their continuing quest for profits and growth. First of all, of course, political pedagogy must seek to deepen and widen public concern with these issues; educational efforts must seek to establish why we should object strenuously to having our own creature comforts secured, even luxuriously, at the cost of depriving others, the less affluent in the world as well as our children's children, of resources needed for their health and basic well-being.

Second, as the task of developing such concern involves the pricking of many people's conscience, we need organizational strategies that are not repugnant to people with conventional moral perspectives. We need strategies that are scrupulously careful not to inflict violence against persons, nor damage against the kinds of property that serve to meet basic human needs, as distinct from property that is widely understood to be used for offensive purposes. A napalm- or bomb-producing factory can serve as an example of property that could well be sabotaged in connection with campaigns against war or armaments policies, provided extreme care is taken not to endanger human lives.

Third, it must be recognized that effective civil disobedience campaigns require a lot of advance education and training; they had better not be attempted at all, rather than be carried out by enthusiastic amateurs, or by people who are prone to respond to government or rightwing violence with counterviolence. Gandhi was far more important as an inventor of effective political strategies than he was as a moralist; all modern emancipatory organizations in struggle need to emulate Gandhi's stress on the necessity of combining a militant struggle against evil practices with an always conciliatory attitude toward the human beings in charge of those practices.[45] Gene Sharp's books have shown what a large reservoir of nonviolent strategies is available for all kinds of purposes and situations.[46] And George Lakey has written a fine manual, *Strategy for a Living Revolution*,[47] in which he contributes a provocative framework for many kinds of agendas for revolutionary struggles on the basis of the Gandhian premise that we must scrupulously follow principles of openness and nonviolence, not for moral reasons (for governments perpetrate or connive with violence on a grand scale, and have scant moral justification for condemning unauthorized violence) but for *practical* reasons: governments, as I have argued, know only too well how to deal with revolutionary violence, at least in our politically stable part of the world; also, revolutionary conspiracies are easily infiltrated by government agents, who may soon be in a position to discredit and sow general confusion about what these conspiracies are up to. In North America our hope for promoting structural changes, over the long run, depends mainly on openly prepared and discussed strategies, like strikes, boycotts, or (other) mass civil disobedience campaigns, perhaps accompanied by acts of "propaganda of the deed,"[48] and by attempts over time to develop parallel institutions with which to challenge openly, when the situation is ripe, the legitimacy of existing hierarchies.[49]

I have been emphasizing ad hoc organizations and environmental issues as the most likely direction from which to challenge and eventually destroy the legitimation of our liberal-corporate economic system. This is not to say that the industrial working class is no longer an important force when assessing the prospects for a radical socioeconomic change; but I do believe that many Marxists remain irrationally fixated on that class as the necessary as well as sufficient agent for the revolution to come. Psychologically speaking, late capitalism has so far succeeded very well in dispersing (by types of work, levels of skills, of pay, and of social status, etc.) as well as depoliticizing the working class, just as other strata have been depoliticized. The traditional core of the industrial working class, the unskilled and semiskilled factory workers, keeps declining in numbers, as automation advances. Nevertheless, the drudgery of their work routines and their daily proximity to one another, as well as their collective power to disrupt production and profits by way of the strike weapon—these are all factors that suggest an important political role for this class, within a broader-based struggle to force changes in the system.

And the history of past labor struggles, even the myth of the proletariat as the crucial revolutionary class, may well help to strengthen the psychological potential of blue-collar workers in future struggles and thus continue to give them an importance disproportionate to their declining numbers, in most First World countries.

They do remain oppressed. North American and West European labor unions have over the years done much to improve their members' pay in many industries but have so far left every industrial workforce remaining under conditions of servitude and drudgery, with a minimum of control, at most, even over elementary matters like sanitation and accident-prevention policies.[50] Almost every kind of worker insubordination can lead to summary dismissal and, with unemployment high, to prospects for long-term deprivation. Until this changes, the bulk of employed workers are, even in our relatively affluent part of the world, trained every day in submissiveness and thus incapacitated for democratic citizenship (see 5 §3 for a discussion of the psychology of powerlessness as it afflicts above all the underprivileged classes, who need political power the most); and it can be reaffirmed, with the Marxists, that wage labor amounts to a modern form of slavery.

Unlike some Marxists, however, I think the struggle for self-management must be carried out piecemeal, from shop to shop. Nationwide strategies for a nonviolent revolution are also required, but as a separate effort, to be carried out independently of the local struggles for industrial self-management. Local struggles need not await national struggles to get started, and vice versa, even though successes at either level will be strengthening efforts at both levels.

Carole Pateman has lucidly shown that worker participation at high levels of managerial decision also is compatible with reasonable standards of industrial efficiency.[51] Yet it needs to be added (and Pateman is aware of this) that it would be justifiable to return the control over their own lives to the workers and other employees even if it could be proved that much inefficiency would result, if we once have decided that the meeting of basic human needs should take precedence over the achievement of optimal efficiency

in corporate production processes, in a world in which perceived scarcity now is mainly a consequence of too much
power for the owners of capital, not of too little capital or
of not enough raw materials for production. Moreover, Ivan
Illich and the late E. F. Schumacher have both made a powerful case for reducing the size and scale of industrial enterprises, utilizing small- and intermediate-size technology, so
that places of work can become decentralized and made more
human, and be turned into places of work where many can
find employment, rather than continuing to pursue growing
labor-efficiency and optimal return on capital.[52]

No North American or West European government is
likely to insist within the near future that the corporate
giants take this advice, either in their home country plants
or in their Third World subsidiaries. The industrial strike
weapon appears to be declining in clout as the multinational
corporations diversify; most of them can afford to close
down specific plants long enough to exhaust their workforce while picking up the slack and replenishing their profits
in other plants in other countries; even threats of massive
strikes are losing some of their credibility, with mounting
evidence, most recently from countries like Britain or Italy,
that recurrent strikes tend to feed rightwing sentiment and
weaken the unions, not the corporations. Realistically speaking, I am afraid we must look mainly to the next generation,
faced with continually higher levels of structural unemployment and more keenly aware of the need to curb economic
growth, to mobilize effective struggles for an "Economics
as if People Mattered."[53]

Meanwhile, the struggle for worker self-management within many plants, in West and East Europe, Commonwealth
countries, and North America, continues at a brisker pace,
aided by increasing problems for management: absenteeism,
higher labor turnover, increasing incidence of sabotage of
production processes within the plants. When bargaining for
new contracts, employers increasingly are tempted to yield
some power as an alternative to yielding more money for
higher wages.

Yet I must conclude this part of my discussion on a som-
ber note: co-optation, being bought off with small favors, is

as constant a hazard in so-called industrial democracy as it is in so-called representative political democracy on the national scene. Those who are privileged with wealth and power will use every available ruse to make the other side mistake empty or near-empty concessions for substantial ones.[54] There is today a great deal of participatory make-believe on the industrial scene, too—also, incidentally, as it applies to supposedly democratically constituted union governments, in many cases. But the size of constituencies is an important variable, with respect to the feasibility of democratic and self-management practices. In small unions' locals, elections can become real contests. In industrial plants of small or moderate size, self-management schemes may become real rather than mainly symbolic, when established. Possibilities for political emancipation are brighter relative to small-sized plants than relative to the state, even in states that are relatively small, as states go. Unlike the citizenries of states, the workforces in relatively small-sized factories can aspire to become what will here be called horizontal communities, a concept that will be discussed in chapter 5.

As of today, and I am most interested in where we are now and where we can go from here, I think André Gorz has contributed the most promising discussions of industrial strategies that will insist on winning revolutionary reforms affecting power relations within each plant, rather than reforms that win immediate pay raises or similar advantages to the workers, at the price of leaving management in unimpaired control of the decision-making processes. The aim of industrial struggles must be, according to Gorz, to gradually weaken management and to strengthen the relative power of the workforce, with future contests in mind, always looking toward the ultimate goal of achieving victory for complete workers' control.[55] A recent account of the rise and then the decline and fall of the Welfare Rights Movement in the United States, by Piven and Cloward, illustrates well how easily a movement can be subtly corrupted and then be made to wither at the grassroots, for lack of such attentiveness as Gorz recommends, to the membership's continuing active involvement in consciousness-raising struggles and in the dialectics of decision-making regarding aims and strategies, locally no less than nationally.[56]

4. THE DEMAND FOR A GUARANTEED ANNUAL INCOME

"Every American should be guaranteed an adequate income as a matter of right whether he works or not, a 32-member group calling itself the Ad Hoc Committee on the Triple Revolution urged today." This is the first paragraph in a front-page news story in the *New York Times* of March 23, 1964. The "Triple Revolution" statement received much publicity at the time, but soon afterwards was all but forgotten by most Americans, who had other pressing matters to think about, like saving Vietnam from communism. The statement argued that three kinds of revolutionary change have been taking place in the real world, like it or not, and that, accordingly, some basic changes have to take place in our political thinking as well. The statement referred to the cybernetics revolution (I shall be using the word automation instead, as it is in more common use today), the weaponry revolution, and the human rights revolution.

Let me cite the three key observations in the diagnosis, in reverse order:

(1) A universal demand for full human rights is now clearly evident ... the civil rights movement within the United States ... is only the local manifestation of a world-wide movement ...

(2) New forms of weaponry have been developed which cannot win wars but which can obliterate civilization. .... The need of a 'warless world' is generally recognized, though achieving it will be a long and frustrating process.

(3) The cybernation revolution has been brought about by the combination of the computer and the automated self-regulating machine. This results in a system of almost unlimited productive capacity which require progressively less human labor.[57]

The statement is boldest, perhaps, in its insistence that there must be a recognition of a universal right for everyone to consume, independently of opportunity to produce. It dramatizes as an inescapable fact of the modern world that our traditional work ethic has become obsolete, for we are now living with a technology that promises an increasing abundance of products but also an increasingly acute scarcity of available jobs.

Naively one might think of this as a blessing: less labor and work will be needed to achieve satisfactory standards of living for everybody. But, with our conventional thinking and training, the automation revolution may easily come to be seen as a disaster, second only to the horrors of the weaponry revolution in a deeply divided world, for under capitalism we are not working in order to live, but living in order to work. The work ethic and our so-called educational system, which trains us for jobs rather than educates us for living, have made most of us define ourselves in effect as intelligent cogs in the system of production; without a full working day, how can we esteem ourselves, how can we find meaning and purpose in life?

Our traditional liberal subservience to the marketplace and to the nation's system of production is an aspect of domination (see chapter 3), but the call to struggle for the principle of a guaranteed annual income is in my view well suited as a key strategy in the struggle against deprivation too, within the nation at first but soon as a worldwide struggle as well. It is a strategy with, potentially speaking, a strong support in many people's common sense, if the diagnosis in the Triple Revolution statement is sound. In fact, both on the left and on the right there have been influential voices calling for a guaranteed annual income as a basic right, though among Manchester liberals the preferred phrase is "negative income tax."[58] A widely influential utopian novel has assumed that this is the way of the future in America but has warned us poignantly that guaranteed welfare payments, housing, health services, etc., without meaningful political participation, could become a nightmare of an affluent but alienated society.[59] I shall leave that issue aside here, however, since I shall be concerned to show that with guarantees of an adequate income to all, unprecedented levels and quality of political participation can become attainable for all.

Most people located on the political right or center today may well fear that a guaranteed annual income could lead to widespread lethargy, idleness being seen as "the root of all evil." I take the contrary view, that spontaneous activity comes naturally to most people, and that lethargy most often comes as a result of chronic frustration or of a basic sense of hopelessness, when culturally prescribed goals come to seem unattainable. I agree that the more dehumanizing kinds of drudgery at poor pay would find few takers. Conceivably, some people might under the new system become shy of all kinds of effort-requiring work; that would be too bad for them, but their families would not be made to suffer; in a transition period, the work-shy might well be seen as benefactors to the many others still hooked on the old work ethic and desperate to find jobs that can make them feel useful and appreciated, according to that old recipe for achieving a sense of personal pride and social acceptance.

The long-term boon of a guaranteed annual income is in my view that it will make it possible to shed the old servant-minded work ethic for a new, free person's action ethic; there will be vast new opportunities to choose life projects that will transcend alienating servitude, freeing most people from dependency on the power hierarchies that govern our industrial, bureaucratic, and political systems. People can come to manage their own lives at last, and live in accord with their own basic need priorities. And to struggle for this right to an annual income can become an important part of our struggle for a rational order of human rights (see 4 §2).

Hannah Arendt in her most influential book, *The Human Condition*, discusses her concepts of labor, work, and action, and takes the position that only the relative few are capable of becoming political actors, men and women who take an active part in shaping our public realm.[60] Advancing technology would have liberated us from the necessity of most kinds of labor, in Arendt's sense, were it not for our economic system, which makes workers into commodities and in effect into appendages to the machines, and which turns all of us as consumers into instruments for the sales machinery that keeps the economy going.

We all have basic physical needs and community needs, I have argued (see 4 §2), which are prior to our subjectivity needs; yet it is our subjectivity needs for differential status that are appealed to by most advertisers, who would have us keep deepening our dependencies on brand-name products and who make it harder for us all the time to remain clear about where our individual basic need-priorities are. To the extent that we become fixated on our artificially inflated consumer needs, we retain less attention and less energy for our more basic affiliation and community needs, let alone for our concern that other people are not to be denied the satisfaction of their most basic physical needs.

Unlike Arendt, I think most people are capable of self-directed work as well as authentic public action, provided we are freed from the double burden of serving, as employees, purposes that may be alien to our own and of being constantly induced to consume commodities that we may be brought to think we want but that we do not need. The point of a system with guaranteed annual income is that, right from the beginning development of our consciousness, we could take charge of our own educational priorities, to find out what kinds of future work and action we think we need and want to prepare for. In short, our education could come to serve our own need for growth to the fullest stature of which we may be capable, rather than serve hypothetical future employers' desire to get the most out of our work or labor, for their own profit. We would know from the outset that we could always afford to be choosy about the kinds of jobs that we would be prepared to take on.

In one sense it can be said that guaranteed annual income plans have been in effect in this country for some time, on a large scale, but applied to some categories of persons only; thus, in 1976, financed by payroll taxes, more than 70 billion dollars was paid out to some 32 million recipients who were pensioners, widowed persons, and/or physically disabled.[61] Our social-security system could be seen as a first stage achieved in the struggle toward the far more ambitious concept of a guaranteed minimal, yet adequate, income for everybody, as a matter of right. Beginning where we are today, I think further advances should be pushed for by stages, to avoid the appearance of a dangerously radical scheme, which could scare off even the many voters who would stand to benefit.

Further advances toward a more adequate guaranteed income for far more individuals could come to liberate great political energies, by enabling many more people to do something worthwhile and self-chosen with their working lives, and I think that the *struggle* for a right to an adequate income for all could come to fit in very well with the broader struggle for rational human rights priorities, a struggle that is in our time clearly spilling across national boundaries and becoming worldwide; a struggle that can create a transnational solidarity against oppression and hopefully come to weaken the ability of governments to prepare to make catastrophic uses of the products of the weaponry revolution.[62]

A guaranteed annual wage would make vast numbers of recruits available for emancipatory organizational efforts of many kinds, the kinds of people who at present are chained to jobs and career constraints and cannot afford the luxury of developing, and living by, a sensitive moral and political conscience. Even the mere fact of becoming engaged in the struggle for such a policy will find a lot of people able to overcome much of their present alienation.

But about overcoming alienation I shall have more to say in the next chapter.

5

To Overcome Alienation:
From Contract to Community

IN THIS CHAPTER I SHALL discuss what I take to be the core problem in any overall strategy of political emancipation: how to overcome the psychologically crippling impact of domination and coercive oppression; how to find ways of reasserting our humanity against political systems with immense powers of oppression—the states and their allied conglomerates of private and public corporations.

Terms like alienation and estrangement—I shall use the two as synonyms—have become trendy in the last couple of decades. This is perhaps a hopeful indicator, suggesting that many have discovered the importance of various kinds of problems in this general area. On the other hand, the vast variety of meanings associated with "alienation" and similar terms could make one wonder whether or not the term has been worn out by now, having been stretched in so many directions.

As my guiding purpose in this work is to explore avenues of political emancipation, I shall not try to sort out the many kinds of usage of "alienation" and similar terms; that would have required a long march through massive libraries of psychology, sociology, and philosophy, and indeed through innumerable works of drama, fiction, and poetry as well. At the obvious risk, then, of overlooking many astute points that various authors and scholars have made about the proper understanding of the term, or about the genesis and nature of the phenomenon, let me limit our journey in this chapter to the following itinerary.

I shall first of all offer a rather broad definition of the term alienation, as I propose to use it; distinguish my concept from another broad one, neurosis; and discuss and justify the direction of my inquiry in this chapter. Second, I shall examine Marx's concept and theory of alienation under

the capitalist system, with briefer mention of antecedent contributions by Rousseau, Hegel, and Feuerbach. It will be
clear that I am heavily indebted to Marx's pioneering insights
in this area, and yet that I think they must be transcended,
in the light of subsequent economic and ideological knowledge, and also in the light of modern socio-psychological
research. Third, I shall briefly report some conclusions suggested by some of this research, and some perspectives on
strategies for emancipation that these conclusions would
seem to suggest. Extrapolating further, I shall argue for the
necessity of moving away from our contractually based,
commodity-oriented, competitive kind of individualistic social order, toward building cooperative, solidary communities as the basis for social life and political commitments.
How can we learn to extricate ourselves from the debilitating
impact of an economic system that reduces people to commodities, both coming and going, as producers and consumers? How can we gradually get acceptance for the idea
that artificial persons like corporations have no inherent
value, and should be granted no legal rights beyond the
quid pro quo of actual service to the common good? How
can we go about building and strengthening the role of
horizontal communities in our social order? In conclusion,
I shall briefly comment on the paradox that the state, as a
pseudocommunity with vast but, I think, on the whole illegitimate claims on our loyalty, is a formidable enemy to
the cause of human emancipation that must be resisted, re-
strained, and eventually checkmated through the strategy
of building self-managing, autonomous communities; and yet
the state provides for now the essential arena for the struggle and must also be seen as an ally or a potential ally in the
struggle against formidable private-corporate enemies of
human emancipation. In chapter 6, finally, I shall discuss the
relationship between autonomous human communities and
the transnational order, or "the human community as a
whole," as mankind is sometimes called—inappropriately, as
I shall argue.

While I do not share the faith of many Marxists in the in-
evitability of socialist revolutions, and much less their con-
fident anticipation of an eventual communist utopia, I am not
a total pessimist. Unlike many Marxists, I think that it is pos-

sible to struggle far more effectively than we have done for aims of political emancipation, even and indeed especially with largely nonviolent means, in our own kind of late capitalist society, and that the time is ripe now for discussing priorities for the immediate as well as the longer future. Moreover, unlike the more apocalyptic varieties of revolutionary I strongly feel that our best thought and action must be given to the struggle for immediate advancements in the cause of human emancipation, or there may not *be* any longer future ahead of us.

The most outrageous evils perpetrated by political and economic oppression, which most urgently call for a determined struggle to resist and overcome them, are surely in the realm of *coercive oppression*; more precisely, in the realm of government-sponsored or government-condoned violence, deliberate or structural; violence that may threaten all of humanity or, more selectively, may be destroying unwanted peoples or individuals. Ecocide, genocide, homicide: this is a quantitative continuum of maximal evils that emancipatory strategies must at any cost seek to prevent. It is in the realm of *ideological domination*, traditional as well as revolutionary, that we must seek explanation for the paradox that most otherwise decent citizens of First World countries up to now have been active or passive accomplices in so many barbaric acts and policies, both domestically and, particularly, transnationally: hence the crucial importance of seeking more effective ways of political education. But we need to study *alienation* in order to understand the most complex obstacles to an effective political education: just what is happening to our minds and emotions when they are reprocessed under the impact of liberal ideological domination in a corporate social order—that paralyzing combination of the democratic makebelieve with the behavioral experience of actual powerlessness.

1. THE CONCEPT OF ALIENATION

One conceptual possibility is to define alienation simply as the opposite of domination: as the psychological dislocation that happens *to the extent that* human beings are deprived of their cultural or potential freedom; "alienation" would then refer to the processes by which human consciousness is made to serve the legitimation of compliance or complicity with oppression, rather than serving the social and individual adaptation and growth needs of each person. I choose instead to make space for an empirical relationship between domination and alienation by making alienation the reverse of psychological freedom, just as domination has been defined as the reverse of cultural or potential freedom.

The amount of alienation will depend, thus understood, not on the extent and weight of domination only, but also on the extent and exploitive severity of the coercive oppression that domination with partial success endeavors to legitimate, and on each individual's "natural" or instinctual propensities, which may vary widely in strength and direction from person to person and from class to class.

Psychological freedom was defined in chapter 2 as degree of harmony between basic needs and overt behavior. This means, too, harmony between basic motives (as needs presumably tend to activate motives) and consciousness; it takes neurotic distortions and disharmonies, as the Freudians are right to insist, to block important instinctual urges or motives from the individual's consciousness.

"Neurosis" in this work will refer to the negation of psychological freedom in the individual person, that is, when we look at the individual in isolation from the social order and are concerned with behavioral symptoms and their origin in the single family's history. "Alienation" will refer to the impairments of psychological freedom that are studied in their social context. While the psychiatrists, psychotherapists, and psychoanalysts properly seek to deal with neuroses (and also with psychoses when that is feasible), it is for social scientists and political theorists to try to understand and deal with alienation.

If I may borrow from C. Wright Mills, who saw it as a main task of political education to enable individuals to translate their personal troubles into social issues, as exercises in gaining political understanding as well as collective strength to resist oppression,[1] I shall argue that a main potential benefit of taking part in radical political inquiry is to come to see individual neuroses in the context of alienation, one's own and that of others; this can lead not only to a gain in social and political self-understanding but also to the mobilization of collective resources of insight and strength with which to overcome alienation and thus reduce the weight of neuroses.

The psychiatrist and the psychoanalyst still have their work to do, with neurotics as well as with psychotics amenable to treatment; in fact for psychotics I doubt that any other source of help my be available. Yet for many neurotics there may be health and freedom in becoming involved, politically, socially, or pedagogically; it is conceivable that task-oriented political work for some present patients might prove a viable alternative to the psychiatrist's couch. According to at least one very persuasive account, hardened criminals and once incurable drug-abusers have, in a supportive community context, been enabled to function as purposive political radicals, practicing militant but nonviolent struggles over periods of several years so far.[2] And it is remarkable that in times of war or other political upheavals, in times that offer great dramas and call for much sacrifice, there appears to be a reduced incidence of many kinds of psychiatric symptoms.[3]

Psychiatric treatment serves one kind of legitimate objective, struggle to overcome alienation by political analysis and action serves another. The professional healer (and the amateur healer, too!) must endeavor to help the individual adjust, with less pain, to alienating circumstances in his or her existing surroundings, if the latter cannot readily be changed; in the tradition of the Hippocratic oath, life and health must be protected and individual suffering must be reduced. At the same time political thought and action face the challenge of change, to reduce the structural origins of much human suffering.

In the interest of *prevention* of neuroses and alienation it is important to seek to explain the suffering not only in terms of infancy and childhood situations, as orthodox Freudians do, but also in terms of present social structures and dominating ideologies. Not only must we be open to the possibility that less alienating patterns of social life may reduce the enduring impact of family-inherited neurotic tendencies; we must also anticipate a strong possibility that some parents, who themselves struggle successfully to overcome alienation, are more likely than other parents to protect their own children's levels of psychological freedom.

A reminder about the nature of psychological freedom is perhaps in order at this point: as human beings we are all born free, in the sense of psychological freedom. For our emerging consciousness is at the outset fully in tune with our basic "natural" need priorities, that is, until we begin to be encumbered with social inhibitions about expressing ourselves freely and learn the fine arts of insincerity, or worse, until we become saddled with fears and anxieties severe enough to make us slip into neurotic repression, by way of amputating some of the links between our consciousness and memories that would testify to now-forbidden motives on our part. The social order and its institutions place us in chains, to continue in Rousseau's metaphor: for the more fortunate, inhibitions can be limited to rationally defensible behavioral accommodations to the perceived requirements of well ordered social life, while to the less fortunate, repression comes to block out important sources of knowledge about our own basic nature and need priorities.

To sum up my exercise in defining alienation and relating this concept to the concept of neurosis, for the purposes of deciding how to struggle to overcome it: while healers of neuroses are just about as important resource persons as are the healers of our bodies, not even the world's best psychiatry and medicine can make up for the damage that is caused by the alienating conditions of an oppressive social order. For prevention of neuroses on a wide scale, as well as to improve the prospects for cure, we need to take up the struggle to understand and then to remove or transcend the major social and political causes of alienation.

2. ESSENTIALS IN THE MARXIST UNDERSTANDING OF ALIENATION

The relatively recent publication in German and English of Marx's *Economic and Philosophical Manuscripts of*

1844 has perhaps been the biggest single influence in spreading the word, in recent decades, that alienation is a major problem, a major malaise, in the life of modern man.

Before Marx, Denis Diderot of the Enlightenment had written about the economic system's tendency to produce superfluous wants, imaginary goods, and artificial needs.[4] More importantly, Rousseau had written eloquently on man's alienation from nature and from his own, God-given nature; this was one of the recurrent themes in Rousseau's thought: man is born free, but is everywhere in the chains of institutions, which serve not the natural needs of man but the requirements of industry and commerce, and of the state. The demands of the state, much like those of the so-called civilized individual, have a tendency toward artificial growth without bounds, as artificial needs are allowed to proliferate. Rousseau charged that the state often takes on new tasks as pretexts for raising new revenues, thus adding to the chains that hold the citizenry down; the citizens, meanwhile, keep acquiring new, artificial needs, thus deepening their dependency on the economic system and the state.[5]

To the theme of proliferating human wants I shall return. First, let me briefly consider other influences on Marx's thought on alienation. Hegel was the first to develop a systematic theory of alienation, in the context of his dialectical view of history. Already at the outset of his intellectual career, in the *Theologische Jugendschriften*, Hegel wrote about man's deepening alienation from nature in the modern era. And it would seem that Hegel's realization that the Christian religion even in its advanced Lutheran version was insufficient to restore the lost harmony was an important influence in making him move on from theology to philosophy in the bulk of his life's work: "The need for philosophy arises when the unifying power [*die Macht der Vereinigung*] has disappeared from the life of men, when the contradictions have lost their living interrelation and interdependence and assumed an independent form."[6]

Schiller, too, had written about the soul-destroying impact of modern specialization, but his strategy for restoration of the soul's harmony was ahistorical, relegated to the realm of ideas. Feuerbach had inverted Hegel's dialectical idealism prior to Marx, but had stopped short of proposing an entirely dialectical-materialist resolution to the problem of alienation, and he had, moreover, limited his inquiry to religious as distinct from political origins of alienation. Feuerbach believed that man has created God in his own image, that is, in man's *essential* or ideal image, as distinct from his actual, everyday attributes and nature.[7] Freud would have called this a process of projection. By attributing the better aspects of his nature to God, Feuerbach believed, man is left with a false and impoverished conception of his own nature and resources.

Marx initially admired Feuerbach, saw him as a truly revolutionary theorist, but before long he moved on and adopted a critical perspective on Feuerbach's materialism, which he came to view as insufficiently dialectical. In the famous *Theses* Marx took Feuerbach to task for failing to see that religious sentiment needs not only to be debunked but to be explained as a social product. And in *The German Ideology* Marx wrote: "As far as Feuerbach is a materialist he does not deal with history, and as far as he considers history he is not a materialist."[8] To Feuerbach man becomes a static "object of the senses"; to Marx man *is* "sensuous activity," a being in dialectical interaction with history, shaped by history and in turn shaping the continuing course of history. Marx's materialism, unlike Feuerbach's, does not reduce products of the human spirit to epiphenomena; instead, Marx insists that material conditions—physical nature, productive resources, and technology—always set the outer limits within which historical processes will determine the course of events: "Men make their own history, but they do not make it just as they please; they do not make it under circumstances chosen by themselves, but under circumstances directly found, given and transmitted from the past."[9]

To return for just a moment to the *Theses on Feuerbach*, presumably an outline for the lengthy and, until the 1930s, unpublished manuscript, *The German Ideology*, Marx writes in the Fourth Thesis:

> Feuerbach starts out from the fact of religious self-alienation, of the duplication of the world into a religious, imaginary world and a real one. His work con-

sists in resolving the religious world into its secular basis. He overlooks the fact that after completing this work, the chief thing still remains to be done. For the fact that the secular basis detaches itself from itself and establishes itself in the clouds as an independent realm can only be explained by the cleavages and self-contradictions within this secular basis. The latter must itself, therefore, first be understood in its contradiction and then, by the removal of the contradiction, revolutionised in practice. . . .

Philosophers, including the revolutionary Feuerbach, have only interpreted the world; for Marx, the point is to change the world![10]

To understand Marx's concept of alienation it is necessary, as Bertell Ollman writes, to understand what Marx would mean by "unalienation": "Without some knowledge of [Marx's conception of] the future millenium alienation remains a reproach that can never be clarified," just as, in the absence of a conception of health, we would consider familiar symptoms of disease as normal.[11] In parenthesis it might be added here that *with* conceptions both of physical health and of "unalienation," empirical studies of disease are nevertheless more manageable and less complex in presuppositions and methods, than are empirical studies of alienation, because physically healthy individuals can be studied in capitalist society, while *entirely* "unalienated" individuals are not as readily identifiable, if they exist at all. This is not to say that empirical research on alienation should be shunned, but that it should be seen as a mighty challenge and, incidentally, one that Marx himself did not find the time to tackle.

In his essays on Bruno Bauer's *The Jewish Question*, Marx for the first time suggested the contours of his conception of the unalienated man, in the context of a blistering critique of liberalism at its highest point: the French Revolution's Declaration of the Rights of Man, as well as the Bills of Rights of American states. These political liberators, Marx wrote, reduce citizenship, the *political community*, to a mere *means* for preserving these so-called rights of man; and consequently, . . . the citizen is declared to be the servant of egoistic 'man,' . . . the sphere in which man functions as a species-being, is degraded to a level below the sphere where he functions as a partial being, and finally . . . it is man as a bourgeois and not man as a citizen who is considered the *true* and *authentic* man.[12]

Marx's unalienated man turns out to be a close relative of Rousseau's future citizen: the free man who embodies the general will, man transformed from an isolated individual into (and this is Marx quoting Rousseau, in the same essay) "a *part* of something greater than himself, from which, in a sense, he derives his life and his being. . . ." And Marx concludes the essay by defining, in effect, "unalienation":

Human emancipation will only be complete when the real individual man has absorbed into himself the abstract citizen; when as an individual man, in his every day life, in his work, and in his relationships, he has become a *species-being*; and when he has recognized and organized his own powers [*forces propres*] as *social* powers so that he no longer separates this social power from himself as *political* power.[13]

Mere political emancipation on the liberal model, by contrast, reduces man to an egoistic moral cripple, much as Christianity as well as Judaism, to Marx, reduces man to a hopeless sinner, unredeemable except by grace.

There are, for Marx, three component determinants of actual human nature, or of human activity, as he would prefer to say: man is a natural being, a species-being, and a historical being. Man's natural needs and powers are biologically determined, as are those of all other animal species. Man's species-being, on the other hand, is shaped by the needs and powers, many of them still dormant under alienating conditions, that are unique to man as a species; self-awareness (as an individual and as a human) belongs to the human species-being. Concrete human beings are, third, historical beings as well, and this is what makes the empirical study of human nature so extremely difficult, for in each period and in each society and community men and women are shaped by unique constellations of historical forces as well as by their own (natural *and* species-being-determined) powers and needs, and are in turn reshaping their own history, within certain objective limits that are set by the physical world and technology, in addition to the objective limits of human needs and powers.

Man is made by history, then, and yet makes himself, in evolution beyond his most distant humanoid ancestor, the merely animal man. Evolution toward what? Marx generally shied away from describing his conception of communist man, or even of communist society, believing that the dialectics of historical processes make long-range prediction hazardous and believing, too, that human aspirations will change with advancing socioeconomic structures. But his occasional statements about communist society suggest that unalienated men and women will find meaningful satisfaction in productive work and will freely exert themselves according to their abilities, while being content to share in the products of work according to priorities of individual and family needs. The end of alienation, then, means the full blossoming of human solidarity and brotherhood.

Marx's most famous statement on the actual processes of alienation, as they affect the working class in the capitalist system, is found in his 1844 manuscripts. He writes that the worker's life becomes fragmented in four ways: (1) he becomes alienated from the products of his labor: commodities as well as fresh capital, both of which are appropriated by the capitalist; (2) he becomes alienated from the process of labor itself, which no longer can express the worker's individuality, as its procedures and aims are dictated by others, serving their interests; (3) the worker also is alienated from his own nature as a species-being, in that his labor power and indeed the laborer as a person is reduced to a commodity subject to purchase and sale on the labor market; last but not least, (4) workers become alienated from one another to the extent that they are forced to compete for scarce jobs; for scarce commodities, including housing; and for advancement in their jobs, let alone for retaining their jobs.[14]

The alienation of the worker must be seen in relation to the basic purpose of production under capitalism: to accumulate capital. With his key concept of surplus value, Marx demonstrated in great detail how the worker's labor power, and indeed the worker himself, or herself, becomes reduced to a means of capital accumulation—and an expendable means whenever an industrial "reserve army" is available.

In our own century it is becoming just as clear, I think, that all of us, and not only industrial workers, have in an important sense been reduced to a means of consumption as well, and not only to a means of production. We are all interchangeable as consumers, too, and therefore expendable, each of us, if we are without sufficient purchasing power and there are other potential buyers of available products around; look at the starvation in many Third World countries, today, or look at the poverty of the majority of our own old people. The market economy, that sacred altar of liberals and free enterprise conservatives, establishes and maintains the *system* of impersonality in all economic relations, guaranteeing that the priorities of human need become irrelevant; indeed, making it certain that prior access to scarce means of consumption is given to people with relatively well satisfied basic needs on account of their greater purchasing power compared to that of needy people. As Edgar Z. Friedenberg has put it, our system is good at accommodating "demands, which are what winners are in a position to make" in a competitive society, but it performs badly in meeting "needs, which are what losers have."[15]

Crucial is the logic of production for exchange under capitalism, as distinct from the more primitive society's system of production for use. Products of labor become *commodities* to the extent that they are produced for the purpose of sale or exchange; it is by the same logic that workers come to be seen, and also to see themselves, as commodities, when they have to sell their labor power to stay alive, or to acquire the basic dignities of life in modern society.[16]

There was plenty of oppression prior to the capitalist age, of course, but peculiar to the age of capitalism is the process of *reification*, the process by which human relationships are made to appear as relationships between things, subject to the same kinds of instrumental calculations as are relationships between other things. For example, "capital," not capitalists, is said to employ workers; "land," not landlords, is said to require rent; it is said that money creates more money, not that moneylenders are in a position to extract interest on loans. For present purposes what matters about reification is that concerns with priorities of human need and with human relationships inexorably become subordinated, by way of the reifying ideology, to concerns with making money by "free trading" in commodities and services. As Lukacs wrote half a century ago:

> Reification requires that a society should learn to satisfy all its needs in terms of commodity exchange. The separation of the producer from his means of production, the dissolution and destruction of all 'natural' production units, etc., and all the social and economic conditions necessary for the emergence of modern capitalism tend to replace 'natural' relations which exhibit human relations more plainly by rationally reified relations. . . . But this implies that rational mechanization and calculability must embrace every aspect of life.[17]

In a recent work William Leiss examines the consequences of reification in modern liberal-corporate societies or, as he calls them, "high intensity market settings," and he emphasizes four categories of social cost: (1) "a fragmentation and 'destabilization' of the categories of needing"; (2) "the difficulty of 'matching' the qualities of needs with the characteristics of goods"; (3) "a growing indifference to the qualities of needs or wants"; and (4) "an increasing environmental risk for individuals and for society as a whole."[18]

My own theory of human needs differs from Leiss's (see 4 §1), but in substance I think his catalogue of costs is valid; I would paraphrase the four kinds of cost as follows: First, human wants and desires, reflecting our manipulated consumer preferences, keep on proliferating and become more haphazard and transitory all the time, less relevant to our basic needs. Second, the satisfaction even of our transitory wants becomes less adequate, as products are produced, not to give lasting pleasure, but to be attractively packaged and advertised so as to attract many buyers over a short period of time; and a built-in obsolescence, in the poor quality of the product or in the manipulation of fashions, makes sure that buyers soon will be in the market for new products. Third, as we become increasingly indifferent regarding the relative attractiveness of one kind (brand) of product compared to another, we become shallower in our perception and articulation of our own wants, too. Last but most important of all, the race between the large corporations striving to outproduce and outsell one another leads to enormous waste, pollution, and depletion of nonrenewable resources, perhaps also to excessive global heat-production, all of which will soon strain the carrying capacity of the earth's biosphere. It is becoming all too clear that enormous deprivation will be suffered by our children's and grandchildren's generations, unless we find ways of slowing down the accelerating madness of runaway corporate commodity production within the next decade or two.

What is missing in Marx's pioneering perspective on alienation can be attributed to the hindsight of a world that has become a century older since he lived. First, Marx defined alienation in the context of his critique of capitalist society, and his concept does not lend itself well to examining the extent and varieties of alienation in other social orders. Second, he discussed alienation only as it affected the working class, as employees engaged in capitalist production; even for purposes of studying the permanently unemployed, his concept of alienation is less than fully appropriate, and the same holds in relation to the study of alienation in other classes.[19] Third, Marx was concerned, even for the working class, with their alienation as workers only, in the context of defining the term in his 1844 manuscripts, not with their alienation as consumers, or as citizens.

Fourth and last, but not least, since the days of Marx there have been important developments in empirical psychology and other social sciences, of which Marx for understandable reasons could take no account. One of my principal reasons for preferring a concept of alienation that is simpler than Marx's is to make it easier to relate it to a broad range of empirical research and theorizing. It will be recalled that in this work "alienation" refers to commonly occurring neuroses whose incidence (because they are commonly occurring) can be attributed to structural properties of the social order; empirically, alienation (as well as neurosis) is indicated by "tensions and conflicts between people's consciousness and some of their basic needs and motives" (see p. 42).

It must be pointed out, though, that this behaviorally oriented, rather simple concept of alienation may seem to miss a most important aspect of Marx's concept of alienation, which is independent of Marx's historicist perspective on the working class of his time: to Marx, alienation is a loss of the objective possibility of becoming more fully human, due to the capitalist system's reduction of the worker to a labor-time–equipped commodity. An objective lack is not necessarily accompanied by or indicated by tensions or other empirically ascertainable, manifest consequences. "Unalienation," to use Ollman's term again, is an open-ended, ideal concept, a hypothetical construct, not an empirical phenomenon.

This apparent dilemma illustrates a most important point about the nature of emancipatory political thought, as I understand "Politics":[20] the Political task is always to reduce discrepancies between rational humanist ideals and empirical realities. In the struggle for psychological freedom, the tensions between authentic needs and a restricted or distorted consciousness not only constitute manifest alienation, as the concept has been defined here; these tensions also provide the motivating energies that prompt us to struggle against domination and other modes of oppression.

If this struggle meets with some success, with accustomed kinds of manifest alienation being partly overcome, then new needs and motives emerge, and tensions and conflicts within the persons, that before were hypothetical ("objective" contradictions between possibilities and realities), now become actual, within the same persons. As individuals grow in moral stature, their alienation becomes more fully humane, until Ollman's and, implicitly, Marx's transempirical ideals of "unalienation" in principle can become approximated empirically: all adult humans can come to be seen as "my brothers and sisters," all children everywhere as "my children." This is the sentiment also expressed by Christ, according to the New Testament, for example in this statement in the Gospel according to Matthew: "Anything you did not do for one of these, however humble, you did not do for me" (Matt. 25:45). Gustavo Gutierrez, the influential liberation theologian, quotes from a poem by León Felipe that Che Guevara is said to have copied and treasured:

> Christ I love you . . .
> Yes! You taught us that man is God
> a poor God crucified like you
> and the one who is at your left on Golgotha
> the bad thief
> is God too.[21]

3. ALIENATION AND POWERLESSNESS: EMPIRICAL PERSPECTIVES

To gain an adequate understanding of the problem of alienation in the modern world it is necessary to draw on certain basic Marxist and neo-Marxist insights into the nature of the late capitalist system and its supporting liberal-democratic ideology. But we also require some knowledge and theoretical perspectives from recent work in psychology and other empirically oriented social sciences; especially if we seek the kind of understanding of alienation that will be helpful in learning how to overcome it by struggle from within our own social order, prior to the promised land that a socialist revolution some day will inaugurate, maybe.

First of all, there is the confusion between alienation and anomie. In much of the literature, these two terms are used very loosely, often as overlapping concepts, and at times even as synonymous terms. "Anomie" is a term that gained its currency with Durkheim's work, and it is a concept that his pioneering research made reasonably clear (clearer than it has been left by subsequent generations of researchers and theorists). Durkheim's term refers to the relative absence of or weakness in the *conscience collective*: the lack of organic solidarity, or the lack of faith in the validity of moral norms, the collective normative convictions that Durkheim held to be essential for social solidarity.[22] In his famous study of suicide he demonstrated that this ultimate act of desperation occurred with frequencies that correlated with economic instability, increasing in times of affluence as well as in times of depression: "Suicide varies inversely with the degree of [moral] integration of . . . society."[23]

Carrying Durkheimian conceptions further, Sebastian de Grazia defines "simple anomie" as the result of "conflict between the directives of belief-systems," and reserves a stronger term, "acute anomie," for the outright disintegration of belief system: he speaks of normlessness, as compared to norm conflict.[24]

What is important normatively for de Grazia and other recent students of anomie (especially Nisbet, though this is not true of the more empirically minded Merton)[25] is to overcome anomie by way of establishing a transcendent belief system that will establish legitimate norms once and for all. De Grazia, after analyzing with deep insight the psychological ravages of unemployment, in effect concludes that the only way we can hope to live with our kind of system is that we all become Roman Catholics: if our industrial system keeps tearing our community solidarity apart, we must have a shared *religious* basis of solidarity to compensate for what the system destroys within and between human beings. It is a deeply conservative orientation: Let us make the best of a bad scene here on earth and seek compensation in the realm of the spirit.

The overcoming of anomie as envisaged by Durkheim and his successors is associated with a commitment to continuing social stratification and with a belief in the necessity for continuing resignation on the part of those in society who must perform the menial tasks. In short, while I grant that the task of reducing anomic suffering is a legitimate concern, therapeutically as well as politically, a society without *some* anomie would in my view be very undesirable; it would be profoundly oppressive, both by my standards of psychological freedom and compared to the visions of overcoming alienation that the Marxists at their best are committed to.

Most leading writers on alienation, all of them at least *influenced* by Marxism, have an emancipatory intent: they seek to identify alienat*ing* forces or circumstances, in the hope that when we understand them we can explore possible strategies for overcoming them, in ways that *universally* (i.e., for all men and women, or for the least free) will liberate an increasingly wide range of species-man's potential capabilities.[26]

Let us now turn away from these long-range visions and consider a few of the many specific empirical research approaches that bear on alienation as I am using that term (see pp. 41-44 and 131-132).

The sociologist Melvin Seeman contributed an influential paper two decades ago, in which he suggested a typology of five varieties of alienation: powerlessness, meaningless, normlessness, isolation, self-estrangement.[27] Actually, normlessness and meaninglessness turn out to be aspects of anomie, as I understand the latter term; Seeman acknowledges this with respect to normlessness but does not see the importance of differentiating anomie sharply from alienation. That still leaves three types or aspects of alienation for empirical research.

More recently Seeman published another paper on alienation in which he revised his initial classification and also summarized the most recent empirical research literature bearing on each variety of alienation.[28] I shall skip over the two that relate to anomie; the remaining three types of alienation have by now become four: powerlessness, cultural estrangement (called "value isolation" in the 1959 paper), self-estrangement, and social isolation. But I hasten to delete one more concept from further consideration: "cultural estrangement" strikes me as a misnomer, or at any rate as not being a variety of alienation as the concept is understood in this paper. The reference is to a sense of antagonism against revolting policies or to a rejection of prevailing cultural norms, claiming personal sovereignty in choice of basic commitments. "Anti-Americanism"—attitudes associated with the rebellion among young Americans in the late 1960s—is suggested as an example. This kind of political rejection of establishment policies strikes me as an indication of high, not low, levels of psychological freedom, at least among most of the leading rebels; many of these young people in their activities seemed to me to indicate an awareness of their own basic need for fairness and integrity as guiding principles in their lives, and found it abhorrent when their government with contempt for law as well as for loss of lives went about trying to subjugate the South Vietnamese population under an American-imposed regime.[29]

That still leaves three component concepts of alienation in Seeman's more recent survey of the empirical literature: powerlessness, self-estrangement, and social isolation. I shall limit my discussion in the main to powerlessness, but first let us take a brief look at the other two concepts, self-estrangement and social isolation. Both terms are subject to varieties of interpretation, and yet I think it makes sense to argue that both are best associated with the phenomenon of loss of community: community as confirmation of a socially rooted identity and as basis for meeting what I have called community solidarity needs, after basic physical needs the needs most crucial for human health and freedom. Self-estrangement is like "the master theme in alienation studies," writes Seeman,[30] and a wide assortment of studies of oppression in the workplace bear on this concept; social isolation is the opposite of community integration, and in this area, too, there are many studies. Relative to Marx's concepts, self-estrangement is close to alienation from our species-being, while social isolation quite explicitly is the same as alienation from our peers; as I have suggested, both kinds of alienation block our awareness of community dependency and solidarity needs.

By contrast, powerlessness may relate more closely to what has been called the most basic subjectivity needs, the need to feel free and to feel competent. In Marx's terms, powerlessness comes closest to his conception of the worker's alienation from the processes of production, as the worker becomes reduced to something much less than a free man or woman: he or she becomes like a cumbersome, perishable appendage to the one human commodity that does have a limited, if fluctuating market value: each worker's labor power. In today's world it must be emphasized, as I have done already, that alienation in the sense of powerlessness applies not only to the products that the worker has had a hand in producing; it applies to all commodities, and it applies to all of us, possibly excepting the superrich, as consumers; as programmed chasers-after-commodities, it is hard to retain even the power to keep a steady conception of our needs- or want-priorities. If brawn, literacy, and intelligence are the alienated workers' assets for employers, so eyes, ears, tastebuds, and stomachs, as well as medical ailments, appear to be what makes alienated consumers valuable to the corporate system of production and sales.

There is by now a very extensive empirical research literature on powerlessness. First of all, how can a sense of powerlessness be measured? The most influential approach in recent years was inaugurated in 1966 by Julian Rotter with his I–E scale, which measures perceptions of internal versus external control: Individuals, even if their social situation and circumstances appear to be much the same, have been found to differ widely in their beliefs about whether or not they have much real influence over their own lives or, conversely, whether or not they see themselves on the whole as being at the continuing mercy of externalities like powerful other persons, "the system," fate, or random chance.[31] More recently there have been some weighty criticisms of Rotter's approach, and alternative approaches to measurement and to concepts and theorizing have been attempted.[32] I shall not discuss any of these controversies here, only observe that research work on internality/externality, or sense of personal power/powerlessness (roughly, at least, the same pair of concepts) has been in rapid development in recent years. Next I turn to a brief discussion of two major lines of inquiry in this research literature which strike me as particularly promising in relation to purposes of political emancipation: one (A) dealing with the genesis of powerlessness in patterns of childrearing and the other (B) dealing with the influence of participatory activity as a way of possibly overcoming the affliction of a sense of being without personal power even over one's own life.

(A) Stanley Renshon has shown the origins of powerlessness to be associated with such aspects of family structure as predictability of rules governing everyday behavior and the child's degree of influence on the contents of such rules, etc.; but, at least according to Renshon's data, by far the most important influence on the development of personal power (the opposite of powerlessness, of course) is the parents' own sense of personal power in *their* lives.[33] Beyond the range of studies included in Seeman's survey, Mantell's data on the family backgrounds of American war resisters compared to Green Berets (I now assume that the former exhibited some independent personal power while the latter more often exhibited subordination to the dominant ideology and to the discipline of strict hierarchy) make it clear that the latter, unlike the former, in most cases came from families in which the father was the boss without open challenge; families, that is, without dialogue regarding rules and decisions.[34] And Melvin Kohn's study of Italian and American families indicated that lower-class families tend to program their children into a sense of powerlessness while middle-class children to a much larger extent are taught to think that they will be able, to a considerable extent, to shape the course of their own lives; correspondingly, the latter also come to feel more of a sense of personal responsibility for the decisions they make about how to live, when to obey, with whom to associate, etc.[35] Obedient soldiers, as epitomized by Lt. William Calley, infamous for his behavior at My Lai, and people who sympathized with him, tend, on account of their lack of personal power, to see themselves as destined to obey their bosses and their government under an implicit contract that absolves them, in return, from any wrongs that their obedience might bring about; it is for others, the Internals, to contemplate possible disobedience, in connection with their own personal judgment about the moral acceptability of their bosses' or their governments' acts and intentions.[36]

How do these kinds of research bear on emancipatory strategies? First, they suggest that one ought to choose parents with personal power; second, that middle- and upper-class parents are more likely to possess it; and third, that one should pick mothers with a feminist spirit of insistence on equal rights, who can produce climates of dialogue within the family, as an alternative to a structure of arbitrary power and submission. But why is it that working-class parents tend to have a relatively limited sense of personal power? Presumably because they have to a large extent been treated as servants in their work situations.

Since it is not as yet practicable to enable infants to

choose their own parents or to equip them to choose wisely, and since there are not enough prospective parents with sufficient personal power around anyway, and certainly not enough strong mothers, perhaps we should settle instead for the following kinds of short-range strategies:

(1) Let us support all practicable worker-control and self-management schemes, not only in industry but in offices and schools and colleges as well, so that more people's daily working lives can become a training ground for self-determination, not for submission.[37] (2) Let us also support the feminist struggle for equal rights, especially as it pertains to work and to family structures, so that more women can become equal partners in the politics of family life and more men can learn to accept their spouses as full equals and, in consequence, more children's first political experience can be as observers of and eventually partners in discussions of common concerns, rather than as objects of commands in the absence of reasoning, or even perhaps in the absence of reasons.[38]

(B) Another recent research approach, this one barely mentioned in Seeman's survey, is attribution research, a line of work that originated with Fritz Heider's 1958 volume, *The Psychology of Interpersonal Relations*;[39] it owes much to Skinner's behaviorism and more still to cognitive dissonance theory and research. Most briefly stated, these researchers assume not only that we learn by doing (that is hardly news), but also that we tend to learn about our own personal qualities less from our intuition than from our accumulating perceptions and cognitions about our own acts and behavior.

It is immediately apparent that this is how we tend to learn what other people are like: when evaluating their behavior, we tend to emphasize its external causation only when it appears that they have been forced into a certain line of action; whenever and only to the extent that we believe another person had a real choice and acted deliberately do we tend to draw inferences from observed acts to conclusions about what the other person is like, or how he or she is disposed toward us, unless, of course, we suffer from prejudice or other varieties of irrationality.

Daryl J. Bem was probably the first to argue that we

arrive at inferences about our own personality and attitudes by exactly the same processes that we apply in appraising other persons, rather than by drawing on some kind of subjective reservoir of intuitive self-knowledge.[40] A great number of experimental research studies have confirmed the validity of Bem's proposition.[41]

This basic insight has important implications that bear directly on the psychological processes that keep on confirming and deepening the widespread sense of powerlessness that afflicts our complex and in many respects conformity-demanding society; that powerlessness afflicts above all those social classes that are most in need of access to political power in order to move toward more equality with less oppressed classes. For we must conclude that actual conformity behavior coupled with the familiar pretension that we live in a free and democratic society makes for a deadly combination, virtually dooming most of us to a continuing incarceration in a psychological jail of utter powerlessness; as we keep hearing that participation in the exercise of political power is ours for the asking, we are made to conclude that it is our own fault if we in fact count for nothing, as most of us do, when it comes to influencing public policies.

What strategies does this construction of the psychology of powerlessness suggest? If it is not feasible over the short run to achieve power for the oppressed, we can at least go to work against the pacifying illusion that we are exercising power now, on the national scene; without this kind of pacifier perhaps we can learn how to begin to exercise personal power in our daily lives and to learn, by doing, the difference between a real participatory influence and a fraudulent ideological attribution of influence.

First of all, then, we need to redouble our educational efforts to puncture that omnipresent myth, the democratic makebelieve, as I have argued above (3 §1): We have in fact *not* been free to elect different political or economic regimes, *not* been free to opt out of the ratrace for jobs and consumer commodities, *not* even been free to choose our own kind of education, not without the constant pressure toward confining our career aspirations within inherited and unjust corporate-interest–dictated kinds of job specifications. Instead of being given the option of fitting future job specifications to our own human needs and requirements, each new generation is asked to compete for whatever existing job descriptions best serve the corporate race for profits, with little inherently meaningful work in prospect.[42]

Second, we must discover experimentally, as cooperating individuals, that we *are* able to struggle to emancipate our consciousness and to conquer new degrees of freedom from alienation, to the extent that we at long last are becoming realistic about what we have been and are up against in our own alienating environment. In other words, the strategy to combat the vicious circle that makes us attribute our lack of power to our personal powerlessness, instead of the other way around, must be exercises in consciousness raising and attempts, with others, to assert ourselves with increasing determination against the continuing pressures on our life which, if we at all analyze them, can be seen to serve indefensible interests of others (say, corporate profits) at the expense of our own authentic needs.

An ontologically radical attribution researcher, Herbert M. Lefcourt, has taken the view that "freedom and control are both illusions, inventions of man to make sense of his experience." Yet he most carefully examines a wide assortment of research on many kinds of animals, including a good number of studies of human beings, and is led to this conclusion: the illusion of freedom and a measure of personal control over one's life probably has a definite role in sustaining life, even to the extent, he suggests, that it "may be the bedrock on which life flourishes."[43]

If an ontological skeptic like Lefcourt is persuaded to adopt this positive view of the value of attributing freedom and personal power to ourselves, then those of use who believe in psychological freedom as a possibility, and not only for the newborn infant, should all the more take heart in our attempts to understand and overcome alienation.

4. TO OVERCOME POWERLESSNESS:
TOWARD HORIZONTAL COMMUNITIES

Political consciousness-raising as a strategy of emancipation is a recurrent theme in this work; but consciousness of what? In part, the task is to raise our consciousness of individual resources of potential personal power and self-management capabilities; therefore, of the possibility that patterns of hierarchy, whether traditional or recently imposed, can be replaced by patterns of participatory democracy in our communities and within our organizations. I have argued for a continuing struggle to make our organizations more "horizontal" and to keep them from slipping back to oligarchy, as organizations tend to do. "Eternal vigilance is the price of liberty" is a most important insight not only in the context of the nation-state where, at best, such vigilance has preserved one system of oppression against alternatives that could well be far worse. It holds in all other social contexts, too. Without a continuing political awareness of power and oppression in our everyday lives and of the moral necessity of upholding the principle of equal human dignity and basic rights for all, we become thoughtlessly complicit in supporting the ever-present tendencies toward oligarchy and exploitation, tendencies that sooner or later will come to victimize us as well as those presently more vulnerable.

But consciousness of oppression and its false justifications is not enough; we also require a self-consciousness that goes deeper than the presuppositions of conventional liberal individualism. In chapter 1 I made reference to Donald Carmichael's critique of the basic liberal premise that men (and women) are individual agents, defined by themselves as separate, socially detachable or even detached, individuals (see 1 §3). This is a false premise, though one that is "exceedingly well established" in our society, as Carmichael writes. He comments, wryly: "I suggest, however, that no one, on reflection, would willingly consider himself and others in these terms."[44] For what matters to us, as real persons, is not only how long we live but how well. Agent-individualists could not meaningfully ask themselves whether to make sacrifices for a worthy cause, not unless some kind of full compensation for each exertion were in prospect, though it need not be monetary—it could even consist of good feelings, so long as this could be anticipated and calculated in advance. In the real world, as Carmichael observes, most of us understand ourselves as continuing projects begun by earlier generations, as sharing these projects with others in the common cause of social existence, and as bequeathing them to be completed by those who survive us. Further, we measure our meanings as persons by the manner in which we meet these tasks, and we expect others to measure us in the same terms.[45]

When Thomas Hobbes published his pioneering works, liberal contractualism was a revolutionary doctrine in a world oppressed by feudal and ecclesiastical authorities. Paradoxically, his own political purpose was to vindicate established (secular) authority and, indeed, to justify almost limitless power for any well established regime, for the evils that he feared were anarchy and civil war, not authoritarian tyranny. But John Locke and other liberals soon reformulated the contractualist doctrines to justify, with great effectiveness, the economic and political emancipation of a new class: the private entrepreneurs or, more broadly stated, the bourgeoisie.

More than a century ago it was clear to Marx and Engels that the newly emancipated class not only had deepened the miseries of the peasantries and the new industrial working class, but that it was gradually destroying itself as a class through merciless competition which resulted in recurring bankruptcies and mergers and increasing concentrations of economic power on ever-fewer hands. Yet the successful few, who fattened at the expense of all the rest of society, have been able to maintain their cultural domination ever since by imposing an alienating consciousness of possessive individualism on all social classes, a consciousness that would make us all repress our human community needs and make us continually competitive with our peers, including the Joneses across the street, but deferential to economic and political power. In other words, the liberal ideology tended to turn the more aggressive and successful or well connected people into avaricious entrepreneurs, while the rest of the population was encouraged to become pliable employees, enthusiastic consumers of commodities, and conformist citizens.

Money thus becomes the focus of individualist consciousness, as Marx wrote in one of his early papers:

Money is the alienated essence of man's work and existence; this essence dominates him and he worships it. ... Just as man, so long as he is engrossed in religion, can only objectify his essence by an *alien* and fantastic being; so under the sway of egoistic need, he can only affirm himself and produce objects in practice by subordinating his products and his own activity to the domination of an alien entity, and by attributing to them the significance of an alien entity, namely money.[46]

This reification of economic relationships that is expressed in the perceived "power of money" in the consciousness of individuals has its counterpart in the "power of institutions." "Institutions" may be taken to refer to all widely accepted expectations of behavior, of dos and don'ts, as they reflect the established division of labor in a given social order and the established distribution of rights and duties, assets and liabilities. If money is what we as agent-individualists are supposed to be striving for, (other) social institutions supposedly lay down the rules of the game, over and beyond the law, assigning to each player specific categories of instructions determined by various skills, training, social connections, etc.

It is in the interest of every ruling class that institutions become as confining as possible in order to prevent the kind of human solidarity that could make ordinary people want to combine forces against those who exploit them and direct their working lives and much of their consciousness. And in a technologically advanced society, which requires intelligent, articulate employees on many levels, a diversification of institutions to match the many levels of training and mental ability is required to keep the system as a whole from being questioned effectively and to make most people define themselves in terms of their specialized roles. Thus many people develop a sense of a stake in their roles, in their careers, and in the system itself. They also become less capable of seeing themselves as whole human beings in search of whole lives in natural human communities, in which they would be free to combine forces to seek ways of achieving rational political self-management.

Robert E. Agger in a recent work contributes a radical

critique of the common notion that institutions actually exist as manifestly as physical things do, instead of being mere reifications, as he argues, of abstract expectations that people have been induced to develop, reciprocally. In the interest of power and domination, technological developments have been utilized to carry the logic of liberal contractualism to its extreme, with proliferating rules of specialization and differentiation to dictate who can do what, how, and when, to whom, and with people programmed to treat each other more and more instrumentally, as bundles of specific wants and assets, with the result that natural, whole person-to-person relationships are becoming the exception rather than the rule.

Agger calls it a very destructive "little white lie" that institutions in modern society are there to meet human needs, rather than being there to prevent self-management and the growth of human communities:

> That little white lie became transformed over time into a major foundation of the modern world. What appears to have happened, quite apart from the often bemoaned or applauded growth in the proportion of public over private space, is the development of institutions to the point that personal, presumably residual, everyday-life space became a shred of what it used to be. Despite a great reduction in working time, giant institutions seem to have moved in and around people until people can hardly breathe in noninstitutionalized everyday-life air.[47]

Agger also develops a general scenario for resisting the whole modern tendency toward extreme role-differentiation, superspecialized career patterns, and partialized, exchange-oriented rather than whole human relationships; the alternative development that he anticipates is the emergence of human communities, that is, "places wherein people relate to each other as relatively total or whole persons."[48] His emphasis is on

> opening, cross-cutting and integrating institutions. This is a mission subversive of our own closed institutions. It

may be more easily accomplished than we might think
if we come to understand how beautiful and sad, dangerous and delightful life can become when we end the
illusion of our being inside some and outside other institutions of a kind that really do not exist.[49]

I am not convinced that it is fruitful to debate whether or
in what sense institutions "exist," but I welcome Agger's call
to assault, in principle, all institutional cutting asunder of
human relationships, even our relationships to ourselves. His
proposed strategies are less than clear in specifics, which I attribute in part to his rejection of a need concept that admits
of rational priorities to guide human rights–extending policies (above, pp. 96-99). However, I agree that the main task
that he sees is indeed a crucial one: opening up all institutions
in the struggle to build what he calls human communities.

My own preference is to speak of "natural communities";
I shall also use the terms horizontal communities, fraternal
communities, and authentic communities. Before discussing
these adjectives, let me define what I take to be the opposite
of community in the strict sense, that is, hierarchy.

Hierarchies, too, can be natural, the traditional human
family being the most obvious example, or they can be deliberately established for some purpose, as in a formal organization. By "hierarchy" I shall understand an interacting
social system, small or large, with asymmetrical power or
authority relations. In the animal world the pecking order
in a chicken coop would be the paradigm (I am not prepared to say whether power or authority is the organizing
force). In the more articulate and self-conscious world of humans, asymmetrical authority and respect is usually ration-
alized and accepted on grounds thought of as in some sense
natural, like differences in age, rank, knowledge, wealth,
moral desert, etc. My intention here is not to reject out of
hand every basis for hierarchy as unjustifiable; I am simply
making the conceptual point that a hierarchy in charge of
political decisions is incompatible with a community of political equals. And in this work I shall speak of *community*
in the strict sense only if, or to the extent that, political
hierarchy does not prevail. By my definition, every authentic

community is fraternal and horizontal, at least to a considerable extent: all members are in fact entitled to influence decisions that may affect the community as a whole.

"Community" will be understood here as any social system, small enough so that individuals can recognize and relate to each other, in which all members are equally free to discuss and to influence decisions affecting the common good. With Rousseau I hold that (democratic) communities are small. On a larger scale the best we can hope for is a federation of communities. What we in fact are up against are hierarchies (the state) that falsely claim to be, or to represent, so-called national communities. Such alleged communities, and all other kinds of alleged communities that are in fact governed by hierarchies, I shall call *pseudocommunities*; I consider this a pedagogically vital distinction.

But first let us consider in what ways communities as well as hierarchies can be considered natural. Reference has already been made to the traditional family as the prototypical natural hierarchy: since the days of our jungle ancestors the physically stronger member has protected and governed the lives of the weaker members. Second, there is the fact that from Stone Age tribes to modern nation-states hierarchies have invariably been in charge, with the majority of members, subjects, or citizens having little say over decisions affecting the common good, or even over those affecting their own well-being. The notion of human rights is a recent invention.

Let me also argue, however, that "natural" in a different sense can be applied to my kind of human communities as well. For in this book I am concerned with finding ways of leaving outlooks and behavior patterns inherited from the jungle behind us to the fullest possible extent;[50] this task is inspired by the vision that human nature is capable of evolving with history, to be sure within the limits of biological and psychological constraints as well as under the impact of changing production technologies and of the dynamics of historical processes. Social institutions are historically determined, and many can be transcended and eventually discarded. As human nature and human activities have evolved, gains toward a fuller consciousness of human capabilities and propensities have been made, compared to the days of life in the jungle: interpersonal trust has become possible outside immediate family ties; aspirations toward a world without war, even a world with security and freedom for all, have been articulated and adopted by growing numbers of individuals. So have ideals of equality and fraternity; in fact these ideals have helped bring about the four major revolutions in the last two centuries, those of the United States, France, Russia, and China, and many others as well (even though it must be conceded that the postrevolutionary societies always have fallen short of the prerevolutionary hopes).

It is in line with this clearly discernible trend in human consciousness that I speak of fraternal or horizontal human communities as *natural*, on this basis: they represent the kinds of social system that men and women, to the extent that they become "unalienated" and free from coercion and fear, will aspire to. As human beings come to "find themselves" in situations giving them security and freedom—and every progressive school educator works with this assumption taken for granted—they tend to seek out human relationships based on equality and mutual trust. I suspect one would have to be some kind of an academic specialist in order to doubt the validity of this proposition: in free and mature men and women there is a *natural* yearning to establish not only cooperative relationships but full friendships, on the basis of equality and reciprocity of caring concern.[51]

Fraternal communities (if I may be forgiven for my continued use of this sexist but convenient term; "fraternal" refers of course also to sisterhood-type relations between women and to brother-sister–type relations between men and women) are natural, then, in the special sense that, as human beings transcend alienation and reclaim their psychological freedom, they will naturally crave to belong to communities of equals, that is, to horizontal communities. People as individuals are of course by nature *unequal* in many ways and may well become more unequal when they become less oppressed, since this will allow their respective individualities to come into fuller bloom;[52] the point is that free adults, and probably most secure and free youngsters as well,[53] will tend to crave human relationships based on equality in dignity, respect, political rights—in short, fraternal, horizontal relationships.

Such communities are "authentic" in that they can be presumed to be based on our spontaneous fraternal affiliation needs; they are not maintained by way of externally imposed rituals and symbols, and they do not require for their cohesion a sense of threat from the outside.

Authentic, horizontal communities are an antidote to alienation first of all in the sense that they enable us humans to gratify our basic community-solidarity needs, which take precedence over our individuality needs as requirements for individual health and freedom, contrary to the conventional liberal wisdom (see 1 §3 and 4 §2). Second, they help us transcend our alienation in the sense that they enable us to develop a real sense of personal power, through the actual practice of participation and the self-attribution that comes with practice, which differs so radically from the tenuous, psychologically unreal self-attribution of political freedom that comes with the so-called political, mainly private interest–oriented behavior within the electoral macrosystem that we are all familiar with: the contests between the "gladiators" in our far from democratically governed liberal-corporate state.[54]

5. THE NATION-STATE AS PSEUDOCOMMUNITY: ENEMY, ARENA, AND ALLY?

It is intrinsically rewarding to belong to an authentic human community; it enlarges the self, and it extends and deepens our social consciousness. Authentic communities are sustained by friendships, common concerns, and spontaneous solidarity; they do not require contrived myths to mark them out as superior to other communities, or barrages of propaganda to remind the members of alleged duties to the common good. Pseudocommunities, on the other hand, are characterized by a requirement of constant reinforcements of such kinds.

The accoutrements of the nation-state come immediately

to mind, for the nation-state is indeed the archetype of pseudocommunity: Imperial Majesty or Imperial Presidency (or Comrade Chairman, in other countries), flags, anthems, prayers, attractively packaged morsels of distorted history—these are some of the most potent ingredients from which hierarchical domination is made, and with a vengeance, in the most violence-prone of all hierarchies, that of the modern nation-state.

If the way to overcome alienation is to substitute a solidarity with our own authentic communities for the misguided loyalties to the authoritarian pseudocommunities that try to run our lives for us, then we must first aim at finding ways of resisting and frustrating the claims of the state. Yet that is not to say that the laws of the state should be disobeyed, and certainly not indiscriminately, for the state is not the only enemy of human emancipation. While the state is indeed an enemy in the struggle for full emancipation, it is also the main arena for that struggle, and in some ways, actually and potentially, an ally as well.

First, consider in what sense the state must be seen as the archenemy of human emancipation, which ultimately must be destroyed if men and women are to become free to live unmolested, physically and spiritually, in their natural communities. Even over the short run we must attempt to weaken the state, for it remains the main engine of political oppression, even in the liberal-corporate First World where, domestically, it is in some ways more benign than other kinds of state, and more benign, at least potentially, than many of the powerful private corporations to which it now affords indiscriminate protection. Every modern state, and especially the states with large populations, have immense arsenals of means of violence on the ready, and the vast resources of indoctrination and domination under their control are in the service of legitimating, in most people's minds, a flagrantly unjust, inhumane, status quo.

New *kinds* of organizations are required if we are to free ourselves from the state's ideological stranglehold, I have argued: horizontal organizations, but above all horizontal *communities* in which people are free to burst out of organizational constraints and to "open up" institutionalized patterns and innovate on many levels. Such natural communities declare their spiritual independence of the state even when they, for reasons of prudence and to promote nonviolence, decide to obey the law; their practice of civil disobedience is likely to be selective, when possible with advance warning systems to the state, which may thereby be encouraged not to overstep certain bounds in abusing its powers.

I mean to make two points with this last statement: advance warnings of civil disobedience may, especially if considerable numbers of protestors are involved, induce the state to scale down actual or intended specific oppressive policies against which the campaign is directed; these early warnings may also motivate the state to avoid extremes of violence in its attempts to put an end to the civil disobedience campaign. As George Lakey argues so well, open and nonviolent campaigns of defiance, if well prepared and well publicized, can make it extremely awkward for the state to employ physical violence in response and equally awkward to persist with the specific policies objected to.[55]

The issue here is not only what horizontal communities can achieve against the state. I also want to emphasize what they can come to mean in the lives of their members. Their main function in that context is to reverse the psychologically debilitating processes of so-called representative democracy, where actual powerlessness is made politically castrating by the accompanying belief that ordinary people are in fact in control of the state, so that the oppression and injustice that is everywhere to be felt is taken to be attributable to the poor capabilities of ordinary people, the supposed masters. Horizontal communities that spiritually defy the state, even while cooperating to the extent of obeying most of its laws, will have their members in fact exercise power over their own lives and yet be conscious of the state as an engine of oppression.

Thus, the oppression is now seen by citizens as external to themselves and as a challenge to be struggled against, rather than as reflecting character defects in themselves. In this way the recognition of the state's oppression comes to strengthen rather than weaken the sense of personal power; it comes to increase the individual's courage to act and persist against unjust policies, in solidarity with others, and thus to reduce the levels of alienation.

Second, let us now consider that the liberal-corporate state can and often does provide an arena that makes nonviolent struggles for emancipation possible, struggles against the state itself and also against other formidable enemies of human emancipation. In the latter context the state in a sense may be seen as an ally of humanist aspirations.

Our kind of state does provide some protection against random as well as vigilante violence. The United States government has in the past decades provided considerable protection for many of the basic civil and human rights, especially those of black people in the traditionally tyrannical states of the Deep South. Also, over the years the poorest people in the United States have gradually achieved some improvements in guaranteed access to food and shelter, even if their relative deprivation, compared to the affluent classes, has not been reduced. The proverbial policeman on the corner, the most visible agent of state power on the domestic scene, has not always been the protector of members of racial minorities, sexual deviants, or young people (especially those with deviant smoking preferences); nevertheless, the police forces undoubtedly offer most people, including revolutionary dissenters, some needed protection against politically and criminally inspired violence. Even convicted criminals are on the whole treated a bit more humanely than in former days, and the death penalty has fallen into disuse in most of the states. The Freedom of Information Act has made it possible for individual citizens to sue Federal agencies that heretofore could harass and punish people in clandestine ways for no legally defensible reason; the secret police is now less likely to invade people's private lives or to blacklist people without well-founded suspicions of crimes committed and a follow-up of criminal prosecutions in open courts.[56] In short, it must be said that the United States government has been improving its track record in recent years when it comes to curbing acts of life-destroying violence as well as policies contemptuous of individual liberties; its behavior abroad is quite a different matter, to be discussed in chapter 6, sections 2 and 3.

I conclude that, in our struggle to overcome alienation, the task for the foreseeable future is not to attempt to destroy the liberal-corporate state but to attempt to tame it and to get it out of our hair, so that we become psychologically resistant to its traditional claims on us. The state must come to be seen as a means only, a means to maintain as nonviolent a social order as is possible at each point of time in the unfolding of history.

Our natural communities must come to replace the nation-state as our end, as the focus of our loyalties. As we overcome our alienation by way of strengthening the natural communities that sustain us, we can progressively come to weaken the state in proportion as the state's services of protection and enforced allocation become less necessary. The more our basic community-solidarity needs come to be met, the less we shall need the state; to this extent the anarchists are right. But I believe that both anarchists and communists invariably tend to underestimate (a) the importance of working to make the liberal-corporate state progressively weaker and yet remain a source of protection for nonviolent political work, and (b) the great possibilities even today for building grassroots political strength within and through politically defiant natural communities.

Eventually the state must be *made* to wither away. It won't go of its own accord, and it won't be destroyed by violent revolution, for mass violence always makes strong oligarchies necessary to restore some kind of social order, old or new. The more we attempt to destroy the state by violence, the more it bounces back, more violence-prone than ever. The only way to destroy the state is a slow way; it is to take the time to build something that can replace it: our natural communities, the authentic communities that can give us all the strength to gradually overcome and discard that most persistent pseudocommunity, that self-imposed hierarchy which emasculates us politically and then feeds on our political impotence: the nation-state.

We need a different kind of patriotism, a two-pronged one, a humane patriotism that relegates the state to oblivion as a moral force—while recognizing of course that it is still a predator *and* a protector, with teeth. In part our loyalty must be directed to our natural communities, our friends, neighbors, and fellow workers who sustain us in our every-day lives. But we are not alone, even as a community; we are parts of mankind. For the rest, and indeed preponderantly, our loyalty must go to the transnational "community" of humanity, of mankind as a whole, present and future, as I shall argue in chapter 6.

In our present world the nation-state's historically contrived claims on our loyalties have come to overshadow these two loyalties, one of which is natural to us as social human beings, and the other of which is necessary to us as members of a species that now appears heading for extinction.

To be sure, there is no "community of mankind," for communities are by definition small. But the welfare of all communities in the long run depends on the welfare of all of mankind, an insight that is now removed from many people's view by the divisive blinders of national patriotisms. It is time to turn our backs on traditional patriotism. This is not to belittle the moral leadership of patriots of the past, nor of patriotic leaders of today's struggles of national liberation from foreign domination; it is the patriotism that is compatible with oppressing others and with suppressing dissent that must be stubbornly resisted and severely condemned. Yet even the most emancipatory national patriotism carries the seeds of oppression within it; it must come to be replaced eventually by the two kinds of patriotism I have described: community loyalty and transnational patriotism.

In proportion as we develop strong natural communities that can make us "unalienated," I think we will come to reach out across present borders toward all human beings in the spirit of brotherhood and sisterhood.

6

Toward a World of Natural Communities

1. MAKING A FUTURE FOR HUMANITY THINKABLE:
   AN OVERVIEW

I HAVE BEEN TOLD THAT the late Groucho Marx once summed up the existential dilemma of liberal man, of man alienated from his species-being, in pursuit of his individual interests in a competitive social order; our American Marx confronted the ecologists and the environmentalists with the question of why should he worry about a future for the human race: "What," he demanded to know, "has the future ever done for me?"

What scares me is that there are respected academics around these days who are in effect asking exactly that question, but in all seriousness, and who in effect assert that they can find no valid answer to it and therefore no valid reason for any profound concern about mankind's long-term future.[1]

Recognizing no moral absolutes and seeing society in terms of a contractual quid pro quo between individuals, rather than in terms of the safekeeping of priceless communities to shelter and give meaning to human lives, these academics, impeccably rational in a formal sense of the term, would seem in principle prepared to accept a possible termination of the human experiment, provided it can be postponed for awhile, if this resignation at the expense of others can save the now living generations from the trouble of cutting down on our standard of living, or save us from having to change our accustomed ways of doing business. Other academics are just as formally rational and as cavalier about sacrificing even on a grand scale the lives of others right now, in faraway Third World countries, countries they apparently classify as being among the undeserving poor. Let me give an example of each of the two orientations.

Professor Wilfred Beckerman, the same authority who was quoted in an earlier chapter to the effect that poverty cannot be abolished in countries like Britain because the poor are too few to have much clout in elections, on another occasion has written as follows, in a paper that makes light of the ecologists' worries about the corporate squandering of the Earth's resources: "Suppose that, as a result of using up all the world's resources human life did come to an end. So what? What is so desirable about an infinite continuation of the human species, religious convictions apart? Do I care what happens a thousand years from now?"[2]

Another unsentimental liberal, University of California Professor Garrett Hardin, has in effect been asking an equally blunt question: what have the Bengalis, or the Sahel Africans, ever done for us Americans? Having found no satisfactory answer, Hardin proposed a new kind of political ethics for the favored nations in the modern world, what he called "lifeboat ethics." He was concerned with the so-called population explosion and with the world's limited supplies of food; comparing the Earth to a lifeboat whose carrying capacity is limited, he recommended that the rich nations should share their wealth only with those poor nations that take effective steps to limit the growth of their populations. Less deserving, less responsible nations should be cut off from foreign aid. Hardin would want the American people to become less softhearted, less morally troubled, by the prospect of letting millions of people in some parts of the world perish from starvation.[3]

Both Beckerman's and Hardin's statements are in the tradition of a new kind of "hardheadedness" inaugurated some years earlier by Herman Kahn, the author of *On Thermonuclear War*, who wanted the American people to learn to "think about the unthinkable"; Kahn's books developed fearless "scenarios" that computed the pros and cons of alternate military strategies estimated to bring about a larger or smaller number of millions of deaths in the United States and in the USSR; he was in favor of as few millions of casualties as possible. Kahn used the more convenient term "megadeaths," to refer to "millions of deaths," and his key point was that we all must face up to the need for cool calculation in such matters, within a cost-benefit perspective. While he took pride in his own boldness in thinking rationally about incurring calculated risks of multimegadeaths, a curious limitation in Kahn's rationality was made evident by his reluctance to think at all about possible policy alternatives that *to him* remained unthinkable, alternatives like surrender to communism, or even risky initiatives toward disarmament. Megadeaths did not seem to scare him, but Soviet communism did. Better dead than red. While the beginning of this nation owed something to the democratic principle of "no taxation without representation," its ending might well come to owe something to the fact that strategic minds like Kahn's seem quite unconcerned about a more elementary version, one would think, of the same democratic principle: "no annihilation without representation."[4]

I don't want to come across as a Manichean, but it does seem to me that the cavalier attitude to human lives that people like Kahn, Beckerman, and Hardin have expressed, at least in the specific contexts referred to, represents a natural culmination of the processes of alienation from our human nature, or from our nature as solidary species-beings, that the liberal ideology of the supremacy of the marketplace has set in motion. Over several generations now, most middle- and upper-class youngsters have been taught that man by nature is a selfish individualist, always trying to get the "mostest for the leastest," a cunning calculator, an optimizing animal, a being without absolute values, without any values not subject to marketplace calculations. If nothing, not even human life itself, is seen as sacred or as infinitely valuable, then it becomes perfectly rational to calculate and recommend policies that could cost millions of lives in warfare, or wipe out allegedly irresponsible nations, or take the gift of life away from future generations of human beings and deed the world back to the cockroaches and the amoebas.

This is not to assert that any liberal, or any other sane person, *wants* any of this to happen. I am saying, rather, that we have been boxed into an economic system and pacified and confused by a political ideology that is going to *make* these things happen, or continue to happen, unless we can find ways of turning things around. I shall show in this chapter how and why the killing of "useless" or "obsolete"[5] indigenous peoples in several countries is continuing unabated; I shall give examples of the kinds of ecological destructiveness on the part of the "power industry," private and public, that will make life "nasty, brutish, and short" for millions of people yet to be born, unless our corporate and political managers soon can be weaned away from nuclear fission as a source of energy; and I shall also show how the corporate world order today dooms millions in the Third World to deprivation and death at an early age.

In the previous chapters, if I may survey the overall course of my discussion once more, I have discussed three modes of oppression in relation to possible strategies of emancipation. After an initial critique of liberalism's concept of liberty and a presentation of my alternate concepts of liberty and of three modes of oppression, I have in three chapters tried to analyze each of these modes of oppression in relation to proposed appropriate strategies of emancipation. If I may attempt to summarize three chapters in three sentences, I have argued, first, that against domination we need a new political pedagogy, and that we should look to democratically transformed colleges and universities as a potentially important recruitment ground for a new breed of political educators (see chapter 3); that against structural violence and other debilitating coercive oppression and deprivation we need a variety of organized efforts to confront the established order with nonviolent acts and strategies of defiance, for the double purpose of sabotaging or undermining existing agencies of oppression and of increasing the powers of self-determining individuals joined together in reasonably horizontal counterorganizations (see chapter 4); and, finally, that against alienation we need to build horizontal communities and to develop strong federations of horizontal communities, again for a double purpose: to overcome our individualist alienation and to defy the nation-state's persistent tendency to take charge of determining our collective purposes and value priorities (see chapter 5).

In this concluding chapter I shall elaborate on my opening charge that the liberal ideology, with its faith in the economic and political marketplace as the arbiter of all values, has served to justify enormous human miseries. Many of the worst agonies, on the largest scale, are in progress in Third World countries. I shall argue that the cited antihumanist perspectives of allegedly hardheaded and rational academics like Kahn, Beckerman, and Hardin are made to appear possible, even respectable, by the modern combination of corporate capitalism on an international (First and Third World–wide) scale and the liberal ideology of acquisitive liberty and democratic makebelieve.

I turn next to a brief assessment of the vision of a corporate world order that appears to be shared by the present President of the United States, Jimmy Carter, and his closest advisors, and by important corporate, academic, and political leaders in this and other rich countries. Then I shall demonstrate how the international corporate system makes at least three categories of human beings expendable: indigenous peoples who occupy desirable lands and whose labor cannot be exploited or is not needed; people of future generations, in any part of the world; and urban and rural Third World populations now living, whose labor or whose potential consumer capabilities are not deemed suitable for "development." I shall show that the alleged worldwide scarcity of food is entirely a result of corporate power and programmed avarice; it is *not* due to lack of adequate world resources. In the same context I shall also demonstrate that this corporate avarice is mindlessly wasteful of the world's nonrenewable resources and is in the process of *making* inevitable future scarcities, at best, and irreversible ecological catastrophes at worst.

What can we do? I shall outline my own conception of an emancipated world: a world of cooperating, federated natural communities rather than nation-states; and then, to conclude, I shall argue that the way toward a communitarian and free world must begin, from where we are today, within our liberal-corporate societies, with a rejection of national loyalties and of the legitimacy of corporate claims to property rights, and with a continuing struggle to strengthen the bonds that will build mutual trust and social responsibility within our natural communities and at the same time facilitate a sense of transnational solidarity with all human communities.

2. THE MULTINATIONAL CORPORATIONS AND
UNITED STATES FOREIGN POLICY

Tommy Douglas, an illustrious member of the Canadian House of Commons (a former Priemier of Saskatchewan and the first national leader of Canada's New Democratic Party) used to compare the free enterprise system to a dance of elephants among chickens: some participants carry more weight than others and are a lot safer and freer than the rest, notwithstanding the formal equality implicit in the freedom to dance around. Inevitably, as Marx and Engels anticipated, larger and stronger firms have been gobbling up or co-opting or killing off smaller and weaker firms, cumulatively over the years and generations, until the major markets in the so-called free and competitive system are now dominated by the corporate giants.[6]

What Marx and Engels did not anticipate was the modern First World/Third World split, in which the deepening immiseration, which they did foresee for the national proletariats in advanced countries, is hitting instead the Third World's peasantries and emerging proletariats. Meanwhile, the bulk of the unionized Western working classes have been given a sense of a stake in the corporate system, as both their access to commodities and their wants for commodities have expanded and as they have come to be programmed, perhaps majorities among them, to believe in the myth of democracy and freedom achieved.

The power of the global corporations, as Barnet and Müller like to call the multinationals, derives from their "unique capacity to use finance, technology, and advanced marketing skills to integrate production on a worldwide scale and thus to realize the ancient capitalist dream of One Great Market."[7]

So profitable have investments in resource-rich but colonially impoverished new nations proved to be, that the assets of the successful multinationals have grown very much faster than the assets of any nation in the last three decades or so, until today each of the one hundred largest corporations have assets and incomes larger than those of many nations.[8] Unlike the First World nations, the multinationals in their Third World operations have no compelling reasons to pay their own workers wages that they can live on, even if some find it wise to do so; none of these corporations, being private rather than public to this extent, have to worry at all about the physical survival of the large unemployed populations in many of the states that they dominate, both economically and politically. They tend to become dominant, for the comparative strength and efficiency of the multinationals gradually push domestically owned businesses out of most of the limited domestic markets within the Third World countries, after first appropriating nearly all of the more lucrative export trade.

Multinationals are by their nature not troubled by national loyalties but, since their vast assets require military and paramilitary protection, they do make deals with national governments. In the United States and other First World countries, whose military might is most essential for their protection everywhere, they willingly pay taxes as well as wages sufficient to ensure domestic tranquillity, while in their Third World operations they pay local or slightly higher wage rates and very limited taxes, sufficient only to keep repressive regimes in power by paying for bureaucracies, secret police, and armed forces, but not sufficient to keep expendable poor people alive.

For many years after World War II things had been going well for the growing multinational corporations; even when conflicts erupted over nationalization of resource industries in some countries, under the impact of new nationalist currents, First World government pressures usually sufficed to make sure that full capital assets were recovered, funds which could then without loss be deployed in less sensitive industries or in "better-behaving," less powerful, more dependent countries. It was only with the OPEC-sponsored oil boycott of Western countries, which began in October, 1973, that the stability was shaken for the established world trade patterns, trade patterns that had been making the multinationals bigger and fatter each year and many Third World nations poorer and hungrier each year, in spite of all the United Nations–sponsored rhetoric about international aid programs and in spite of all the manifold small-scale aid programs that had in fact been instituted.

Price fluctuations, which more often than not tended to favor the rich countries, usually had an impact that far outweighed the contributions of foreign aid efforts.

In the years following 1973 some of the Third World countries have made efforts to organize in OPEC fashion, hoping to push up prices of specific crops like coffee, tea, bananas, etc., but all these efforts have come to naught, for a number of reasons. First, only foodgrains have a potential clout comparable to oil if cross-national bans on exports below certain price levels can be implemented; but grains for export are of course mainly a First World resource these days. Second, one-crop Third World economies could hold back their crops only at the cost of enormous suffering by desperately poor populations. And third, many Third World regimes outside the so-called socialist orbit are so corrupt and/or so completely dependent on multinational subventions and other First World support that they could not in fact pursue any independent economic policies, even though they may find it politically expedient from time to time to make rhetorical noises to that effect.

In short, in spite of the one major irritant of the OPEC cartel among oil-exporting governments (which of course has hurt poor nations far more than either the rich nations or most of the multinationals, which have been hurt least), the giant private cartels, whose deepening impact on world food consumption I shall discuss shortly, have been continuing their growth. What are the prospects for the future? David Rockefeller, Chairman of the Chase Manhattan National Bank, has called for a "crusade for understanding," that is, understanding why global corporations should be given even *more* freedom "to move goods, capital, and technology around the world without the interference of nation-states. . . ."[9] And Zbigniew Brzezinski, an academic with excellent corporate connections picked by President Carter as his National Security Advisor, in an influential 1970 book on the coming "technetronic era" called for a close alliance between the three rich groups of "free nations" in the world, nations based on private corporate economic systems: those in North America, in Western Europe, and Japan.[10] Soon afterwards the so-called Trilateral Commission was established, with Brzezinski as Director, and with a membership of powerful corporate executives from the three groups of rich countries, as well as a number of well connected academics and politicians, including a former Governor of Georgia who aspired to high office in Washington, Jimmy Carter.

Leaders of many Third World countries in the so-called "Group of 77" have in conference after conference under U.N. auspices called for a new international economic order, one that could reduce the mounting gap between what these countries receive for their exports and what they have to pay for their imports; that is, a way to end the free-for-all bargaining between the strong and the weak over world commodity prices, which has kept on deepening the poverty, the dependency, and the debt burdens of most Third World countries.[11]

While apparently upset over some signs of beginning Third World unity, interest in Chinese and Soviet economic models, and possible economic ties with the USSR, the West's prevailing response has been an adamant refusal to tamper with the so-called free international market; instead, modest alms-increases have been proposed—that is, more, or expanded, foreign aid programs. Meanwhile, the Trilateral Commission's strategy appears to be to try to weaken the poor countries' international bargaining position by way of welcoming some of the most fortunate Third World countries—notably some of the OPEC nations—into the charmed circle of the rich nations, thus further bolstering their bargaining position against the majority of poor nations. Trilateral associates of Dr. Brzezinski in a 1976 paper were quite candid in stating their view that this is the way to promote the combined interests of the Trilateral nations and of the multinational corporations (which include, of course, the largest banks) in the years to come.[12]

This Trilateral vision brought back to me a memory from a good number of years ago, from the days when this country still had the draft and a major war going on in Asia. I was watching television in San Francisco as the then Director of Selective Service, General Lewis B. Hershey, was explaining how it was that America needed a draft program permanently, even after the anticipated subjugation of the foreign aggressors from North Vietnam. The gist of his argument went as follows: Americans today eat three or four meals a day while much of the rest of the world has to get along on one meal a day; to protect our advantages, other peoples being envious, we will need to keep our powder dry, and lots of it.

It no more occurred to the General that sharing some of America's wealth might be an alternative than it seems to have had occurred to Herman Kahn, when he wrote *On Thermonuclear War*, that reaching an accommodation with the Soviet Union might be a viable alternative to scenarios involving millions of deaths on both sides. Contrary to Kahn, it could be that the Russians had been arming so frantically *because* the NATO countries had initiated a threatening arms race on a grand scale. Contrary to Hershey it could be that Third World peoples are starving or suffering from malnutrition today *because* American-based corporations are extracting immense wealth from them, while at the same time de facto military alliances protect their long-suffering populations from communism or, in fact, from any rebellious forces that would hope to change the established feudal or liberal-corporate system.

During the Carter presidency the vision of a viable liberal-corporate world, as represented by Brzezinski and presumably by the President himself, was manifestly at odds with another political posture for which President Carter had become much better known: his public determination to make the achievement of human rights, more and better protected human rights, all over the world, a primary aim of U.S. foreign policy. This was a public stance that I, for one, very much welcomed, regardless of the apparent inconsistencies in actual foreign policy, for I think there is power in words, especially when good words are proclaimed by persons in authority, even if deeds fall far short of matching them. Good words can feed our political aspirations and help to create political forces strong enough to come back and haunt those who uttered them, for whatever reason. The clearer the discrepancies between good words and not-so-good deeds, the better armed will the critics of illegitimate authority become.

As critics of President Carter's actual foreign policy we were bound to note that he appeared to have forged an

alliance with the Trilateral Commission interests; of all people he chose to appoint Mr. Brzezinski, as I have mentioned,
as his chief national security advisor; some have even suggested that it was Mr. Brzezinski and his friends within the
corporate elite who chose Mr. Carter as the Democratic
presidential candidate to receive their favor and their funds
in the spring of 1976.[13] Mr. Brzezinski, as I have documented,
is a man whose vision for the future is to build an even better world for the wealthiest corporations, a man who most
probably, with his Trilateral associates, had been hoping to
coax the Shah's Iran, Saudi Arabia, and other oil-rich countries not famous for their human rights achievements to
make common cause with the Trilateral countries, in order
to make sure that the poorest of the Third World countries
will remain unable to force a restructuring of world trade
arrangements in their own favor. Some human rights policy
that was, that worked to keep multinational corporate profits
healthy at the expense of deferring indefinitely every humanist's hope of seeing food, shelter, and work provided for
the world's most destitute populations!

It has been estimated by a respected British scientist that
70 percent of the world's next generation "seriously risks
permanent damage" to their mental or physical growth po-
tentials as a result of malnutrition. This is particularly true
for infants and children in the Third World: "Countries
sapped by chronic food shortages or thrown into despair by
sudden devastating famines have burned those images [of
bloated bellies, stick-thin arms, and sad listless eyes] into
our conscience. But less dramatic, and therefore more insidious, are the effects of long-term undernutrition, which
more than 300 million children already suffer."[14] The late
President Salvador Allende, in an address to the United
Nations General Assembly, placed the welfare and health
of his own country's children in the context of foreign corporate domination:

> These same firms that exploited Chilean copper for
> many years made more than $4,000 Million in profits in
> the last 42 years alone, while their initial investments
> were less than $30 Million. A simple and painful exam-
> ple, an acute contrast: in my country there are 600,000

children who can never enjoy life in normally human terms, because in the first eight months of their existence they did not receive the elementary amounts of protein. Only a small part of this amount would assure proteins for all the children of my country once and for all.[15]

President Carter cannot be blamed for the bloody military coup that destroyed President Allende's democratically elected regime on September 13, 1973, and put an end to more than a century of constitutional governments in Chile, as well as to Mr. Allende's life and to his struggle over several decades to achieve a regime devoted to social justice by way of scrupulously democratic methods. Mr. Kissinger and the Republican regime he served must take the blame.[16] But their corporate friends were largely the same, and even if we assume the best of personal intentions we must wonder whether a human rights–oriented President Carter would have had the power to act otherwise in a Chilean-type situation. For from a liberal-corporate point of view, the crime of President Allende and his regime had indeed been heinous: copper mines had been nationalized without payment of full monetary compensation at current market value. As if this were not enough, President Allende also had the temerity to claim that *reasonable* compensation had been paid:

> We want everyone to clearly understand that we have not confiscated the large foreign copper mining firms. In keeping with constitutional provisions, we have righted a historic injustice by deducting from the compensation all profits above 12 percent a year that they had made since 1955. Some of the nationalized firms had made such huge profits in the last 15 years that when 12 per cent a year was applied as the limit of reasonable profits, they were affected by important deductions.... However, the application of the constitutional norm has kept other copper firms from suffering deductions because their profits did not exceed the reasonable limits of 12 percent a year.[17]

All Third Word regimes today are in a bind, when capital is needed to improve their countries' earning capabilities or even to keep their populations alive: Unless they remain subservient to foreign corporate interests, they are deemed poor credit risks and no loans will be made available, either from the World Bank or from the International Monetary Fund.[18] A "climate hospitable to free enterprise" is a prerequisite for international loans; a policy like Allende's, that would seek to make health and nutrition available to all, is abhorrent to the world's money lenders. For Third World regimes to stay in power under an international economic system that keeps draining their countries' wealth away from their own populations, they must employ increasingly repressive methods; there is little wonder that arms sales to Third World regimes have been booming in recent years.[19]

While it would be entirely false to charge the Carter Administration with deliberately encouraging repression and brutality on the part of Third World regimes, it is all too evident that it was content to use American and allied power to preserve a "Free World" order in which structural deprivation as well as brutal repression is inevitable in many Third World countries. I think Assistant Secretary of State Patricia M. Derian was right to insist, nevertheless, that the Carter posture on human rights introduced a tangible change of emphasis, compared to the lack of any visible humane purpose for U.S. foreign policy under the previous Administrations, from Truman's through Nixon's and Ford's. Yet she ludicrously overstated her case when she concluded that "a fundamental change in the tone and direction of U.S. policy has occurred, placing this country alongside those who speak for human dignity."[20] To be sure, it would appear that American influence in the last few years has reduced the use of torture and the number of politically motivated executions in some countries in Latin America, and perhaps in some other parts of the Third World as well. This must of course be welcomed; to the extent that this is so, it is good news indeed. Compared to their more colorful predecessor, Henry Kissinger, Secretaries of State Cyrus Vance and Edmund Muskie have been far more credible and creditable spokesman for a civilized nation with some humane aspirations.

Perhaps it may even be asserted that humane intentions

during the first years of the Carter presidency may have been one modest yet real influence in guiding some aspects of American foreign policy. But intentions are ephemeral, we do well to remember; realities of power and ideology are more persistent. It is clear that Jimmy Carter, Cyrus Vance, and Edmund Muskie have remained the prisoners, if not the willing accomplices, of the liberal-corporate world order, for they take its legitimacy, let alone its power, for granted. Even their constitutional responsibilities dictate that America's power, prosperity, and military security must remain their prime concern. If the terms of world trade enforced by the multinational corporations mean continuing deprivation and loss of life in much of the Third World, and if this requires repressive regimes to keep desperate populations from looking for emancipatory political movements and strategies, then no amount of human rights idealism in the White House or in the State Department will help, in terms of bringing relief to those in the Third World who need protection of basic human rights most badly.

Correspondingly, if social stability in First World liberal-corporate society requires high employment, and if the maintenance of high employment with modern technology requires enormous industrial waste, then vast military budgets will remain necessary, with much power for professional warriors and a violence-prone world the likely result. This is hardly compatible with a world order that aspires toward a rational humanist scheme of priorities for the most basic human rights. What are other human rights worth if there is no protection for the right to live in peace? The most extreme kinds of deprivation, I have argued (4 §2), are those that involve loss of health or of life itself. Therefore, any stated commitment to human rights that does not include, even begin with, a right to live in peace is in my view profoundly suspect.[21]

3. THE COST OF CORPORATE POWER: MAKING PEOPLE EXPENDABLE

The violence of warfare, including the various kinds of internal war that many regimes today wage against parts of the domestic population, and the structural violence of suffering due to starvation and malnutrition, are two of the legacies of the liberal-corporate system that today governs the so-called Free World; these kinds of violence tend to occur together and to be more extreme in some countries than in others, depending on internal and external circumstances at different times.

I shall not discuss the arms race and the danger of international war in this book, beyond making the simple observation that since the 1950s the United States has consistently been leading the international arms race, in terms of levels of arms expenditures and in terms of accumulated arms hardware as well as arms technology (only in the first few years after World War II, when this country had a monopoly control over nuclear weapons, and the credibility of its readiness to use them had been demonstrated over Hiroshima and Nagasaki, did the arms budgets of the USSR apparently exceed those of the United States). I think the front runner in any kind of race must be held mainly responsible for the fact that there is a race, for its speed, and for its costs.

Wars treat people as expendable; preparations for war assert that people are expendable, relative to other values. That is obvious. In this section I shall argue, instead, that peacetime conditions also make vast numbers of people expendable, in the liberal-corporate world order that this country's might endeavors to uphold. I shall particularly emphasize this system's role in bringing about artificial scarcities of food, leading to starvation with loss of life and health in many Third World countries. But first let me briefly review a couple of other categories of extreme violence that our kind of world order inflicts on the most defenseless of all populations: the "primitive" indigenous peoples and future generations.

In neither case is there necessarily an evil intent on anybody's part. American liberals and conservatives, including executives in our most powerful corporations, may well wash their hands and feel free of any criminal or even moral responsibility, for they presumably are, like most of us, kindly disposed toward children, born and unborn, and wish no harm to illiterate peoples who want to continue to subsist according to the ways of their ancestors, in faraway places. The major failing that this work attributes to conventional liberals and conservatives in general, and to corporation executives in particular, is complacency, along with a tendency to look the other way when the system that provides for their creature comforts, their ample standards of living, inflicts severe suffering on unfamiliar kinds of people.

The private enterprise system has brought some nations and some social classes many commodities and comforts, but it is time to face up to some of its enormous costs to other populations. In the Amazon region of Brazil, for example, enterprising individuals and corporations in search of wealth have inflicted heavy casualties on the many kinds of native peoples who lived there prior to the European invasion; four hundred years ago they numbered probably at least 2 ½ millions, or possibly twice that number.[22] Today there may be a mere 100,000 or so survivors, and most of the remaining tribes, too, are facing decimation and extinction, as the frontiers of "civilization" keep moving closer. In neighboring eastern Bolivia there appear to be plans underway today to encourage large numbers of Rhodesian farmers to settle in traditional indigenous lands; it appears that the prospective settlers are being promised more docile servant populations than they have had to deal with in Zimbabwe lately.[23]

To return to Brazil for a moment, vast regions of the Amazon basin are now being deforested and turned into giant cattle ranches operated by multinational agribusiness corporations or by diversifying industrial corporations, for example, the Volkswagen corporation. Not only does this mean continuing inroads on the remaining territories that have offered sanctuaries for some still surviving indigenous peoples; because the ecological system itself is precarious in much of the basin, deserts have been spreading rapidly where the rain forests used to support human, animal, and plant life of astounding variety.

Shelton Davis in a recent book shows what our transnational corporate system of business is doing to Brazil at an accelerating pace, with the vast highway-building programs, the floating woodpulp factories, and the enormous ranching operations established to produce beef exports for First World markets, from a country with rampant malnutrition.[24] Davis quotes Paulo de Alameida Machado, director of Brazil's National Institute for Amazon Research, who a few years ago pointed out how the Indian peoples for centuries lived in the Amazon valley, raising hundreds of kinds of crops not used by white people and keeping the ecological system itself intact; the tragedy, as Mr. Machado put it, "is that the Indian is one of the main keys to the successful occupation of the Amazon, and as he disappears his vast wealth of knowledge is going with him."[25]

Mankind, like every other animal species, is equipped with certain instincts of self-preservation, individually and in relation to our own youngsters, our brood. But there are no instincts to make sure that there will be efforts toward collective self-preservation, and there is certainly no inherited guidance to protect us from the dangerous consequences of the deadly hazardous technological innovations of the last decades, which for the first time have made man mortal as a species. B. F. Skinner is right to observe, therefore, that human behavior is severely deficient in that most of us are not effectively reinforced today for behavior that serves our future needs, however basic and crucial these needs may be. The practical question for the reformer, he writes, is "how remote consequences can be made effective," effective as reinforcers with impact on our behavior at the present time.[26]

Our liberal individualism undercuts rational incentives toward an active concern with our collective survival as a class or a nation, let alone as a species; in another context Skinner writes that "it is not difficult to demonstrate a connection between the unlimited right of the individual to pursue happiness and the catastrophes threatened by unchecked breeding, the unrestrained affluence which exhausts resources and pollutes the environment, and the imminence of nuclear war."[27] Unfortunately, Skinner has not been reinforced by critical studies of the economic and ideological roots of our liberal individualism, and his proposed emancipatory remedies have so far produced only the occasional utopian community, without appreciable impact on the larger society.[28] It appears that Skinner's scientistic positivism has no place for a continuing dialectics between linear scientific progress and the evolving normative priorities of purpose and meaning; priorities rooted in the far from linear human aspirations, ancient and evolving, toward freedom and dignity, and also, even in a liberal society, toward brotherhood and solidarity.

The central defect in human instinctual equipment that Skinner is right to lament is nowhere more apparent, or more menacing to our future as a species, than in our apparent incapacity to empathize with future generations. *Their* stake in life and health is nowadays being treated as if they were expendable people, it seems to me, by our nuclear energy planners and their commercial and political sponsors; as even less worthy of human concern than the indigenous peoples of the Amazon Basin, for example, appear to be. Our generation of corporate entrepreneurs and associated scientists, politicians, and bureaucrats have in three short decades saddled the coming generations with large and rapidly growing arsenals of nuclear waste, the toxicity of which is bound to lead to catastrophes that will dwarf, by comparison, such recent calamities as Hiroshima and Nagasaki, Dresden, and even the Holocaust. And the buildup of additional nuclear-fission power plants is continuing at an accelerating pace. As of early 1979, according to the usually reliable research department of *Der Spiegel*, 230 nuclear power plants were in operation, in 22 countries; in the process of being built, or having been ordered, were an additional 274 plants, in 35 countries.[29]

At the time of this writing there is perhaps a flicker of hope that the near catastrophe that occurred in a nuclear plant near Harrisburg, Pennsylvania, on March 28, 1979, will have a sobering effect on energy planning in the United States, the leading fission-energy producer and user, to slow down the pace for a while and thus buy a little time. For the first time the media were given access to a major nuclear accident and did a creditable job in reporting on what happened, and for the first time the American and other Western publics (unlike the publics in the so-called socialist world) were exposed to at least a budding recognition of what nuclear accidents will come to mean, concretely.[30] In the past, nuclear accidents and even near catastrophes on the same order of magnitude had been given very little truthful coverage in the mass media; witness for example John G.

Fuller's belated but most important book, *We Almost Lost Detroit*, reporting on the extremely hazardous accident that took place in 1966 in a nuclear plant near Detroit and on how the story then was suppressed and thus caused no alarm and no widespread concern and reflection.[31] This time the news story could not be suppressed; even in faraway Hamburg *Der Spiegel* asserted in a headline: "After Harrisburg the World Has Changed."[32]

However, I fear that it will take a major *real* catastrophe before any substantial change in energy policy will come. How many additional environmental time bombs will have accumulated by then? My intention in what follows is not to attempt a technical discussion of the major energy policy options, for which I do not feel well equipped. I shall say nothing further about probabilities of nuclear-power plant catastrophes in the next few years, beyond asserting that some are likely to happen, in some places, due to human error, equipment faults, and/or faulty design; I will hardly be challenged on this assertion. My main point in this context is to stress the lack of responsible concern for the life and health of *future* generations that is clearly in evidence, given (1) everybody's awareness of the long-term radioactive toxicity of waste from every current kind of nuclear-power plant, and (2) the disinclination of those in power within our liberal-corporate establishment to give weight to alternate options toward nondestructive energy-development programs, with the generation now living paying for its own energy instead of charging its major costs to future generations.

(1) The risks and the costs of storing mounting quantities of radioactive waste are staggering; I think it requires a certain quality of madness to treat this as a challenging technological problem to be tackled, rather than as an option to be emphatically rejected, although in an age of space travel the minds of many professional and amateur engineers are apparently open to the assumption that nothing is technologically impossible to achieve if it can be made economically feasible and profitable. Yet the fact remains, and it is as disturbing from an ethical as it is from an empirical point of view, I think, that some highly toxic by-products of nuclear fission production will remain deadly radioactive for more than 10

million years, and most other toxic elements will remain so for at least a thousand years.[33] It takes an extraordinary recklessness with the lives and health of others to be willing, for the sake of present energy convenience, to saddle innumerable future generations—more generations than have existed so far since the Stone Age—with the burden of struggling for safety against this enduring menace through times perhaps of earthquakes and ice ages and other temperature changes, or perhaps through periods of wars and insane tyrannies as well as more politically benign epochs. And I find it particularly aggravating when otherwise intelligent establishment scientists blithely ignore these perils for the future generations in their learned papers on energy policy options, even, at times, in papers directly addressing comparative security problems associated with alternate categories of energy-producing processes and installations.[34]

(2) There are many benign options for coping with the world's energy crisis. The most obvious one, if perhaps the least palatable one to the liberal-corporate rules of our society, is a planned gradual reduction of energy use for wasteful purposes like military armaments, new-model cars, and for the promotion of endless numbers of electric gadgets that perform tasks that people are well equipped to perform mechanically (electric can-openers, carving knives, shavers, will serve as examples). But there is also the "soft energy path," of which Amory Lovins is the most convincing but by no means the only qualified advocate: the approach that involves an increasing and eventually complete reliance on such potential energy sources as the sun, the winds, the tides, and wood, plant-oil, cowdung, etc., either indefinitely or until it becomes feasible to produce nuclear energy by fusion processes without harm to mankind or to our natural environment.[35]

Many "soft," renewable sources of energy have the added advantage that they tend to facilitate political and economic decentralization and local community self-sufficiency. Thus according to Lovins some 4.5 million cowdung gasplants were installed in China between 1972 and 1978.[36] The great variety of soft-energy processes available with present technology (let alone with a modest investment in future developments of such alternatives), along with the low cost of many of them, is another factor that favors local decisions about how each community can live within its own means with respect to energy consumption, neither being dependent on foreign suppliers nor living at the expense of future generations who are not yet here to defend *their* basic requirements for life and health.[37]

For many North Americans, however, such options may well seem unrealistic. In an individualistic society, in which competitive self-assertion is deemed a prime virtue, it is not necessarily taken for granted that future generations must be protected, any more than it is assumed that rich countries and wealthy classes ought to stop exploiting their advantages over poor and weak countries and classes. Instead, most appear to take it for granted that the corporate system of hierarchies and concentrations of private power must be continued indefinitely, unhampered by considerations of social justice, along with the allegedly democratic processes of general elections that serve to legitimate the present social order.

The one liberal philosopher in recent years who has raised the issue of justice between the generations is John Rawls, who argues persuasively that a just social order must incorporate a "just savings principle" to protect future generations. In a just universe there must be no systematic advantage in belonging to one generation rather than another. Rawls asserts that "every generation, except possibly the first, gains when a reasonable rate of saving is maintained."[38] The first one also gains, I should like to add—and this is also in reply to the question attributed above to Groucho Marx. The hope and the peace of mind associated with a faith in a (more) viable future for our community, if not for the world, is a potential source of deep satisfaction for most people, possibly excluding only some of the archliberals that Groucho Marx presumably intended to caricature.

Rawls's thought, too, as has been observed (1 §3), is limited by his own liberal assumptions about considerable inequalities, even a hierarchy of social classes, being required to ensure adequate levels of production. But he deserves much credit for his "unliberal" willingness to do justice to future generations, even though, as he concedes, a just savings principle could scarcely be adopted democratically, assuming that most people think like liberals.[39] What we are up against today is a social order that not merely fails to save for the benefit of posterity, but insists on using up at an accelerating rate the earth's remaining fossil fuels and other nonrenewable resources; not only that, it proceeds to prepare for radio-active havoc to be visited on many of our descendants. In the words of Jacques Madaule, it is extraordinary "when human beings value the products of their work more highly than their own lives, and are willing to throw their own children into Moloch's jaws. The monster is within us."[40]

Having considered how those who direct our liberal-corporate world order in effect treat "useless," unemploy-able, indigenous people as expendable, and having then seen how the energy crisis has induced the same corporate managers and politicians to treat our own people's future generations as well as expendable, let us now turn to a considera-tion of their treatment of contemporary Third World popu-lations in general.

I shall not attempt a general treatment of Third World economics but will select one aspect of corporate behavior within the transnational commodity market system as it af-fects the meeting of basic needs in Third World countries. I could have chosen to focus on how the energy crisis affects poor countries, or I could have discussed corporate depletion of nonrenewable resources in the Third World, along with the destruction of wildlife and fragile natural environments, in relation to the scramble for big returns on corporate in-vestments. Let me instead pick the food crisis, or the apparent worldwide scarcity of foodstuffs. By a few examples I hope to convince the reader that there is no natural basis for shortages of food; I shall show that the large corporations have been creating artificial food shortages on a widening scale, at the cost of severely depriving mounting numbers of millions of Third World people. Lives and health have been and are being lost, on a vast scale, in many countries. These murderous corporate policies do not prove that corporate leaders or corporate stockholders are vicious people; they prove only what we ought to have known all along: that the laws of the market take no interest in saving human lives or in meeting human need-priorities; that the large corporations in search of optimal profits are guided by the laws of the market, not by a moral concern for human life; and that this is precisely why we can never hope to build a humane world unless we learn to face up to the necessity of destroying the political powers and immunities of the large corporations.

As late as 1973 American farmers were paid over $3 billions by the U.S. government for holding agricultural lands out of production.[41] The purpose, of course, was to keep grain prices from falling, a perfectly rational purpose from a corporate point of view, even though I think this amounts to cheating on the official liberal commitment to letting the market freely establish all price levels. In making allowances for our own farmers and for agribusiness, the American government chose to play down the fact that high grain prices mean starvation in many poor countries, unless people in those countries are allowed to grow their own food.

The trouble is that in many poor countries most people are nowadays barred from access to most of the good soil, outside the so-called socialist world. Not that food is always abundant in those countries, either; the Russians, especially, have not done very well as grain producers. On the other hand, other so-called socialist countries, including Bulgaria, China, and Cuba appear to have been success stories in wiping out hunger while achieving, over short periods of time, self-sufficiency in food production. But then there are success stories in some densely populated capitalist countries as well, with respect to self-sufficiency in food production, for example France and Taiwan. But let me now focus on the general picture in the First and Third Worlds, to show how and why it is that Third World people to such a large extent are not in a position to grow their own food.

How and why is it that large Third World populations nowadays are denied access to the land, or to sufficient amounts of land to be self-sufficient? First, there are the large landowners, who have no incentives to use their lands effectively unless they can be used to produce profitable export crops; nor have their laborers any incentives to work effectively at starvation wages. Second, and increasingly more important, multinational agribusiness corporations have in recent decades accumulated control over increasing percentages of the best agricultural lands for the purpose of producing profitable export crops; depending on climates and soil, these crops could consist of tomatoes, bananas, peanuts, cotton, tobacco, or—as in food-starved Senegal—enormous quantities of iceberg lettuce for American cities. After Cesar Chavez's troublemaking among California's once so dirt-cheap farm workers, lettuce can now be grown much more cheaply in Senegal than in Southern California.[42]

A third and most basic reason why most Third World people are not allowed to grow their own food is the collusion between multinational corporations, American social scientists and politicians, and corrupt and/or oppressive Third World regimes. Every regime wants to enlarge its nation's money economy and to increase its population's dependency on its dictates. Most American social scientists, including those who advise the State Department and the foreign aid program administrations, were until recently committed to what they called "modernizing development," which to them meant moving people off the land and into the growing urban centers, out of a subsistence economy into a budding (so they believed) industrial economy, and out of traditional tribal ties and identities into emerging national ties and identities. The multinational corporations were more than happy to receive industrial reserve armies too desperate to demand living wages and too weak and divided to attempt to organize unions. From the perspective of most Third World regimes, peasants who can grow their own food are too self-reliant, too disposed to take a dim view of governmental authority; while urban slum dwellers in abject poverty make willing recruits for military and police forces, and it is easy to tax those urban residents who are able to earn money.

Now, there are often some troublemakers around, like educators or clerics with a social conscience, but they can usually either be done away with, or intimidated, or co-opted. Sometimes Marxist revolutionaries emerge, but with Washington-trained army officers and police interrogators loyal to the powers that be, they, too, can usually be destroyed or checkmated.

What are the results of all these so-called modernizing forces and circumstances? Instead of citing fifty examples that illustrate the real causes of the alleged world food crisis, a crisis that is real enough for those who starve, I shall relate only one fairly typical example, and leave it to the reader to do the multiplying, after consulting such well documented sources as Barnet and Müller's *Global Reach,* Susan George's *How the Other Half Dies,* and Lappé and Collins's *Food First: Beyond the Myth of Scarcity.*[43]

Ethiopia's climate makes possible several cuttings of alfalfa a year, compared to only two or three in the United States. In the early 1970s, the Ethiopian government granted a concession to the Italian firm MAESCO to produce alfalfa to feed livestock in Japan. MAESCO's plantation is in the area where thousands of people, evicted by such commercial plantations from their best grazing lands, starved to death in 1973 along with their herds of camels, sheep, cattle, and goats. That year MAESCO started to raise cattle and sheep for export.[44]

Lest the reader should believe that the multinationals are cultivating exclusively First World markets, writing off as too unprofitable all prospective markets in the Third World itself, let me give an example of some of the most imaginative multicorporate minds at work, those of the Swiss-based Nestle corporation; several years ago these gentlemen launched a major effort to convert African mothers in several countries to feed their babies with its formula product instead of their own breastmilk. Let me quote from Susan George's book:

Dr. Henri Dupin who has spent much of his career teaching public health in Africa was amazed in 1970 to see mothers in the Ivory Coast giving Nescafé to 19/20-month-old toddlers. His students came to the rescue, explaining that the following message was broadcast thrice daily over the national radio: 'Nescafé makes men stronger, women more joyful and children more intelligent.' These African mothers were simply putting this 'advice' into practice. Dr. Dupin sometimes feels he is waging a losing battle—Nestle's advertising budget is far greater than the total annual budget of the World Health Organization.[45]

Nestle, and other formula-milk companies like Unigate, use posters, radio advertisements, and loudspeaker vans to push their products.

> They also use saleswomen, *dressed as nurses*—and who may even *be* nurses—to go around maternity hospitals and clinics to demonstrate the use of Nestle's products. 'The mothers are not to know that they are not paid by the government. They go into the clinics and try to sell their products.' In some hospitals, every mother is given a free tin of milk and a feeding bottle before she leaves for home with her new baby. [Two doctors with long experience in Africa] report increasing malnutrition—marasmus, kwashiorkor, gastro-enteritis—in Africa, and although they are cautious scientists, they do not hesitate to say that 'undoubtedly, the increase of malnutrition in the young baby and the many deaths which occur from this must have some relationship to the increased mis-use of artificial feeding.'

One of the doctors cited estimates that, with the high cost of formula milk relative to most family incomes, "probably less than 10% of [the mothers converted to formula feeding, in one African country] buy sufficient milk to really adequately feed their babies."[46] Subsequently, some African governments have outlawed advertising that recommends formula feeding to mothers whose own milk supply is adequate, but most Third World governments would not presume to meddle with free enterprise in such a blatant manner (in parentheses: the United States government has at long last become a large-scale meddler, now insisting that pharmaceutical drugs that can be dangerous for your health must carry warnings on their labels when sold in the United States; but some large American companies producing hazardous drugs are continuing to sell them without warnings on the labels in Mexico and other countries with less finicky legislation).[47]

Before I turn to a discussion of my vision of a community-based world that hopefully some day will replace our present liberal-corporate world, which in fact has a system of government of, by, and for the large corporations (I shall save till the end what I have to say about possible strategies), let me hastily list just a very few statistics that will further demonstrate the extent to which the liberal-corporate international order in effect makes human populations expendable, whenever market conditions make it more profitable to serve objectives at variance with requirements to meet basic human needs:

(1) Fertilizers are expensive and therefore Third World customers, except for the multinational agribusiness firms, have very limited access to them, although the so-called "green revolution" has provided the means for some large farmers in some countries to gain privileged access to fertilizer products. While the great majority of Third World subsistence farmers must do without fertilizers, beyond what their animals may produce, in the United States at least two million tons of fertilizers "are used for beautifying lawns, golf courses and other non–food-producing greenery."[48]

(2) In 1974 the total grocery bill for pet foods in the United States was estimated at $2.1 billion. Meanwhile, while large numbers of Third World people have been starving to death or suffer severe malnutrition, it has been calculated that "the livestock population of the United States alone (leaving out dogs and cats) consumes enough food material to feed 1.3 billion people."[49]

(3) Between 1940 and 1972 beef consumption per person doubled in the United States and increased over three and a half times in Japan. To produce a pound of beef requires from four to seven pounds of cereals.[50]

(4) Over 60 percent of the total U.S. grain production, around 140 million tons a year, is consumed entirely by cattle, sheep, pigs, and poultry,[51] purchased at prices that Third World people could not afford; American consumers want grain-fed, not range-fed beef.

(5) About 40–50 percent of the world's fish products and 25–40 percent of the world's milk products are fed to livestock in First World countries, and over one-third of the world's grain crops is fed to livestock each year.[52]

To end this part of my discussion, let me cite Lappé's and Collins's concluding reply to their own question, "Why is it that many Third World peoples no longer can feed them-

selves?" Their answer stresses the historical background of
colonialism: Indigenous agricultural developments were actively suppressed in many colonies, for two reasons. First,
plantation owners and foreign investors did not want competition from independent, highly motivated, and therefore
more effective farmers; second, driving them off their land,
the best farming lands, ensured cheap supplies of labor. In
summary, colonialism "forced peasants to replace food crops
with cash crops that were then expropriated at very low
rates; took over the best agricultural land for export crop
plantations and then forced the most able-bodied workers to
leave the fields to work as slaves or for very low wages on
plantations; encouraged a dependence on imported food;
blocked native peasant cash crop production from competing
with cash crops produced by settlers or foreign firms."[53]

The First World has through its colonialist heritage gained
an economic stranglehold on the Third World, resulting in
untold miseries on a vast scale in the many urban and rural
slums that blight virtually every country in Latin America,
Africa, and Asia; only in a few allegedly socialist countries
like Cuba have priorities of public health and welfare made
it possible for even the poorest to feed their own children
adequately. In every liberal-corporate or feudal Third World
country a radically new deal, assisted from the outside, is
necessary to make blighted areas fit for human life.

Unfortunately, as successive UNCTAD sessions have
demonstrated, the rulers of the major First World countries
have remained adamantly opposed to any structural changes
in international trade that could benefit the poorest nations.[54]
President Carter and Dr. Brzezinski, like many of their com-
patriots, are in this sense America Firsters, even if their rhetoric is more sophisticated on occasion than that of Mr.
Reagan, or President Nixon; as, for example, when a few
years ago Mr. Nixon commented on the fact, embarrassing
to some of us, that with 5½ percent of the world's population the United States was consuming a full third of all the
world's energy: " 'That isn't bad; that is good,' exclaimed
Mr. Nixon: 'That means we are the richest, strongest people
in the world, and that we have the highest standard of living
in the world. That is why we need so much energy, and
may it always be that way.' "[55]

The human costs inflicted on much of the rest of humanity did not seem to matter to the man who was then President, as long as his country kept on winning all the major contests. He seemed to see the world much like a sports arena. In actual fact it is, of course, much more like a jungle, as it is now governed: the losers are mostly predestined to lose, and they don't live to compete again. While the language of Dr. Brzezinski and of President Carter has been less crude than was President Nixon's, this is the kind of liberal world order that the military forces of the United States, regardless of whether Republicans or Democrats are in power, will be committed to defend. The early Carter years undoubtedly introduced a new element in U.S. foreign policy, with the posture of championing the world's poor and downtrodden while at the same time working to preserve and expand the corporate might of the world's financial elite. It was a brave posture indeed, and it probably did help bring down a couple of the most vicious former U.S. client regimes, including those of the Shah and of General Somoza.

4. A CONCEPTION OF A FREE WORLD

In what is frequently referred to today as the Free World, the governments are in the business of protecting property rights indiscriminately, so that their chief beneficiaries are the corporate rich. I take this to be a statement of fact, beyond dispute; what can rationally be disputed, of course, is whether there is any viable alternative. The strong have always been oppressing and exploiting the weak; this keeps happening also in the countries today governed by professed Marxists. I am not prepared to say, with Lincoln Steffens some sixty years ago: "I have seen the [nonoppressive] future, and it works." There have been far worse systems to contend with than the liberal-corporate system that we know today. However, the present inquiry has proceeded on the assumption that we shall never know whether viable alternatives are possible until we take the trouble to analyze as incisively as we can the parameters of oppression and the nature and origins of oppression in our own kind of society.

Responsible Politics deals with the discrepancies between realities and possibilities; alternate possibilities must be chosen according to well considered ideals that reflect our humane values. Political inquiry must be dialectical: research-based (where possible, empirically tested) factual propositions must be confronted, constantly and cumulatively, with well analyzed normative imperatives and priorities, in order to determine at each time what might be possible and what directions and choices for policy are required.

My main emphasis in this brief work has been on analyzing the nature of the real world in relation to ideals of liberty or freedom that have been defined, but only abstractly, without clear reference to historical contexts. A much longer work would be required to situate my ideals of emancipation in a systematically developed historical perspective; all I have offered is the occasional glance backward.[56] In this section I shall now attempt a brief glance forward.

My own conception of the optimally free world is of a world as different as possible from the world of the jungle: its antithesis.[57] In my kind of free world the governments will function to protect primarily those who are weak and only secondarily and conditionally those who are strong. Progress will be measured in terms of expanding the protected human rights for those who are most vulnerable and in safeguarding the equal life opportunities for those not yet born; while corporate rights and even private rights to disproportionate amounts of property, and to kinds of property that yield power over others, will be narrowly restricted by democratically constituted assemblies. Every corporation will be required to have public-interest advocates on its board who will publish annual reports that detail and evaluate the overall benefits and costs of all operations over the past year, the fiscal but also the social costs, and the costs inflicted on nature by way of extraction and waste disposal and pollution.

Corporations will no longer *own* capital or natural resources; they will be given continued access to both kinds of assets only to the extent that it is found that they keep operating in the public interest. There will be no stockholders; the governing boards to whom the administrators report will represent the workforce and the local community constituencies, in addition to the professionally trained local, national, and supranational public-interest representatives. The mandate of the public-interest representatives will explicitly include responsibility for protecting resources for future generations and for the survival of the animal and plant species of the region.

The conservationist emphasis will not be limited to the kinds of economically oriented calculations having to do with ensuring adequate supplies of raw materials for future years as well, or even for future decades. As John Rodman has suggested, there are at least three other aspects to a responsible environmentalist concern for the future: the preservationist perspective, that seeks to preserve "natural" nature for its aesthetic and inspirational values; the anti-homocentric view, which holds that members of other animal species should be treated as if they had rights also, rather than continue to be subjected to wanton destruction when this will suit the convenience or whimsy of men (some would have this perspective apply only to the "higher," or "sentient," animals); and finally there is the inherent value of natural variety and diversity, an orientation that Rodman incidentally associates with John Stuart Mill's philosophy of nature, the view that every diminution of the earth's diversity of plants, animals, and human cultures must be seen as an irreparable loss to mankind, if not to the earth itself; an orientation that considerably antedates the modern ecological argument about the interdependency among all species which asserts that the loss of any one species will have incalculable repercussions on many, possibly all, species in the same general environment.[58]

While I am personally empathetic with the animal rights perspective, I have chosen to limit my argument in the present work to the issues of *human* emancipation. To conclude my brief sketch of some features of my transnational utopia, before taking a parting shot at the most basic issues of strategy, let me emphasize that small communities will be the building blocks, the essential units, of my kind of free world. Neighborhoods, occupational groups, religious and political aggregations, all small enough to make direct democracy possible and a large and specialized legal profession unnecessary—not to mention professional politicians—

will form federations with coordinating secretariats, whose directors will be elected for at most two-year periods and be subject to recall either by their own constituencies or by a majority of constituencies.

Communities will be in charge of most production; even at the loss of past achievement levels in economic efficiency, most processes of industrial production will eventually be reduced in scale, "as if people mattered": "Small is beautiful."[59] Even steelmaking is possible on a relatively small, communal scale, as the Chinese of Mao's days demonstrated. Nevertheless, some industries, including most steelmills I believe, will remain predominantly large scale. These must come to be governed in the public interest by boards that actively represent their workforces, their neighborhoods and surrounding areas, and the regional and transnational public interest.

The new kind of free world will come to resemble what Ivan Illich has called the convivial society, a society "in which modern technologies serve politically interrelated individuals rather than managers."[60] It will be based, not on independent nations capable of international exploitation and warfare, but on interdependent federations of small, natural, horizontal communities, so small in size and so numerous that it will take sophisticated computers to keep track of all of them.

With modern computer technology, however, it will be quite feasible to make the various transnational authorities (each with worldwide or regional scope but with strictly delimited functions) aware of problems of deprivation and violence that may still occur in a few communities, so that advice and aid, and forcible intervention if necessary, can be made to arrive speedily.

I believe that people with deep roots in natural communities, people who are basically without fear, because they live in convivial social surroundings based on the practice of solidarity and trust, will develop creative individual imagination with unprecedented foresight and compassion, even anticipatory compassion, and will achieve levels of spiritual emancipation unmatched at the present or any previous time.

But let me now return to the real world, *anno* 1981. Where do we go from here?

5. A COMMUNITARIAN BASIC STRATEGY

The late dean of American pacifists is often quoted as having said, "There is no way to peace. Peace is the way." I am not a pacifist in A. J. Muste's sense, for I cannot follow him all the way; as one who thought the war against fascism necessary I suspect I might well be a fair target for another consistent pacifist's, the late Ammon Hennacy's, reproach: "To be a pacifist between wars is like being a vegetarian between meals."[61] But so would the late Bertrand Russell be; he once remarked that he wanted to "pick his wars," for he said he saw nothing wrong with having supported the war effort in World War II while having resisted World War I and being just as adamant in resisting even the very idea of serving in a World War III. In his (and my own) defense we should recall that even Thomas Hobbes, for all his authoritarianism, defended the individual's right to choose not to die, if he could; for myself, I can't think of any human right more fundamental in terms of human need hierarchies than the right to decide for what cause, if any, one would choose to kill, or to die.

I will make my most basic point regarding strategies toward a world of natural communities, though, in parallel fashion to Muste's point about peace: There is no way toward a world of natural communities except through nurturing here and now the development of viable natural communities. At least in the First World this must be the most basic constructive strategy, accompanied, to be sure, by strategies of nonviolent resistance and sabotage of the existing system when that seems possible and productive (see 4 §3).

Let us look again at the concept of "natural" communities; I have called small communities of political equals "natural," since they both reflect and in turn serve to meet a basic category of human needs, a part of our species-nature: our affiliation needs, belongingness needs, community solidarity needs, needs which corporate contractualism and the liberal ideology tend to suppress.

It may be objected, however, that hierarchies, not horizontal communities, are natural. I have acknowledged the traditional family to be an obvious example of a natural hierarchy (see 5 §4). Indeed, the family and the clan are the proto-types of prehistorical and historical social formations which put their stamp on the tribe and the state as well. In the long struggle for survival and for control over nature's hazards and resources, discipline and even the sacrifice of individual lives have been deemed necessary; before modern times, there were no human rights, only obligations, and the notion was unheard of that there would be anything wrong with sac-rificing human lives when this was deemed necessary, by the sovereign or by other allegedly authorized interpreters of God's will. Yet, what this whole argument adds up to is really a rather trite point, that the jungle style of life is eminently natural. That is, "natural" in a purely descriptive sense.

Yet I have been arguing that in a second sense of the term, which is normative as well as descriptive, it is also "natural" for man to want to move out from the jungle, so as to ad-vance toward realizing the species-nature that characterizes man, at least in embryo, man as distinct from other predatory animals. Man's vocation, wrote Paulo Freire, is humaniza-tion,[62] or, in Marx's terms (see 5 §2) to overcome alienation. That is to say that we can and should aspire to nothing less than to *make* human rights and self-governing horizontal communities *natural*: natural in the sense of corresponding to our evolving human nature and needs, the needs that tend to become activated as our basic physical-safety and sustenance needs are being met. Our community or affiliation needs are next in the natural need hierarchy after the basic physical needs, I have argued (see 4 §2); what is *unnatural* about the contractual liberal society is that alienated consumption, alienated commodity wants, get in the way of our commu-nity needs and their satisfaction, thus crippling our ability to be dependable and solidary members of our human communities.

There is a special, third sense, of "natural," in which it is possible to speak of humankind as a whole as a natural entity, in that we all belong to the same species, not only with vari-ous physical characteristics and psychological propensities in common, but with shared objective potentialities for realiz-ing aspirations evolving from within our species-being—

overcoming alienation and becoming more fully human. Moreover, in modern times we have for the first time become conscious of our common mortality as a species, and of our common stake in solidarity against ecocide and humanicide.

Nevertheless I shall carefully avoid referring to humankind as a *community*, for it is of crucial importance to keep it clear that real as distinct from phony communities are always small, small enough to make direct democracy based on face-to-face contact possible. If the nation-state is too big to constitute other than a phony community, a pseudo-community, so is humankind as a whole. The ideal of some kind of a community of mankind has, to be sure, existed for a long time in the imagination of humanistic philosophers and dreamers, but as practical men and women the most we can work for, I think, are strong transnational federations of large numbers of natural human communities, or perhaps federations of federations.

In the last three chapters I have successively argued for three basic strategies corresponding to three modes of oppression. Against ideological domination I have argued for a radical political pedagogy, inside and outside institutions of formal schooling, but always insisting on politically horizontal dialogues in which the emancipation of the key political terms from their status quo–oriented uses must be the first objective. Against violence, deprivation, and other coercive oppression I have argued for the development of horizontal organizations with imaginative nonviolent strategies, arrived at and formulated in open discussion, calculated to resist and sabotage oppressive policies with maximal impact at minimal cost and to frustrate the powers that be and to enhance the sense of potential power among all participants in the struggle for freedom. Against alienation, my proposed remedy is in a struggle to develop natural, horizontal communities, from friendship circles to local grassroots movements, intent on declaring ourselves sovereign in the choice of how to live together and how to conduct our daily lives; making concessions, to be sure, to the realities of legal obligation, but considering laws that protect corporate rights, for example, as temporary (we hope) facts to which we object, rather than as morally binding norms.

This last aspect of the struggle for total emancipation, the struggle to overcome alienation by making communities more important in our lives and making laws and contracts as well as commodity affluence less important, is the part of the struggle against the state that is most constructive; for the stronger the bonds of solidarity that hold our natural communities together, the less do we become willing or even able to give loyalty to the state.

According to early democratic theory the state should protect the weak against the strong and the freedom of individuals against other powerful organizations; yet every First and almost every Third World state is nowadays in liaison with the predatory corporations and in fact functions as their police force and sometimes as their executioner as well. In any event, most of the massive violence in the world today is perpetrated either by or with the connivance of the state; therefore, to the extent that we are serious in being committed to the superior value of human lives and consistently deem violence as the greatest evil, the state must be seen as enemy number one, whose powers to commit or enforce violence must be curbed at all cost.

Natural communities are the prime instrumentality, I believe, not only to undermine the moral claims of the state and to reduce even its legal effectiveness, as when political strategies of resistance are successful; in communities we can also bypass the state in seeking close ties with fraternal communities in other societies, including societies toward which the state would have us feel antagonistic. In the various professions this process is well on its way; there are already many examples of transnational organizations that have exerted pressure on national regimes, in all three "Worlds," to free prisoners, or to give visas to aliens or exit visas to dissident citizens. I hope this is only a beginning, and I would like to see transnational radical caucuses developing, as national ones have done in this country. Some day I would hope to see international associations of journalists go to bat transnationally to defend the integrity and dignity of hardpressed colleagues; that is, the integrity of the political word, the political dialogue, in countries blessed with newspapers of the "Official Gazette" variety as much as in countries with newspapers of the "Daily Scream" variety.[63]

For us political scientists I hope that once again we will find our way back to our most ancient calling: to serve as fearless and energetic critics of every establishment, intent on showing the glaring differences between what is and what ought to be, as well as on trying to project what *can* be. By extension, our calling in the modern world must be to seek to establish, for the first time, a powerful dialogue among political equals on the worldwide political arena; or, to leave the imagery of our ancestral world of gladiators behind, let us call it our worldwide political forum.

But equality as well as personal power and the commitment to the common good must begin at home: in the family and in the small community. As we act as equals in our daily lives, to that extent we come to develop our capabilities for seeing all humankind as entitled to equal treatment; and we come to hate the injustice of the unnatural corporate system with its exploitation and violence, as well as the basic fraudulence of the democratic makebelieve in our kind of state, the "white lie"[64] that has done so much to make us morally comfortable with our corrupting First World comforts in our evildoing kind of world order.

Notes

INTRODUCTION

1. See my *Structure of Freedom* (Stanford, Calif.: Stanford University Press, 1970) (1958), p. 15.
2. This formulation is indebted to Paulo Freire's concept of "problem-posing" education. See his *Pedagogy of the Oppressed* (New York: Seabury Press, 1974) (1970; in Portuguese original 1968), especially chapter 2.

CHAPTER 1

1. Karl Mannheim, *Ideology and Utopia* (New York: Harcourt, Brace, 1946), especially chapters 2 and 4.
2. Daniel Bell, *The End of Ideology* (Glencoe, Ill.: Free Press, 1960); William Kornhauser, *The Politics of Mass Society* (Glencoe, Ill.: Free Press, 1959); Seymour Martin Lipset, *Political Man* (Garden City, N.Y.: Doubleday, 1960), Epilogue.
3. Lipset, *Political Man*, p. 403. But see also Lipset's rejoinder to critics of the end-of-ideology literature in his "The End of Ideology and the Ideology of the Intellectuals" in Joseph Ben-David and Terry Nichols Clark, eds., *Culture and Its Creators* (Chicago: University of Chicago Press, 1977), pp. 15–42 and 286–291.
4. Cf. my "The End of Politics? A Review," *Journal of Conflict Resolution* 5 (1961), pp. 326–335.
5. Harold D. Lasswell and Abraham Kaplan, *Power and Society* (New Haven: Yale University Press, 1959), p. 123.
6. In David Apter, ed., *Ideology and Discontent* (New York: Free Press, 1967), pp. 206–261.
7. Joseph Tussman, *Obligation and the Body Politic* (New York: Oxford University Press, 1960), p. 107.
8. F. A. Hayek, *The Road to Serfdom* (London: George Routledge, 1944). For a recent tract in the same vein, see Milton and Rose Friedman, *Free to Choose* (New York: Harcourt Brace Jovanovich, 1980).
9. F. A. Hayek, *The Constitution of Liberty* (Chicago: University of Chicago Press, 1960).

10. Ibid., p. 12. Cf. Hayek, *The Road to Serfdom*, p. 19.

11. Hayek, *Constitution of Liberty*, p. 133.

12. Ibid., p. 99.

13. Ibid., pp. 231–233.

14. Cf. my "Hayek's Liberalism: The Constitution of Perpetual Privilege" in *The Political Science Reviewer* 1 (1971), pp. 93–124.

15. C. B. Macpherson, *The Political Theory of Possessive Individualism* (Oxford: Oxford University Press, 1962), chapter 5.

16. John Stuart Mill, *On Liberty* (New York: Library of Liberal Arts, 1956) (1859), p. 13.

17. Ibid., p. 64.

18. See Isaiah Berlin, *Four Essays on Liberty* (London: Oxford University Press, 1969), chapter 3. "Two Concepts of Liberty" was first published in 1958.

19. Ibid., p. 171.

20. Ibid., pp. 171–172.

21. T. H. Green, "Liberal Legislation and Freedom of Contract" in John R. Rodman, ed., *The Political Theory of T. H. Green* (New York: Appleton-Century-Crofts, 1964), pp. 51–52. This lecture was delivered, and first published, in 1881.

22. Ibid., p. 52.

23. Berlin, *Four Essays on Liberty*, especially p. 133, note 1.

24. Ibid.

25. See C. B. Macpherson, "Berlin's Division of Liberty" in his *Democratic Theory: Essays in Retrieval* (Oxford: Clarendon Press, 1973), pp. 95–119, at pp. 108–109.

26. John Rawls, *A Theory of Justice* (Cambridge, Mass.: Harvard University Press, 1971), p. 250 and p. 302.

27. Ibid., pp. 42–44.

28. Ibid., p. 302.

29. Ibid., p. 303.

30. Ibid., pp. 204–205.

31. Ibid., p. 205.

32. See Robert Paul Wolff, *Understanding Rawls* (Princeton: Princeton University Press, 1977), p. 91. Also see H. L. A. Hart, "Rawls on Liberty and its Priority" in Norman Daniels ed., *Reading Rawls* (New York: Basic Books, 1975), pp. 230–252.

33. Rawls, *A Theory of Justice*, p. 92.

34. Wolff, *Understanding Rawls*, p. 93.

35. See C. B. Macpherson, "Rawl's Distributive Justice" in Macpherson, *Democratic Theory*, pp. 87–94.

36. Cf. John Plamenatz, *The English Utilitarians* (Oxford:

Blackwell, 1949), p. 52.

37. See Donald J. C. Carmichael, "Agent-Individualism: A Critique of the Logic of Liberal Political Understanding" (PhD. diss., University of Toronto, 1978). I quote from Carmichael's own explication of the concept, pp. 1–2 and p. 3: "This conception, which I shall call '*agent-individualism,*' combines two commitments. First, persons are understood mainly as agents, as beings who pursue ends. These ends are thus the fundamental terms through which any agent's nature and conduct are understood. Second, each person is understood to have a separate self in this respect. He is conceived as an individual, not only as a distinct physical being, but also, and more radically, through the ends of his basic nature and self-understanding. Individual agents are thereby conceived as the several substances of the socio-political order. . . . The fundamental limitation of this logic is its non-dialectical character. It fails to grasp the social tranformation of man's nature, through a process deeper than mere 'social determination' into ends which to a significant extent are indentifiable only relationally, by reference to those of others and to specific relations with them. It thereby ignores the inherently socio-political character of human nature, as well as the possibilities for human excellence within an enriched social existence. Above all, it fails to appreciate the fact that each person, through the ends of his basic nature is implicated with others in the relations, history, and destiny of his social formation."

38. See Rawls, *A Theory of Justice,* p. 127, and Carmichael, "Agent-Individualism," p. 310.

39. Carmichael, "Agent-Individualism," p. 317.

40. Ibid., pp. 319–320.

41. See Mill, *On Liberty,* p. 141. The essay was first published in 1859.

42. Carmichael's chapter 5 discusses representative literature in the field of international relations; his chapter 6 discusses representative works from the political behavior field.

CHAPTER 2

1. George Orwell, *1984* (New York: Harcourt, Brace, 1949).

2. Saul D. Alinsky's best-known books are *Reveille for Radicals* (New York: Vintage, 1969) (University of Chicago Press, 1946), and *Rules for Radicals* (New York: Vintage, 1972) (Random House, 1971). Also see Marion K. Sanders, *The*

Professional Radical: Conversations with Saul Alinsky (New York: Harper & Row, 1970). Saul Alinsky died in 1972.

3. See Bertell Ollman, *Alienation: Marx's Conception of Man in Capitalist Society* (Cambridge: Cambridge University Press, 1971), chapter 23, at p. 157.

4. Andrew Hacker, "What Rules America?" *New York Review of Books,* May 1, 1975, pp. 9–13, at p. 13.

5. Joe Conason and Jack Newfield, "Remember the Greediest: 100 Cases of Avarice," *Village Voice* 223, no. 50 (December 18, 1978), p. 1. See also the two immediately subsequent issues.

6. Edgar Z. Friedenberg, *The Disposal of Liberty and Other Industrial Wastes* (Garden City, N.Y.: Doubleday, 1975).

7. William Leiss, *The Limits to Satisfaction* (Toronto: University of Toronto Press, 1976), p. 7.

8. See Alan Wolfe, *The Limits of Legitimacy* (New York: Free Press, 1977).

9. Murry Edelman, *The Symbolic Uses of Politics* (Urbana, Ill.: University of Illinois Press, 1964), p. 39 and passim. Also see his *Politics as Symbolic Action: Mass Arousal and Quiescence* (Chicago: Markham, 1971).

10. C. Wright Mills, *The Power Elite* (New York: Oxford University Press, 1956), especially chapter 13, "The Mass Society."

11. See C. B. Macpherson, *The Political Theory of Possessive Individualism* (New York: Oxford University Press, 1962).

12. Wilfred Beckerman, "Are the Poor Always With Us?" in *New Statesman,* September 10, 1976, pp. 334–336.

13. "Those conscious activities that refer to the organism form the data for what we shall here call the self. The self is the phenomenal representation of the ego, the ego become conscious. . . . The ego is prior to the self and far wider than it. The self is not the mirror image of the ego; there is between them the same kind of relation as between the physical object and its psychological representation." Solomon Asch, *Social Psychology* (New York: Prentice-Hall, 1952), pp. 277–278.

14. Morris Rosenberg in a recent work discusses empirical work bearing on the contrast between our "two selves: an overt or revealed self and a covert or concealed self." See his *Conceiving the Self* (New York: Basic Books, 1979), p. 195 and pp. 195–223. See also Kenneth J. Gergen, *The Concept of Self* (New York: Holt, Rinehart and Winston), especially pp. 80–86. My own discussion is only concerned with the "covert or concealed" self, the interior self, not with the external, role-playing self. Both are shaped in part by inner processes

and in part by external experience.

15. Cf. *The Structure of Freedom* (Stanford: Stanford University Press, 1970) (1958), p. 15.

16. I say "unsophisticated tyrant" because modern strategies of oppression are far more resourceful than old-time tyrannies, drawing on the many new or improved techniques of domination. Edgar Z. Friendenberg illustrates this point well with respect to much of the exploitation taking place in our society: "Exploitation therefore assumes a peculiarly degrading quality in the modern state, for the victim must not only be used and often ill-used; he must be kept persuaded that such usage is in his best interests as a citizen—a refinement in mystification that would not have occurred to Attila the Hun." Friedenberg, *Disposal of Liberty*, p. 69.

17. See my *Structure of Freedom*, p. 83.

18. Sigmund Freud, *A General Introduction to Psychoanalysis* (New York: Permabooks, 1957) (1920), p. 442.

19. Karl Marx, "Critique of the Hegelian Dialectic and Philosophy as a Whole" in his "Economic and Philosophical Manuscripts of 1844," in Robert C. Tucker, ed., *The Marx-Engels Reader*, 2nd ed. (New York: W. W. Norton, 1978), pp. 106–125, at p. 114.

20. Cf. Marx's essay on "Estranged Labour" in Tucker, *Marx-Engels Reader*, pp. 70–81.

21. *The Structure of Freedom*, pp. 189–217.

22. Ibid., p. 88.

23. While the weight of the law as a restraining force may be lighter in England than in most other European countries, Mill wrote, "the yoke of opinion is perhaps heavier." Mill, *On Liberty*, p. 11.

24. Cf. Alkis Kontos, "Domination: Metaphor and Political Reality" in Alkis Kontos, ed., *Domination* (Toronto: University of Toronto Press, 1975), pp. 211–228, at p. 218.

25. *The Structure of Freedom*, p. 95.

26. Alexis de Tocqueville, *Democracy in America* (New York: Vintage, 1954, vols. 1 [1835] and 2 [1840]), at vol. 1, p. 273. Quoted in *Structure of Freedom*, p. 96.

27. M. Brewster Smith in a recent paper reproduces a "Gestalt prayer" by the late Fritz Perls which expresses sentiments that appealed to many young people on the New Left in the 1960 and, below it, a more recent parody of the same prayer, attributed to Jon Carroll:

Perls: I do my thing and you do your thing.
          I am not in this world to live up to your expectations,

And you are not in this world to live up to mine.
You are you and I am I;
If by chance we find each other, it's beautiful.
If not, it can't be helped.
Carroll: I do my laundry, and you do yours.
I am not in this world to listen to your
    ceaseless yammering,
And you are not in this world for any
    discernible reason at all.
You are you, and I am I, and I got the better deal.
And if by chance we find each other,
    it will be unspeakably tedious.
Fuck off.

See M. B. Smith, "Psychology and Values," *Journal of Social Issues* 34, no. 4 (1978), 181–199.

CHAPTER 3

1. " 'Arise ye prisoners of starvation' is to become, in the context of late capitalism, 'Liberation through communication, not technocratic domination,' " writes a student of Habermas; he continues: "Analogous to Marx's theory of the *possibility* of proletarian action within the context of the crisis of nineteenth century market relations, Habermas demonstrates that enlightened speech and action against technical rationalization also become *possible* within the context of late capitalism's legitimation/motivation problems and the limits they place upon an already-burdened state apparatus. Those unintended developments, that is to say, are rich in possible political consequences, and highlight structural and ideational weaknesses of late capitalist societies hitherto not widely recognized. To the extent that the managers of late capitalist rationalization undermine the very *bases* of their legitimacy, they also create a sensed *need* for unrestricted public discussion about a wide range of issues and maxims; but this sensed need for a truly universal public sphere (within which individuals could come to develop their uniquely human capacities) is unsatisfiable within the confines of late capitalism's organizational principle. This is the fundamental point of weakness of *late* capitalism." John C. Keane, "The Problem of Technical and Moral-Practical Progress in Modernity: A Critique of Jürgen Habermas." Ph.D. diss., University of Toronto, 1977, pp. 208–209. Author's italics. Also see Habermas, *Toward a Rational Society* (Boston:

Beacon, 1970) (in German, 1968), and "On Systematically Distorted Communication," *Inquiry* 13 (1970), pp. 205–218.

2. Karl Marx, "The German Ideology" in Robert C. Tucker, ed., *The Marx-Engels Reader*, 2nd ed. (New York: W. W. Norton, 1978), pp. 146–200, at p. 172.

3. Ralph Miliband, *The State in Capitalist Society* (London: Weidenfeld and Nicolson, 1972) (1969).

4. See my "Foundations of the Liberal Make-Believe," *Inquiry* 14 (1971), pp. 213–243.

5. Here I do not have a hostile attitude to individual politicians in mind. There are plenty of such attitudes now; politicians and taxes serve as convenient targets, as they take the heat off corporate executives, low wages, and high profits as contentious issues. What I anticipate is a wider awareness of the extent to which the political and legal *system* operates in the interest of the corporate rich, at the expense of all who are dependent on employment or (other) social assistance.

6. Herbert Marcuse, *One-Dimensional Man* (Boston: Beacon, 1964), p. 6.

7. Jean Jacques Rousseau, "The Social Contract," bk. 3, chap. 4 in *The Social Contract and Discourses* (New York: Dutton, 1950) (1762), p. 66.

8. See *The Republic of Plato*, trans. Allan Bloom (New York: Basic Books, 1968) and *Plato's Gorgias*, trans. W. C. Helmbold (New York: Liberal Arts Press, 1952).

9. H. Mark Roelofs, *Ideology and Myth in American Politics* (Boston: Little, Brown, 1976).

10. *Republic of Plato*, 389b, p. 67.

11. The best recent work in this category is Richard E. Flathman, *Political Obligation* (New York: Atheneum, 1972). I think this literature is now at a watershed. Three subsequent books make it clear that it is time to leave behind the assumption that there is a prima facie moral obligation to obey the state. See Mortimer R. Kadish and Sanford H. Kadish, *Discretion to Disobey* (Stanford: Stanford University Press, 1973); Burton Zwiebach, *Civility and Disobedience* (Cambridge: Cambridge University Press, 1975); and Ronald Dworkin, *Taking Rights Seriously* (Cambridge, Mass: Harvard University Press, 1978).

12. Kenneth E. Boulding, *The Organizational Revolution* (New York: Harper, 1953), pp. xxxi–xxxii.

13. Robert Michels, *Political Parties: A Sociological Study of the Oligarchical Tendencies of Modern Democracy* (Glencoe, Ill.: Free Press, 1949) (1915), p. 401.

14. Philip Selznick in a classic, highly influential paper written three decades ago discusses categories of deviant or dissenting behavior that are particularly likely to provoke strongly oppressive countermeasures from the organization's leadership. See his "Foundations of a Theory of Organization," *American Sociological Review* 13 (1948), pp. 20–30.

15. Geoffrey Shields here refers to research by Howard V. Perlmutter of the University of Pennsylvania. See Shields, "The Multinationals," *World Issues* 2, no. 5 (December 1977/ January 1978), pp. 3–6, at p. 3.

16. Michels, *Political Parties,* p. 391.

17. Karl Marx, "Wage Labour and Capital" in Tucker, *Marx-Engels Reader,* pp. 203–217, at p. 204.

18. Marx and Engels, "Manifesto of the Communist Party" in Tucker, *Marx-Engels Reader,* pp. 469–500, at p. 485.

19. On at least one occasion, in a private letter, Marx described the discovery of what he thought of as the scientific basis for his revolutionary prophecy as his most important contribution to knowledge.

> And now as to myself, no credit is due to me for discovering the existence of classes in modern society or the struggle between them. Long before me bourgeois historians had described the historical development of this class struggle and bourgeois economists the economic anatomy of the classes. What I did that was new was to prove: 1) that the existence of classes is only bound up with particular historical phases in the development of production, 2) that the class struggle necessarily leads to the dictatorship of the proletariat, 3) that this dictatorship itself only constitutes the transition to the abolition of all classes and to the classless society.

This excerpt from Marx's letter of March 5, 1852, to Joseph Weydemeyer is reprinted in Tucker, *Marx-Engels Reader,* p. 220.

20. William Leiss, *The Limits to Satisfaction* (Toronto: University of Press, 1976).

21. For some recent evidence of the extent of public concern in the United States, see Luther J. Carter, "Public Support for Environmental Protection Remains Strong," *Science,* 203 (12 January 1979), p. 154; and Robert C. Mitchell, "Silent Spring/ Solid Majorities," *Public Opinion,* 2, no. 4 (August/September 1979), pp. 16–20 and 55; and Lester W. Milbrath, "Using En-

vironmental Beliefs and Perceptions to Predict Trade-offs and Choices Among Water Quality Plan Alternatives," to appear in *Socio-Economic Planning Studies* (1980). A comparative four-nation (United Kingdom, Federal Republic of Germany, Australia, and the United States) study of environmental beliefs and values is now under way; the American component of the study is directed by Dr. Lester M. Milbrath of the Environmental Studies Center of the State University of New York in Buffalo. Dr. Milbrath tells me that findings from the American study indicate that popular environmental concern appears to be considerably wider and deeper than most of the elected political leaders tend to assume.

22. See Ivan Illich, *Deschooling Society* (New York: Harper & Row, 1971). Also compare Alan Gartner et al, eds., *After Deschooling, What?* (New York: Harper & Row, 1973). For a splendid essay on Illich and his career, see Francine du Plessix Gray, *Divine Disobedience* (New York: Knopf, 1970), pp. 231–322.

23. Ivan Illich, *Energy and Equity* (London: Calder & Boyers, 1974). See also his *Tools of Conviviality* (New York: Harper & Row, 1973).

24. Ivan Illich, *Limits to Medicine* (New York: Pantheon, 1976). The subtitle is *Medical Nemesis: The Expropriation of Health.*

25. Ibid., p. 33.

26. Ibid., p. 122.

27. Ibid., pp. 127–128.

28. Ibid., pp. 131–132.

29. Ibid., p. 220.

30. Ibid., p. 154.

31. Ibid., p. 166.

32. Ibid., pp. 168 and 260.

33. Ibid., p. 207.

34. Ivan Illich, *Medical Nemesis: The Expropriation of Health* (London: Calder & Boyars, 1975), p. 161. This book was published as a draft, and readers were asked to send their critical comments to the author, who promised to publish a revised edition subsequently.

35. Illich, *Limits to Medicine*, pp. 273 and 270.

36. R. D. Laing, David Cooper, and Thomas Szasz are among the most articulate critics of professional psychiatry. There have also in recent years emerged political movements of self-help among people labeled mentally ill; for example, the Mental Patients Association of Vancouver, Canada, publisher of a

most impressive newsletter/journal with the most appropriate name, *In a Nutshell*. Another self-help movement is well described in Charles Hampden-Turner, *The Sane Asylum* (San Francisco: Jossey-Bass, 1976).

37. The influential *Journal of Conflict Resolution* has developed from the initially modest but highly action-oriented *Research Exchange on the Prevention of War* and is now a medium for many kinds of scientific reports, some of which strike this observer as more calculated to display clever research technologies than to help improve our knowledge on how to prevent or reduce the incidence of international violence.

38. See Abraham Kaplan, *The Conduct of Inquiry* (Scranton, Pa.: Chandler, 1964), pp. 405–406.

39. See C. Wright Mills, *The Sociological Imagination* (New York: Oxford University Press, 1959).

40. Hans J. Morgenthau, "The Purpose of Political Science" in James C. Charlesworth, ed., *A Design for Political Science: Scope, Objectives, and Methods*, The American Academy of Political and Social Science, Monograph 6 (Philadelphia: 1966), pp. 63–79, at p. 73.

41. Harold J. Laski, *The American Democracy* (New York: Viking, 1948), p. 165.

42. Heinz Eulau, *The Behavioral Persuasion in Politics* (New York: Random House, 1963), pp. 9 and 137.

43. Max Horkheimer and Theodor W. Adorno, *Dialectic of Enlightenment* (New York: Seabury Press, 1972) (1944), pp. xiv-xv.

44. "Sovereigns . . . very well know that . . . the increase of artificial wants only binds so many more chains upon the people. Alexander, wishing to keep the Ichthyophagi in a state of dependence, compelled them to give up fishing, and subsist on the customary food of civilized nations. The American savages, who go naked, and live entirely on the products of the chase, have been always impossible to subdue. What yoke, indeed, can be imposed on men who stand in need of nothing?" See "A Discourse on the Arts and Sciences" in Rousseau, *The Social Contract and Discourses* (New York: Dutton, 1950) (1759), pp. 143–174, at p. 147, note 1.

45. Herbert Marcuse, *Reason and Revolution* (Boston: Beacon Press, 1960) (1941), pp. vii-viii.

46. Marcuse, *One-Dimensional Man*. It would lead too far afield here to discuss Marcuse's views, and those of others, on whether modern technology by its own nature tends to serve political oppression, or whether it is by its own nature neutral

but is put to oppressive uses in a capitalist system.

47. See Paulo Freire, *Pedagogy of the Oppressed* (New York: Seabury Press, 1974) (1970; in Portuguese original, 1968). Also see his *Education for Critical Consciousness* (New York: Seabury Press, 1973) (1969) and his *Cultural Action for Freedom* (Harmondsworth: Penguin, 1972) (first published in the *Harvard Educational Review* in 1970).

48. Freire, *Pedagogy of the Oppressed*, p. 75.

49. See Clark Kerr, *The Uses of the University* (New York: Harper & Row, 1964).

CHAPTER 4

1. "... there are two kinds of mastery [of Nature]: a repressive and a liberating one.... Civilization produces the means for freeing Nature from its own brutality, its own insufficiency, its own blindness, by virtue of the cognitive and transforming power of Reason..... Civilization has achieved this 'other,' liberating transformation in its gardens and parks and reservations. But outside these small, protected areas, it has treated Nature as it has treated Man—as an instrument of destructive productivity." See Herbert Marcuse, *One-Dimensional Man* (Boston: Beacon, 1964), pp. 236, 238, and 240. Also see his "Nature and Revolution" in Marcuse, *Counter-Revolution and Revolt* (Boston: Beacon, 1972), chapter 2. See also Peter Singer, *Animal Liberation: A New Ethics for Our Treatment of Animals* (New York: Random House, 1975) and John Rodman, "The Liberation of Nature?" *Inquiry* 20 (1977), pp. 83–145.

2. See Joy Adamson, *Born Free: A Lioness of Two Worlds* (New York: Pantheon, 1960).

3. Frank M. Andrews and Stephen R. Withey, *Social Indicators of Well-Being: Americans' Perceptions of Life Quality* (New York: Plenum Press, 1976), p. 319, note 6.

4. For a preliminary report on an ongoing, very ambitious research project in this area, see Johan Galtung, "World Indicators Program," *Bulletin of Peace Proposals* 4, no. 4 (1973), pp. 354–358, and "Measuring World Development," *Alternatives* 1, nos. 1 and 4 (1975); also see Johan Galtung and Anders Wirak, "Towards New Indicators of Development" in "Human Needs, Human Rights, and the Theory of Development," Paper no. 10 in the World Indicators Program, mimeographed (University of Oslo: Chair in Conflict and Peace Research, 1976), pp. 57–66. Also see Erik Allardt, *Att Ha Att Älska Att Vara: Om Välfärd i*

Norden (To Have To Love To Be: About Welfare in the Nordic Countries) (Lund: Argos, 1975); and Erik Gurgsdies and Klaus Wieser, *Wohlfahrtsforschung in Schweden* (Berlin: J. H. W. Dietz Nachf., 1975).

5. It is easier and less costly to study in depth how the least advantaged in a society fare and to assess trends in their health and welfare than it is to assess the well-being or satisfaction of the majority, or of the population as a whole over given time periods, even with modern sampling techniques.

6. In another paper I have defined human rights as "all categories of individual claims (including claims in behalf of individuals or groups) which *ought to have* legal protection, as well as social and moral support, *because* the protection of these claims is *essential to meet basic human needs." Universal Human Rights* 1, no. 1 (1979), pp. 9–14.

7. See H. L. A. Hart, "Are There Any Natural Rights" in A. I. Melden, ed., *Human Rights* (Belmon, Calif.: Wadsworth, 1970), pp. 61–75, at p. 61.

8. See Alasdair MacIntyre, *Marcuse* (London: Fontana/Collins, 1970), pp. 63–65.

9. Cf. my "Wants, Needs, and Political Legitimacy," *Canadian Journal of Political Science* 1 (1968), pp. 241–260.

10. "Those issues about which members of a given society seem to feel strongly all reveal a conflict one side of which is strongly emphasized, the other side as strongly (but not quite successfully) suppressed." See Philip Slater's very insightful treatment of this theme in his *The Pursuit of Loneliness: American Culture at the Breaking Point* (Boston: Beacon, 1970), especially chapter 1, cited at p. 10. Also see below, chap. 4, p. 98.

11. Frank Pinner in a seminal paper draws a distinction between consensual and dissensual academic disciplines (the latter are "all disciplines whose value or procedures are widely questioned among the public, either explicitly or implicitly"). See his "The Crisis of the State Universities: Analysis and Remedies" in Nevitt Sanford, ed., *The American College* (New York: John Wiley, 1962), pp. 940–971, at p. 943.

12. William Leiss, *Limits to Satisfaction: An Essay on the Problem of Needs and Commodities* (Toronto: University of Toronto Press, 1976).

13. See C. B. Macpherson, *The Real World of Democracy* (Toronto: Canadian Broadcasting Corporation, 1965).

14. I had called the paper "A Liberation of 'Violence.'" It appeared as "Violence as a Negation of Freedom," *American Scholar* 40 (1971), pp. 634–641.

15. Albert Camus took this position: "Absolute non-violence is the negative basis of slavery and its acts of violence; systematic violence positively destroys the living community and the existence we receive from it. To be fruitful, these two ideas must establish final limits." See his *The Rebel: An Essay on Man in Revolt* (New York: Vintage, 1958) (1956; in French, 1951), p. 291.

16. Maslow's ranking represents no substantive difference from my initial ranking that places the meeting of crucial safety needs ahead of crucial sustenance needs: in positive terms, we agree that whatever is required to sustain life itself, and then basic health, represents the most basic need. But in Maslow's *motivational* theory it is assumed, quite realistically, that a starving person, or one with a starving family, will jeopardize his or her physical safety, if necessary, in the search for food. More important, in his best-known early paper Maslow discusses sustenance needs in the context of extreme deprivation, while it appears that safety needs are discussed with less stark extremes in mind. See his "A Theory of Human Motivation" (1943) in A. H. Maslow, *Motivation and Personality* (New York: Harper, 1954), chapter 5.

17. See Slater, *Pursuit of Loneliness*, p. 5 and chapter 1. Also see Kenneth Keniston, "The Dictatorship of the Ego" in his *The Uncommitted: Alienated Youth in American Society* (New York: Harcourt, Brace & World, 1965), chapter 12.

18. See A. H. Maslow, *Toward a Psychology of Being* (Princeton, N.J.: Van Nostrand, 1962), p. 25, where the terms "deficiency-needs" and "growth-needs" are introduced. Most often in this work Maslow uses the related terms, D- and B-values, and D- and B-realms.

19. Cf. David J. Baugh, "Trends toward Community and Liberty after the Limits to Growth" (Unpublished paper, University of Toronto, 1976).

20. His italics deleted. In the same context Goodwin also quotes from D. H. Lawrence: "Men are not free when they are doing just what they like.... Men are only free when they are doing what the deepest self likes. And there is getting down to the deepest self! It takes some digging." Both statements would have been endorsed by T. H. Green (above, chapter 1). See Richard N. Goodwin, *The American Condition* (New York: Bantam, 1975) (1974), pp. 12 and 14.

21. Maslow's latest book, published in the year following his death, is entitled *The Farther Reaches of Human Nature* (New York: Viking, 1971).

22. According to Maslow's theory of motivation, less basic needs become activated only when needs at more basic levels have been satisfied, to some extent at least. The deficiency needs are, of course, more basic than the being needs. But note that, once the "higher" needs have become activated, they may take charge, even at the price of sacrificing "lower" needs, or life itself. Mahatma Gandhi, for example, was capable of fasting to death for his causes.

23. See Ivan Steiner, "Perceived Freedom," *Advances in Experimental Social Psychology* 5 (1971), pp. 187–248, and Herbert M. Lefcourt, "The Function of the Illusions of Control and Freedom," *American Psychologist* 28 (1973), pp. 417–426.

24. "Our theory ventures to suggest that value change, and attitude and behavioral change ... can be initiated only by inducing an affective state of self-dissatisfaction concerning contradictions with self-conceptions and are motivated by the desire at least to maintain and if possible to enhance conceptions of oneself as a moral and competent human being." And the research reported on in this work is ingenious in its conception and most impressive and weighty, in my judgment, in its results, in support of basic themes in Rokeach's theory of value change. See Milton Rokeach, *The Nature of Human Values* (New York: Free Press, 1973), cited at p. 328.

25. In this context belongs John Rawls's espousal of what he calls the Aristotelian Principle, as a basic assumption in his theory of "goodness as rationality": ". . . other things being equal, human beings enjoy the exercise of their realized capacities (their innate or trained abilities), and this enjoyment increases the more the capacity is realized, or the greater its complexity." See John Rawls, *A Theory of Justice* (Cambridge, Mass.: Harvard University Press, 1971), section 65, at p. 426.

26. Robert Nozick, *Anarchy, State, and Utopia* (New York: Basic Books, 1974), especially pp. 150–153.

27. John Locke, the "Second Treatise" in *Two Treatises of Government*, ed. Peter Laslett (New York: Mentor, 1965) (1960; 1689-1690), chapter 5.

28. Ibid., section 49, p. 343.

29. Ibid., section 50, pp. 343–344.

30. A recent doctoral dissertation contributes a closely reasoned argument for the necessity of a clean break with the liberal premise shared by Hobbes and Locke—the individual's right to limitless acquisition of property—if liberal political theory is to be made compatible with the necessity in our modern world of achieving a steady-state economic system, soon. See George

Arras, "Liberal-Democratic Political Theory and the Steady State" (Ph.D. diss., University of Toronto, 1978).

31. See C. B. Macpherson, "Liberalism and the Political Theory of Property" in Alkis Kontos, ed., *Domination* (Toronto: University of Toronto Press, 1975), pp. 89–100; his "Human Rights as Property Rights," *Dissent* 24 (1977), pp. 72–77; and his own beginning and concluding chapters in C. B. Macpherson, ed., *Property: Mainstream and Critical Positions* (Toronto: University of Toronto Press, 1978).

32. E. F. Schumacher, "Roots of Inflation," *Catholic Worker* 41, no. 1 (January, 1975), pp. 1 and 6.

33. Mr. Justice Thomas R. Berger, *Northern Frontier, Northern Homeland: The Report of the Mackenzie Valley Pipeline Inquiry*, vol. 1 (Ottawa: Minister of Supply and Services, 1977).

34. Ralph Nader is our most effective critic of corporate assaults, and of institutions that condone corporate assault, on the public interest. He is an advocate of the concept of "social bankruptcy": even if a company makes a profit, he asked in one interview, "why shouldn't it be thrown into bankruptcy for making thousands of people sick and destroying and depleting other people's property without compensation, which is what contamination and pollution do?" Of course, he advocates a duty of full public disclosure for all corporations, not only of their financial transactions, but of what each does to our environment. See Eileen Shanahan, "Reformer: Urging Business Change," *New York Times*, January 24, 1971, section 3, pp. 1 and 8, at p. 8. Also see Ralph Nader, Peter Petkas, and Kate Blackwell, eds., *Whistle Blowing: The Report of the Conference on Professional Responsibility* (New York: Bantam, 1972) and Mark J. Green, with Beverly C. Moore, Jr., and Bruce Wasserstein, *The Closed Enterprise System: Ralph Nader's Study Group Report on Antitrust Enforcement* (New York: Bantam, 1972).

35. See James Petras and Morris Morley, *The United States and Chile: Imperialism and the Overthrow of the Allende Government* (New York: Monthly Review Press, 1975) and James Petras, *Critical Perspectives on Imperialism and Social Class in the Third World* (New York: Monthly Review Press, 1978).

36. In Kant's own words (translated): "Act so that the maxim of your action might be elevated by your will to be a universal law of nature." Immanuel Kant, "Fundamental Principles of the Metaphysics of Morals" in H. J. Paton, ed., *The Moral Law, or Kant's Groundwork of the Metaphysics of Morals* (London: New York: Harper & Row, 1964) (1785), section 2.

37. See Frances Fox Piven and Richard A. Cloward, *Poor*

People's Movements: Why They Succeed, How They Fail (New York: Vintage, 1979) (1977), pp. 96–97. Their italics. For another study of the experience of emancipatory organizations, more on the behavioral research model and, perhaps inevitably with these kinds of data, more superficial and less insightful, see William H. Gamson, *The Strategy of Social Protest* (Homewood, Ill.: Dorsey, 1975).

38. Seymour Martin Lipset, *Political Man: Where, How and Why Democracy Works in the Modern World* (Garden City, N.Y.: Doubleday, 1960), chapter 12, see especially p. 396: "Employers know well that the more democratic a union—that is, the more opposition in it to the incumbent leadership, the more factions, the more turnover in office—the more irresponsible the union will be." Come to think of it, is it conceivable that among the world's great powers, too, those that have liberal-democratic constitutions and practice elections that lead to turnover in office might tend to be more bellicose, less responsible in their foreign policy postures and decisions than other great powers?

39. "Modern capitalism has thus evolved a system of domination in which people have no democratic control over their political parties, their elected assemblies, or their labor unions; in which 'democracy' is but a method of manipulating the atomized masses into accepting decisions they do not share in making, of preventing citizens from organizing themselves, from shaping, expressing, and exerting their will collectively." André Gorz, *Strategy for Labor: A Radical Proposal* (Boston: Beacon, 1968) (1967, 1964), p. viii.

40. See especially Santiago Carillo, *'Eurocommunism' and the State* (London: Lawrence and Wishart, 1977) (1976). Also see Fernando Claudin, *Eurocommunism and Socialism* (London: New Left Books, 1978); Ernest Mandel, *From Stalinism to Eurocommunism* (London: New Left Books, 1978); and André Gunder Frank, "Eurocommunism: Left and Right Variants," *New Left Review*, no. 108 (1978), pp. 88–92.

41. I have seen an Italian cartoon strip somewhere, in which a new-style Communist Party leader explains to a prospective voter, first, that you don't have to be a Leninist to be a communist; then, that you don't have to be a Marxist to be a communist; and finally, as the clincher: "You don't have to be a communist to be a communist!"

42. Cf. Ralph Miliband, *The State in Capitalist Society* (London: Weidenfeld and Nicolson, 1972) (1969) and Frank Parkin, *Class Inequality and Political Order* (Frogmore, St. Albans: Paladin, 1975) (1971), chapter 4.

43. These are excerpts from President Johnson's closing remarks in his Address to the Nation of March 31, 1968, according to the "unofficial text" distributed by the United States Information Service in Ottawa: "... a house divided against itself by the spirit of factions, parties, regions or religion or race, is a house that cannot stand. There is a division in the American house now. There is divisiveness among us all tonight. . . . I would ask all Americans, whatever their personal interests are concerned, to guard against divisiveness and all of its ugly consequences. . . . Accordingly I shall not seek and I will not accept the nomination of my party of another term as your President."

44. See Udo Bermbach, "On Civic Initiative Groups," *German Political Studies* 3 (1978), pp. 227–240, at p. 227.

45. Cf. Raghavan Iyer, *The Moral and Political Thought of Mahatma Gandhi* (New York: Oxford University Press, 1973), chapters 10–14, H. J. N. Horsburgh, *Non-Violence and Agression: A Study of Gandhi's Moral Equivalent of War* (New York: Oxford University Press, 1968), Joan Bondurant, *Conquest of Violence: The Gandhian Philosophy of Conflict* (Berkeley: University of California Press, 1965), Arne Naess, *Gandhi and the Nuclear Age* (Totowa, N.J.: Bedminister, 1965), and Arne Naess, *Gandhi and Group Conflict* (Oslo: Universitetsforlaget, 1974).

46. Gene Sharp, *Exploring Nonviolent Alternatives* (Boston: P. Sargent, 1970) and *The Politics of Nonviolent Action* (Boston: P. Sargent, 1973).

47. George Lakey, *Strategy for a Living Revolution* (New York: Grossman, 1973).

48. Ibid., chapter 5.

49. Ibid., chapter 7.

50. The most important work of documentation, interpretation, and analysis of this continuing state of affairs is a book by Harry Braverman, *Labor and Monopoly Capital: The Degradation of Work in the Twentieth Century* (New York: Monthly Review Press, 1975). Also see André Gorz, ed., *The Division of Labor: The Labor Process and Class Struggle in Modern Capitalism* (Atlantic Highlands, N.J.: Humanities Press, 1976) (1973). Swedish labor today appears in the forefront, within liberal-corporate systems, of efforts to wrestle control over physical health and safety protection in the workplace from the employers: "A revised Work Safety Law gives union safety stewards the right to halt any process they regard as imminently and seriously dangerous, pending a judgment from a state safety inspector. It guarantees the safety stewards' job secur-

ity and right to do whatever they regard as necessary to perform their duties, including any training and time they need, without loss of pay." Andrew Martin, "In Sweden, a Union Proposal for Socialism," *Working Papers for a New Society* 5, no. 2 (1977), pp. 46–58, at p. 56. Also see, on the Swedish advances in comparison to advances in other West European countries, G. David Garson, ed., *Worker Self-Management in Industry: The West European Experience* (New York: Praeger, 1977).

51. See Carole Pateman, *Participation and Democratic Theory* (Cambridge: Cambridge University Press, 1973) (1970).

52. See Ivan Illich, *Tools for Conviviality* (New York: Harper & Row Perennial Library, 1973) and *Energy and Equity* (London: Calder & Boyars, 1974); also see E. F. Schumacher, *Small is Beautiful: Economics as if People Mattered* (New York: Harper & Row, 1973).

53. This is the subtitle of Schumacher's influential book; cf. note 52.

54. On the political use of symbolic pseudosatisfaction in exchange for economic privilege and exploitation, consult Murray Edelman, *The Symbolic Uses of Politics* (Urbana: University of Illinois Press, 1964) and *Politics as Symbolic Action: Mass Arousal and Quiescence* (Chicago: Markham, 1971).

55. See André Gorz, *Strategy for Labor: A Radical Proposal.*

56. Piven and Cloward, *Poor People's Movements*, chapter 5.

57. "Triple Revolution: Complete Text of the Ad Hoc Committee's Controversial Manifesto," *Liberation* (April 1964), pp. 9–15, cited at p. 9.

58. Milton Friedman, our most articulate Manchester-liberal economist, came out in favor of a negative income tax, if with some hesitation (and also wondering whether the recipients had not best be disenfranchised), in 1962; see Milton Friedman, *Capitalism and Freedom* (Chicago: University of Chicago Press, 1964), chapter 12; see also Milton Friedman and Rose Friedman, *Free to Choose* (New York: Harcourt Brace Jovanovich, 1980), pp. 97 and 120-126. Mr. Nixon favored a sort of negative income tax plan in the early years of his Presidency; cf. Daniel P. Moynihan (then a member of Nixon's cabinet), *The Politics of a Guaranteed Income* (New York: Random House, 1973) and Kenneth Bowler, *The Nixon Guaranteed Income Proposal* (Cambridge, Mass.: Ballinger, 1974).

On the liberal or conservative right, an important concern has been to find ways of scaling down the current social welfare expenditures, and it has been a principal argument for the negative income tax that it can reduce the tax burden. On the left, advocates of a guaranteed annual income have had other priorities in mind, of course: above all the hope of achieving a more just redistribution of income, to reduce deprivation and dependency. Cf. "Triple Revolution." See also Robert Theobald, *Free Men and Free Markets* (Garden City, N.Y.: Doubleday Anchor, 1965) (1963) and Robert Theobald, ed., *The Guaranteed Income: Next Step in Socioeconomic Evolution?* (Garden City, N.Y.: Doubleday Anchor, 1967) (1966).

59. Kurt Vonnegut, Jr., *Player Piano* (New York: Avon, 1971) (1952).

60. Hannah Arendt, *The Human Condition* (Garden City, N.Y.: Doubleday Anchor, 1959) (1958).

61. See Barry R. Chiswick and June A. O'Neill, eds., *Human Resources and Income Distribution* (New York, W. W. Norton, 1977), chapter 4, at p. 41.

62. See my "Peace and Critical Political Knowledge as Human Rights," *Political Theory* 8, no. 3 (August 1980).

Chapter 5

1. See C. Wright Mills, *The Sociological Imagination* (New York: Oxford University Press, 1959), pp. 8–13.

2. Charles Hampden-Turner, *The Sane Asylum* (San Francisco: Jossey-Bass, 1975).

3. Newspaper reports out of the U.S. South in the days of the acute phases of the Civil Rights struggle of the 1960s indicated a relative dearth of violent crime and of incidence of psychoses, especially among the black populations.

4. Cf. Istvan Meszaros, *Marx's Theory of Alienation* (London: Merlin, 1970), p. 41.

5. See Jean Jacques Rousseau, "A Discourse on Political Economy," pp. 318–319, and "A Discourse on the Arts and Sciences," p. 147, in *The Social Contract and Discourses* (New York: Dutton, 1950); cf. Meszaros, *Marx's Theory of Alienation*, pp. 48–55.

6. Cited from Hegel's first philosophical paper, "Differenz des Fichteschen und Schellingschen Systems," *Erste Druckschriften* (Leipzig: 1913) (1801), p. 14, in Herbert Marcuse, *Reason and Revolution* (Boston: Beacon, 1960), p. 36.

7. Cf. Richard Schacht, *Alienation* (Garden City, N.Y.: Doubleday Anchor, 1970), p. 76.

8. Robert C. Tucker, ed., *The Marx-Engels Reader*, 2nd ed. (New York: W. W. Norton, 1978) (1972), p. 171.

9. Karl Marx, "The Eighteenth Brumaire of Louis Bonaparte"

in Tucker, *Marx-Engels Reader*, p. 595.

10. See Tucker, *Marx-Engels Reader*, p. 144. Compare Joachim Israel, *Alienation: From Marx to Modern Sociology* (Boston: Allyn & Bacon, 1971), pp. 31–33.

11. See Bertell Ollman, *Alienation: Marx's Conception of Man in Capitalist Society* (Cambridge: Cambridge University Press, 1971), p. 132.

12. Karl Marx, "On the Jewish Question" in Tucker, *Marx-Engels Reader*, p. 43. Marx's italics.

13. Ibid., p. 46. Marx's italics.

14. Cf. Marx's essay "Estranged Labor" in his "Economic and Philosophic Manuscripts of 1844" in Tucker, *Marx-Engels Reader*, pp. 70–81.

15. See Friedenberg's review of Richard M. Titmuss, *The Gift Relationship*, in the *New York Review of Books* 19, no. 9 (May 20, 1971), p. 8.

16. "What is characteristic of the capitalist age is that in the eyes of the labourer himself labour-power assumes the form of a commodity belonging to him. On the other hand, it is only at this moment that the commodity form of the products of labour become general." Karl Marx in *Capital* (Moscow: Foreign Languages Publishing House, 1961) (1867), vol. 1, p. 170. Quoted in Georg Lukacs, *History and Class Consciousness* (London: Merlin, 1971) (1923), p. 87.

17. Lukacs, *History and Class Consciousness*, p. 91.

18. William Leiss, *The Limits to Satisfaction* (Toronto: University of Toronto Press, 1976), p. 88.

19. Bertell Ollman, *Alienation*, chapter 23.

20. I discuss my conception of Politics briefly in the Introduction (pp. 1–6; on p. 3 I explain why I sometimes capitalize the term).

21. Gustavo Gutierrez, *A Theology of Liberation* (Maryknoll, N.Y.: Orbis, 1973), p. 21, note 45.

22. Emile Durkheim, *The Division of Labor in Society* (Glencoe, Ill.: Free Press, 1947) (1893), pp. 353–373.

23. Emile Durkheim, *Suicide* (Glencoe, Ill.: Free Press, 1951) (1897), p. 208.

24. Sebastian de Grazia, *The Political Community: A Study of Anomie* (Chicago: University of Chicago Press, 1948), pp. 71–74.

25. See Robert A. Nisbet, *The Quest for Community* (New York: Oxford University Press, 1953); and Robert K. Merton, *Social Theory and Social Structure* (Glencoe, Ill.: Free Press, 1957) (1949).

26. An interesting if inconclusive attempt at studying empirical interrelationships between measures of alienation and of anomie (and of external/internal control; cf. below chap. 5, p. 148) is found in David Loye, *The Leadership Passion: A Psychology of Ideology* (San Francisco: Jossey-Bass, 1977).

27. See Melvin Seeman, "On the Meaning of Alienation," *American Sociological Review* 24 (1959), pp. 783–791.

28. Melvin Seeman, "Empirical Alienation Studies: An Overview" in R. Felix Geyer and David R. Schweitzer, eds., *Theories of Alienation: Critical Perspectives in Philosophy and the Social Science* (Leiden: Martinus Nijhoff, 1976), pp. 265–305. Also see other papers in this valuable collection. For another useful stocktaking, see Frank Johnson, *Alienation: Concept, Term, and Meanings* (New York: Seminar Press, 1973).

29. There is much empirical evidence to confirm the proposition that politically critical and rebellious students tended to be psychologically healthier and also academically more competent, statistically speaking, compared to apolitical or conservative students. See my "Political and Apolitical Students: Facts in Search of Theory," *Journal of Social Issues* 23, no. 3 (1967), pp. 76–91. Also see Charles Hampden-Turner, *Radical Man: The Process of Psycho-Social Development* (Cambridge, Mass.: Schenkman, 1970) and Kenneth Keniston, *Young Radicals: Notes on Committed Youth* (New York: Harcourt, Brace & World, 1968), and *Youth and Dissent: The Rise of a New Opposition* (New York: Harcourt Brace Jovanovich, 1972). For a contrary, though in my view more speculative and less convincing, interpretation of activist students on the left, see Lewis Feuer, *Conflict of Generations* (New York: Basic Books, 1969). A subsequent survey of the literature on student radicals is found in Keniston's *Radicals and Militants* (Lexington, Mass.: D. C. Heath, 1973).

30. Melvin Seeman, in Geyer and Schweitzer, *Theories of Alienation*, p. 282.

31. Julian B. Rotter, "Generalized Expectancies for Internal Versus External Control of Reinforcement," *Psychological Monographs* 80, no. 609 (1966), pp. 1–28.

32. For example, see David Loye, *The Leadership Passion*, pp. 180 and 192–193. Also see B. E. Collins, "Four Components of the Rotter Internal-External Scale: Belief in a Difficult World, a Just World, a Predictable World, and a Politically Responsive World," *Journal of Personality and Social Psychology* 29 (1974), pp. 381–391; a significant attempt at theorizing and research that draws on Rotter's work as well as

on the work of Rokeach is found in Stanley A. Renshon, *Psychological Needs and Political Behavior: A Theory of Personality and Political Efficacy* (New York: Free Press, 1974).

33. Renshon, *Psychological Needs and Political Behavior*, p. 151 and chapters 10 and 11.

34. See David Mark Mantell, *True Americanism: Green Berets and War Resisters. A Study of Commitment* (New York: Teachers College Press, 1974).

35. Melvin L. Kohn, *Class and Conformity: A Study in Values* (Homewood, Ill.: Dorsey Press, 1969).

36. See Herbert C. Kelman and Lee H. Lawrence, "Assignment of Responsibility in the Case of Lt. Calley: Preliminary Report on a National Survey," *Journal of Social Issues* 28 (1972), pp. 177–212. Work toward a more complete report is now (Summer, 1980) in progress; the authors' intention is to call their book *Crimes of Obedience*.

37. Carole Pateman writes: "the millions who had formally been given the franchise, who had formally been given the means to self-government had in fact been 'trained to subservience' and this training had largely taken place during their daily occupation. Cole argued that 'the industrial system . . . is in great measure the key to the paradox of political democracy. Why are the many nominally supreme but actually powerless? Largely because the circumstances of their lives do not accustom or fit them for power or responsibility. A servile system in industry reflects itself in political servility.' " See Carole Pateman, *Participation and Democratic Theory* (Cambridge: Cambridge University Press, 1973) (1970), p. 38, and G. D. H. Cole, *Labour in the Commonwealth* (London: Headley Bros., 1918), p. 35.

38. Cf. my "Gentleness and Politics: The Case for Motherhood Reconsidered," *Politics* 10 (1975), pp. 125–138.

39. Fritz Heider, *The Psychology of Interpersonal Relations* (New York: John Wiley, 1958). I am indebted to my friend Joseph F. Fletcher who has kindled my interest in the attribution research literature and has helped me to find my initial bearings in this field.

40. See Daryl J. Bem, "Self-Perception: An Alternative Interpretation of Cognitive Dissonance Phenomena," *Psychological Review* 74 (1967), pp. 183–200, and "Self Perception Theory," *Advances in Experimental Social Psychology* 6 (1972), pp. 1–62. Also see Harold H. Kelley, "Attribution Theory in Social Psychology" *Nebraska Symposium on Motivation* 15 (1967), pp. 192–238, and "The Processes of Causal Attribution," *American*

Psychologist 28 (1973), pp. 107–128.

41. In addition to works cited in the previous note, see Edward E. Jones et al., eds., *Attribution: Perceiving the Causes of Behavior* (Morristown, N.J.: General Learning Press, 1972); Kelly G. Shaver, *An Introduction to Attribution Processes* (Cambridge, Mass.: Winthrop, 1972); Bernard Weiner, *Theories of Motivation: From Mechanism to Cognition* (Chicago: Markham, 1972); John H. Harvey and William P. Smith, *Social Psychology: An Attributional Approach* (St. Louis, Mo.: C. V. Mosby, 1977); and John H. Harvey, William Tikes, and Robert F. Kidd, eds., *New Directions in Attribution Research* vols. 1 and 2 (Hillsdale, N.Y.: Lawrence Erlbaum, 1976 and 1978).

42. See the two classic statements of this problem: Paul Goodman, *Growing Up Absurd: Problems of Youth in the Organized System* (New York: Random House, 1960) and Edgar Z. Friedenberg, *Coming of Age in America: Growth and Acquiescence* (New York: Vintage, 1967) (1963).

43. See Herbert M. Lefcourt, "The Function of the Illusions of Control and Freedom," *American Psychologist* 28 (1973), pp. 417–425, cited at pp. 417 and 425.

44. See Donald J. C. Carmichael, "Agent-Individualism: A Critique of the Logic of Liberal Political Understanding" (Ph.D. diss., University of Toronto, 1978), cited at p. 39.

45. Ibid., pp. 41–42.

46. Karl Marx, "On the Jewish Question" in Tucker, *Marx-Engels Reader*, pp. 26–52, at pp. 50 and 52. Marx's italics.

47. See Robert E. Agger, *A Little White Lie: Institutional Division of Labor and Life* (New York: Elsevier, 1978), p. 88.

48. Ibid., p. 128.

49. Ibid., p. 164.

50. On this aspiration, see my "What it Means to be Human," Ross Fitzgerald, ed., *What It Means to Be Human* (Rushcutter's Bay, Australia: Pergamon, 1978), pp. 128–141.

51. Generally speaking, I think this is true of sexual relationships and of sexually oriented love relationships as well, even though I am aware that some otherwise apparently mature women like to be bossed around by a strong man, and that some otherwise mature men prefer submissiveness in their woman or women; the same kind of phenomenon appears to occur in homosexual love-relationships, both male and female.

52. This vision is well articulated and turned into a powerful argument for a socialist society in Richard H. Tawney, *Equality* (London: Putnam, 1961) (1931).

53. "Students in America are rarely treated with respect; both in high school and college they almost always find themselves in the custody of officials who oscillate between trying to win their good will and betraying their confidence in order to retain that of the public which supports and controls the institution. ... The basic intent is still to control the young and prevent them from becoming a threat to good public relations, rather than to cherish them and further their growth." Edgar Z. Friedenberg, *The Dignity of Youth and Other Atavisms* (Boston: Beacon, 1967) (1965). Also see John R. Seeley's superb essay on the destruction of the psychological freedom of the young in the interest of preserving our "poverty system": "Progress From Poverty" in his *The Americanization of the Unconscious* (Philadelphia: J. B. Lippincott, 1967), pp. 280–295.

54. Cf. Lester W. Milbrath and M. L. Goel, *Political Participation*, 2nd ed. (Chicago: Rand McNally, 1977) (1965), p. 11.

55. See George Lakey, *Strategy for a Living Revolution* (New York: Grossman, 1973).

56. There is already a voluminous literature (interpretive, critical, and polemical) on the 1966 Freedom of Information Act in the United States, on how it has been administered, and on the changes it has wrought. See Carol M. Barker and Matthew H. Fox. *Classified Files: The Yellowing Pages* (New York: Twentieth Century Fund, 1972), and Norman Dorsen and Stephen Gillers, eds., *None of Your Business: Government Secrecy in America* (New York: Viking, 1974). A comprehensive recent symposium, edited by Harold C. Relyea, "The Freedom of Information Act a Decade Later," is found in *Public Administration Review* 39 (1979), 310–332. Also see H. C. Relyea, "Freedom of Information, Privacy, and Official Secrecy: The Evolution of Federal Government Information Policy Concepts," *Social Indicators Research* 7 (1980), 137–156. Another discussion of principles is found in Morton H. Halperin and Daniel N. Hoffman. "Secrecy and the Right to Know," *Law and Contemporary Problems* 40 (1976), 132–165.

CHAPTER 6

1. Robert Heilbroner addresses the same question, as well as the question of what kind of a climate of ideas it takes to ask it, from a humanist perspective, in his "What Has Posterity Ever Done for Me?", a postscript to his *An Inquiry into the*

Human Prospect (New York: W. W. Norton, 1975) (1974), pp. 169–176.

2. Wilfred Beckerman, "The Myth of 'Finite' Resources," *Business and Society Review* 12 (1974/75), pp. 21–25, at p. 22.

3. See Garrett Hardin, "Lifeboat Ethics: The Case Against Helping the Poor," *Psychology Today* 8 (1974), pp. 38–43 and 123–126. Paradoxically, the same author has written one of the most brilliant and influential essays on the diré consequences of free enterprise and private acquisitiveness in a world of finite resources: see "The Tragedy of the Commons" in Garrett Hardin, *Exploring New Ethics for Survival: The Voyage of the Spaceship Beagle* (Baltimore: Penguin, 1973) (1968), pp. 250–264. This essay was originally published in *Science* 162 (December 13, 1968), pp. 1243–1248. By the time he published his "Lifeboat Ethics" in 1974, Hardin had evidently decided that, if liberalism and humanism cannot be reconciled, humanism must go.

4. See Herman Kahn, *Thinking About the Unthinkable* (New York: Horizon, 1962) and *On Thermonuclear War* (Princeton, N.J.: Princeton University Press, 1961) (1960).

5. Our mass media tend to depict impoverished indigenous peoples as quaint and interesting, and at the same time to assert that these peoples are doomed to extinction by "history" or by the necessity for "development" and "progress"; it is hardly ever asked, when indigenous tribes are too weak and inarticulate to pose the question themselves, by what right their traditional lands are invaded and exploited by outsiders. We are rarely encouraged to reflect on our own complicity in the continuing decimation and destruction of indigenous peoples in foreign countries, as citizens and as consumers who with our votes and dollars help to keep predatory corporations and corrupt and brutal foreign regimes free from most kinds of civilized restraints, above all on their "wilderness frontiers." To cite one example among many, consider the ongoing genocide in Paraguay. See Mark Münzel, *The Aché Indians: Genocide in Paraguay*, International Work Group on Indigenous Affairs Document no. 11 (Copenhagen, 1973) and *The Aché: Genocide Continues in Paraguay*, International Work Group on Indigenous Affairs Document no. 17 (Copenhagen, 1974); also see Richard Arens, ed., *Genocide in Paraguay* (Philadelphia: Temple University Press, 1976).

6. According to TRB, the *New Republic's* well informed commentator: "The top 500 corporations in America have in-

creased their share of all US manufacturing and mining assets from 40 to 70 percent in 15 years and they are virtually all global. Interlocking directorates tie them in with the top dozen or so banks, nearly all of which are global too.... General Motors' yearly operating revenues exceed those of all but a dozen nation-states; it has 127 plants at home and 43 abroad. And for the first time in history these superbly efficient organizations, whose simple and supple goal is the maximization of profits, make plans on a global scale, and move from one country to another, slipping between the cracks of national jurisdictions." *New Republic* (February 22, 1975), p. 3.

7. See Richard J. Barnet and Ronald E. Müller, *Global Reach: The Power of the Multinational Corporations* (New York: Simon and Schuster, 1974), p. 18.

8. According to Professor Howard V. Perlmutter, "by 1985, two hundred companies will control eighty percent of all productive assets of the non-Communist wrold. The average growth rate of many of the largest corporations is two to three times that of the most advanced industrial countries." Cited from Geoffrey Shields, "The Multinationals," *World Issues* 2, no. 5 (December 1977/January 1978), pp. 3–6, at p. 3. Also see note 6 above.

9. See Barnet and Müller, *Global Reach*, p. 21. The phrase "crusade for understanding" is David Rockefeller's; the remaining words cited are Barnet's and Müller's.

10. Zbigniew Brzezinski, *Between Two Ages: America's Role in the Technetronic Era* (Harmondsworth: Penguin, 1977) (1970), especially pp. 293–309.

11. By late 1979 the so-called Group of 77 actually numbered 117 "developing countries," as they have come to be called. See *North-South: A Programme for Survival. The Report of the Independent Commission on International Development Issues under the Chairmanship of Willy Brandt* (London: Pan, 1980), p. 262. Also see Karl P. Sauvant and Hajo Hasenpflug, eds., *The New Economic Order: Confrontation or Cooperation between North and South?* (Boulder, Colo.: Westview, 1977); Gerald K. Helleiner, ed., *A World Divided: The Less Developed Countries in the International Economy* (Cambridge: Cambridge University Press, 1976); Guy F. Erb and Valeriana Kallab, eds., *Beyond Dependency: The Developing World Speaks Out* (New York: Praeger, 1975); Khadija Haq, ed., *Equality of Opportunity Within and Among Nations* (New York: Praeger, 1977); and Jagdish N. Bhagwati, ed., *The New International Order: The*

North-South Debate (Cambridge, Mass.: Massachusetts Institute of Technology Press, 1977).

12. "The advanced countries are counting on what Roger Hansen, an official of the National Security Council, called the *embourgeoisiment* of the richer OPEC countries. As the OPEC countries accumulate a larger share of the world's wealth, the advanced countries hope they will become less interested in a new international order and more interested in preserving their stake in the old order. The Trilateral Commission, which Zbigniew Brzezinski directed before moving to the National Security Council, has even suggested that countries like Saudi Arabia, Iran [This was when the Shah was still in power— C.B.], Brazil, and Mexico be brought into the 'inner circles' of international decision-making." See Orlando Letelier and Michael Moffitt, *The International Order*, part 1 (Washington: Transnational Institute, 1977), p. 53 and C. Fred Bergsten, Georges Berthoin, and Kinhide Mushakoji, "The Reform of International Institutions," *Triangle Papers*, no. 11 (1976), pp. 1–31. Also see C. Fred Bergsten (former United States Assistant Secretary of the Treasury for International Affairs), "The Threat from the Third World," *Foreign Policy* (Summer, 1973), pp. 102–124.

13. That Jimmy Carter as a member of the Trilateral Commission had been a humble and impressionable, indeed a model student of the learned Dr. Brzezinski and his fellow advocates of the corporate interests, is suggested by the following excerpt from Mr. Carter's autobiographical book, published in 1975: "In order to insure the continuing opportunity for penetrating analyses of complicated, important, and timely foreign policy questions, there is in operation an organization known as the Trilateral Commission. A group of leaders from the three democratic developed areas of the world meet every six months to discuss ideas of current interest to Japan, North America and Europe. Subjects like the world monetary system, economic relations between rich and poor nations, world trade, energy, the future of the seas, aid to less developed countries, and other possibilities for international understanding and cooperation are first studied by scholars, then debated by members of the commission, and finally analyses are published and distributed to world leaders. Membership on this commission has provided me with a splendid learning opportunity, and many of the older members have helped me in my study of foreign affairs." See Jimmy Carter, *Why Not the Best?* (Nashville: Broadman Press, 1975). For a fuller perspective on the relationship between Presi-

dent Carter and the Trilateral Commission, see Holly Sklar, ed., *Trilateralism: Elite Planning for World Management*, (Boston: South End Press, 1980).

14. See Roger Lewin, "Starved Brains," *Psychology Today* 9, no. 4 (September, 1975), pp. 29–33. Mr. Lewin was at that time Science Editor at the *New Scientist*, and is the author of *Child Alive: New Insights into the Development of Young Children* (London: M. T. Smith, 1975).

15. See Salvador Allende, "Speech to the United Nations" in Hugo Radice, ed., *International Firms and Modern Imperialism* (Harmondsworth, Penguin, 1975), pp. 233–247, at p. 236.

16. Cf. James Petras and Morris Morley, *The United States and Chile: Imperialism and the Overthrow of the Allende Government* (New York: Monthly Review Press, 1975).

17. Allende, "Speech to the United Nations" in Radice, *International Firms and Modern Imperialism*, p. 235.

18. Cf. Teresa Hayter, *Aid As Imperialism* (Harmondsworth: Penguin, 1971) and Cheryl Payer, *The Debt Trap: The IMF and the Third World* (Harmondsworth: Penguin, 1974); also see Stephen Hymer, "The Multinational Corporation and the Law of Uneven Development" in Radice, *International Firms and Modern Imperialism*, pp. 37–62.

19. See the Special Issue on "Arms Trade and Transfer of Military Technology," *Bulletin of Peace Proposals* 8, no. 2 (1977). Also see *The Arms Trade With the Third World* by the Stockholm International Peace Research Institute (London: Holmes and Meier, 1975) and the review article by Emma Rothschild, "The Boom in the Death Business," *New York Review of Books* 22, no. 15 (October 2, 1975), pp. 7–12. Further, see Richard A. Falk, "Militarization and Human Rights in the Third World," *Bulletin of Peace Proposals* 8, no. 3 (1977), pp. 220–232, Ernie Regehr, *Making a Killing: Canada's Arms Industry* (Toronto: McClelland & Stewart, 1975), and Robin Cook, "The Tragic Cost of Britain's Arms Trade," *New Statesman* (June 30, 1978), pp. 874–876.

20. Patricia M. Derian, "Human Rights and American Foreign Policy," *Universal Human Rights* 1, no. 1 (1979), pp. 3–9, at p. 9.

21. See my "Positive Peace and Rational Human Rights Priorities," *Bulletin of Peace Proposals* 10, no. 2 (1979), pp. 160–171; and "Peace and Critical Political Knowledge as Human Rights," *Political Theory* 8, no. 3 (August 1980), pp. 293–318.

22. See John Hemming, *Red Gold: The Conquest of the*

Brazilian Indians (Cambridge, Mass.: Harvard University Press, 1978), pp. 487–501.

23. Norman Lewis, *Eastern Bolivia: The White Promised Land*, International Work Group on Indigenous Affairs Document no. 31 (Copenhagen, 1978).

24. Shelton Davis, *Victims of the Miracle: Development and the Indians of Brasil* (Cambridge: Cambridge University Press, 1977).

25. Ibid., pp. 156–157.

26. B. F. Skinner, *Beyond Freedom and Dignity* (New York: Bantam Vintage, 1972) (1971), p. 165.

27. Ibid., p. 204; cf. p. 201.

28. See Kathleen Kinkade, "Commune: A Walden-Two Experiment," *Psychology Today* 6, no. 8 (January, 1973), pp. 35–42 and 90–93; cf. B. F. Skinner, *Walden Two* (New York: Macmillan, 1972) (1948).

29. See *Der Spiegel*, no. 15 (April 9, 1979), p. 30.

30. Writing in the *Washington Post*, Stephen S. Rosenfeld suggests that the Harrisburg accident might improve the prospects for an American acceptance of the proposed SALT II (the second Strategic Arms Limitations Treaty with the USSR): "The accident at Harrisburg gives the U.S. public the most authentic taste it has yet had of the sort of nuclear disaster war could bring. It is our scariest public nuclear encounter. Its political fallout cannot fail to touch the SALT atmosphere." Quoted from his article "Harrisburg Fallout on SALT," as reprinted in the *International Herald Tribune*, April 10, 1979, p. 6.

31. The most frightening part of the story of how Detroit and surrounding districts nearly were "lost" to a nuclear holocaust is that, in the absence of public awareness and public concern, those responsible for operating the Fermi breeder soon were all set to get it going again; in 1970 it was back in operation! However, corporate funding soon afterwards dried up and 'went for new kinds of fission-energy plants instead; only the highly radioactive carcass of the plant now remains: "The dead Fermi breeder had spawned a $130 million ghost—a ghost that cannot be laid to rest." See John G. Fuller, *We Almost Lost Detroit* (New York: Reader's Digest Press, 1975), quoted at p. 234.

For a not dissimilar story of another near-catastrophic "incident" that was effectively concealed from most of the people whose lives had been gambled with, see David Dinsmore Comey, *The Incident at Brown's Ferry* (Washington, D.C.: Friends of the Earth, 1975). Yet another revealing story about the same corporate conspiracy to conceal nuclear power-production hazards is found in Ralph Nader et al., eds., *Whistle Blowing: The Report of the Conference on Professional Responsibility* (New York: Bantam, 1972), chapter 6, and in John W. Gofman and Arthur R. Tamplin, *Poisoned Power* (Emmaus, Pa.: Rodale Press, 1971).

The liberal-corporate world has no monopoly, however, on corporate recklessness with human lives for the sake of nuclear energy production. See Zhores A. Medvedev, *Nuclear Disaster in the Urals* (New York: Norton, 1979).

32. "Nach Harrisburg hat sich die Welt verändert" is the headline in *Der Spiegel*, no. 15 (April 9, 1979), p. 21.

33. See Amory B. Lovins, "Nuclear Power: Technical Bases for Ethical Concern" in Amory B. Lovins and John H. Price, *Non-Nuclear Futures: The Case For an Ethical Energy Strategy* (Cambridge, Mass.: Ballinger, 1975), pp. 1–104, at pp. 33–34.

34. For example, see Herbert Inhaber, *Risk of Energy Production* (Ottawa: Atomic Energy Control Board, 1978) and "Risk with Energy from Conventional and Nonconventional Sources," *Science* 203 (23 February 1979), pp. 718–723. One of the clearest and most persuasive statements against nuclear-fission-energy plants to date, which also accounts for the corporate incentives to push ahead and to disregard the risks involved, is found in Ralph Nader and John Abbotts, *The Menace of Nuclear Energy* (New York: W. W. Norton, 1977). One particularly telling point emphasized in the book is the incongruity between the nuclear energy corporations' claim that the risks involved in the production of fission energy are infinitesimal, and their insistence on the need for legislation to limit their legal liability for nuclear accidents: "If a reactor incident is really as improbable as the industry claims, why does the industry continue to insist on limited liability? Why will the industry not accept liability for an accident that it contends, in practical terms, will not occur? To these questions the industry has never had a satisfactory answer." Ibid., p. 61 and p. 125.

35. For a recent discussion of the prospects for fusion energy, see John P. Holdren, "Fusion Energy in Context: Its Fitness for the Long Term," *Science* 200 (14 April 1978), pp. 168–180. Proponents of the "soft energy path" tend to reject the principle of fusion-energy development, even if environmentally relatively benign, on account of its expensiveness and its requirement of giant rather than small-scale technology; cf. the next paragraph

in the text; also see Amory B. Lovins, "Energy Strategy: The Road Not Taken," *Foreign Affairs* 55 (October 1976), pp. 56–96, at pp. 91–94.

36. Amory B. Lovins, "The Soft Energy Path," *Center Magazine* (September/October 1978), pp. 32–45, at p. 40.

37. The Lovins paper referred to above in note 35 has been countered by ten critical essays, in my fallible judgment more shrill than convincing, in Charles B. Yulish, ed., *Soft vs. Hard Energy Paths* (New York: Charles Yulish Associates, 1977). The most characteristic statement is found on the last page in the concluding essay by Arnold E. Safer, a vice-president in Irving Trust Company: "For government to force radical change, of the kind Mr. Lovins advocates, would require a major uprooting of the socioeconomic framework within which the United States has prospered." (p. 138.) Maybe so. Must we therefore, rather than question the merit of our liberal-corporate institutions, persist in a course that will inflict veritable holocausts on future generations, if not on large numbers of the now living as well?

A pro-Lovins, quite comprehensive account of some of the major arguments on both sides is found in Hugh Nash, ed., *The Energy Controversy: Soft Path Questions and Answers* (San Francisco: Friends of the Earth, 1979). Other relevant works that stress the hazards of nuclear energy development, and raise ethical issues, include John W. Gofman and Arthur R. Tamplin, *Poisoned Power: The Case Against Nuclear Power Plants Before and After Three Mile Island* (Emmaus, Pa.: Rodale Press, 1979) (1971); Anna Gyorgi *et al*, *No Nukes: Everyone's Guide to Nuclear Power* (Boston: South End Press, 1979); Fred H. Knelman, *Nuclear Energy: The Unforgiving Technology* (Edmonton: Hurtig, 1976); K. S. Shrader-Frechette, *Nuclear Power and Public Policy: The Social and Ethical Problems of Fission Technology* (Dordrecht: D. Reidel, 1980); and Lee Stephenson and George R. Zachar, eds., *Accidents Will Happen: The Case Against Nuclear Power* (New York: Harper & Row, 1979) (1976). For a series of academically weighty papers that stress technical and economic rather than ethical issues, see Robert Stobaugh and Daniel Yergin, eds., *Energy Future: Report of the Energy Project at the Harvard Business School.* Another "balanced" study is found in James J. Duderstadt and Chihiro Kikushi, *Nuclear Power: Technology on Trial* (Ann Arbor: University of Michigan Press, 1979).

For another powerful recent argument for a soft energy strategy, see Barry Commoner, *The Politics of Energy* (New York: Knopf, 1979).

38. John Rawls, *A Theory of Justice* (Cambridge, Mass.: Harvard University Press, 1971), pp. 284–295, at p. 288.

39. Ibid., p. 288.

40. Jacques Madaule is quoted (from a recent article in *Le Monde*, date unspecified) in the lead article in *Der Spiegel* of April 9, 1979, pp. 19–20, at p. 20; the heading of the *Der Spiegel* article is "Atomkraft: 'Das Ungeheuer ist in uns.' "

41. See Geoffrey Barraclough, "The Great World Crisis I," *New York Review of Books* 21, nos. 21 & 22 (January 23, 1975), pp. 20–29, at p. 24. Also see Frances Moore Lappé and Joseph Collins, *Food First: Beyond the Myth of Scarcity* (Boston: Houghton Mifflin, 1977), pp. 22–26.

42. Frances Moore Lappé and Joseph Collins, "Turning the Desert Green for International Agribusiness," *In These Times* (January 5–11, 1977), p. 5.

43. Lappé and Collins, *Food First*; Richard J. Barnet and Ronald E. Müller, *Global Reach: The Power of the Multinational Corporations* (New York: Simon and Schuster 1974); and Susan George, *How the Other Half Dies* (Harmondsworth: Penguin, 1977) (1976). In addition, see the most recent work by Richard J. Barnet, *The Lean Years: Politics in an Age of Scarcity* (New York: Simon and Schuster, 1980).

44. Lappé and Collins, *Food First*, p. 261.

45. George, *How the Other Half Dies*, pp. 180–181.

46. Ibid., cited at pp. 179–180. For further reading on this issue, see Barbara Garson, "The Bottle Baby Scandal: Milking the Third World For All it's Worth," *Mother Jones* 2, no. 10 (December, 1977), pp. 32–34, 38–40, and 60–62; and Nora Booth, "Western Milk Scandal: Sour Story," *Mother Jones* 3, no. 10 (December, 1978), p. 9. Also see Andy Chetley. *The Baby Killer Scandal: A War on Want Investigation Into the Promotion and Sale of Powdered Baby Milk in the Third World* (London: War on Want, 1979).

47. For example, after having been forced to insert strict warnings on the labels of a certain drug marketed in the United States, Parke, Davis, Inc. continued to market it indiscriminately in Mexico. Cf. Ivan Illich, *Limits to Medicine* (Toronto: McClelland & Stewart, 1976), p. 68.

48. George, *How the Other Half Dies*, p. 305.

49. Ibid., p. 173, and Barraclough, "Great World Crisis I," p. 26.

50. Barraclough, "Great World Crisis I," p. 26.

51. Ibid.

52. See Frances Moore Lappé, "Fantasies of Famine: The Case for Modest Optimism about a Man-Made Disaster," *Harper's* 250, no. 1497 (February, 1975), pp. 51–54 and 89–90, at p. 87; see also Lappé and Collins, *Food First*, p. 26.

53. Lappé and Collins, *Food First*, p. 85.

54. See the works cited above in note 11. See also David B. H. Denoon, ed., *The New International Economic Order: A U.S. Response* (New York: New York University Press, 1979).

55. This quotation is from a speech by then President Nixon to the Seafarers' International Union toward the end of 1973, when he was still at the height of his high-profile posture of moral leadership; it is quoted in the opening paragraph of the "Talk of the Town" section in the *New Yorker* (December 15, 1973).

56. See pp. 24–25, 34–35, 62–64, and 110–117.

57. I have developed this theme in "What It Means To Be Human" in Ross Fitzgerald, ed., *What It Means To Be Human: Essays in Philosophical Anthropology, Political Philosophy and Social Psychology* (Rushcutters Bay, N.S.W.: Pergamon, 1978), pp. 128–141.

58. See John Rodman, "Ecological Resistance: John Stuart Mill and the Case of the Kentish Orchid" (Paper presented at the 1977 Annual Meeting of the American Political Science Association, Washington, D.C., September 1977), especially pp. 1–15. Also see his "The Liberation of Nature?" *Inquiry* 20 (Spring, 1977), pp. 83–145.

59. E. F. Schumacher, *Small is Beautiful: Economics As If People Mattered* (New York: Harper & Row, 1973).

60. Ivan Illich, *Tools for Conviviality* (New York: Harper & Row Perennial, 1973), p. xii (italics deleted); compare pp. 12, 25, and passim.

61. This statement was made by Ammon Hennacy in a speech to students at the University of California in Berkeley some time near the beginning of the 1960s.

62. Paulo Freire, *Pedagogy of the Oppressed* (New York: Seabury, 1974) (1970), p. 28 and passim.

63. I owe these epithets for the major species of modern newspaper to J. B. Priestley's eloquent essays on democracy in his *Out of the People* (New York: Harper, 1941).

64. Robert E. Agger's use of the same phrase is not dissimilar when he refers to the myth that institutions are real in the sense that they necessitate role-specified behavior and fragmented

people, even a contractual society. See his *A Little White Lie: Institutional Division of Labor and Life* (New York: Elsevier, 1978), p. 88.

Index of Names

Index of Subjects

DATE DUE

JY 22 '87		
JY 28 '87		
AG 3 '87		
AG 11 '87		
AG 19 '87		
AG 25 '87		
SE 2 '87		
SE 9 '87		
GAYLORD		PRINTED IN U.S.A